Contents

Chronology

EUROPEAN TREATIES AND ENLARGEMENTS
1951–2008

1950	Schuman Declaration, 9th May 1950
1951	**Treaty of Paris** (European Coal and Steel Community)
1957	**Treaty of Rome** (European Economic Community)
1957	**Euratom Treaty** (Euratom)
1958	EEC Established (Belgium; France; Germany; Italy; Luxembourg; Netherlands)
1967	**Merger Treaty** (Establishing Single Council and Commission)
1973	Enlargement (Denmark; Ireland; UK)
1981	Enlargement (Greece)
1986	Enlargement (Portugal; Spain)
1987	**Single European Act** (Extension of scope of QMV; Single Market)
1992	**Treaty on European Union** (Maastricht; Pillar Structure of CFSP and JHA)
1995	Enlargement (Austria; Finland; Sweden)
1997	**Treaty of Amsterdam** (Extended Co-decision; Inclusion of Schengen)
2001	**Treaty of Nice** (Provision for Enlargement)
2004	**Constitutional Treaty** (Not ratified)
2004	Enlargement (Cyprus; Czech Republic; Estonia; Hungary; Latvia; Lithuania; Malta; Poland; Slovenia; Slovakia)
2007	Enlargement (Bulgaria; Romania)
2007	Fiftieth Anniversary of Rome Treaties
2007	**Lisbon / Reform Treaty**

Editor's Foreword

This is the fifth volume in the IIEA series of explanatory texts on successive European treaties. The first – *Maastricht and Ireland: What the Treaty Means* – appeared in 1992 with Patrick Keatinge as editor and has been followed by volumes on Amsterdam, Nice and the Constitutional Treaty.

In fulfilment of the Institute's role as an independent forum, with the aim of providing objective analysis of the process of European integration, this study *Lisbon: What the Reform Treaty Means* is published as a contribution to informed public debate within Ireland on the meaning and implications of the latest treaty text.

It consists of fourteen chapters, dealing with aspects of the Treaty's origins, content and implications, written by twelve contributors from a wide field of disciplines. Professor Brigid Laffan reflects on the failure to ratify the Constitutional Treaty and on the debate among academic observers which followed. The views expressed in this volume are those of the individual authors and do not represent the opinion of the Institute. They are intended, individually and collectively, as an objective examination of a Treaty which holds out the prospect of an institutional settlement permitting the European Union to deal effectively with the global challenges of the early 21st century.

As editor I must pay tribute to my fellow contributors who have produced this text in a period of just over ten weeks, despite busy work pressures and a most unusual pattern of holiday breaks. This is a further proof of the voluntary commitment which has always been the great strength of the Institute. Their expertise, flexibility and readiness to deal with my impatient demands have been exceptional and merit the gratitude of the Institute and, I am sure, of their readers.

This volume should be read in conjunction with the Consolidated and Annotated versions of the Treaty published by the Institute of International and European Affairs. These timely volumes, widely welcomed and praised at both national and international levels, are the outcome of outstanding scholarly work by the IEA Researcher, Peadar ó Broin.

In this endeavour I have benefited from the support of Brendan Halligan, Chairperson of the Institute, and of all my colleagues in the Institute's reconstituted Publications Committee. In particular I must express my gratitude to Jill Donoghue, Acting Director General, for her vision and wise counsel. Margaret Ahearne, Victor McBrien, Elizabeth MacAulay and Ann Dwyer have made significant, and crucial, professional contributions to the technical process of publication. The Institute's small, highly talented Research Staff have provided enthusiastic support throughout. I am grateful for the assistance provided by Liz Rafferty, Lynn Fitzgerald and Bebe Nolan.

TONY BROWN
May 2008

Notes on Contributors

Gavin Barrett is Senior Lecture and President's Research Scholar, School of Law, University College, Dublin and Visiting Scholar, Institut des Hautes Études Européenes, Universite Robert Schuman, Strasbourg. He is editor of *National Parliaments and the European Union: The Constitutional Challenge* (2008, Clarus Press, Dublin).

Tony Brown is Chairman of the IIEA Publications Committee. He was an advisor to the Oireachtas Delegation to the European Convention. He was a Director of the European Bank for Reconstruction and Development 1997-2000. He is author of *From Dublin to Mostar: Irish Involvement in the Reconstruction of the Balkans* (2007, IEA, Dublin).

David Croughan is Head of Economics and Taxation at the Irish Business and Employers Confederation (IBEC) and serves as Chairman of the Economic and Financial Affairs Committee of the EU employers' umbrella organisation BUSINESSEUROPE. He is editor of the IBEC quarterly *Economic Trends Newsletter*.

Joseph Curtin is Senior Research Officer at the Institute of International and European Affairs with responsibility for Climate Change and Energy Policy. He edits the IIEA Energy and Climate Change Newsletter and Policy Briefs.

Paul Gillespie is Foreign Policy Editor of *The Irish Times*. He lectures at the UCD School of Politics and serves on the Advisory Council of the European Policy Centre in Brussels. He edited *Britain's European Question: the Issues for Ireland* (1996, IEA, Dublin) and *Blair's Britain, England's Europe* (2000, IEA, Dublin).

1

Brendan Halligan has been Chairman of the Institute of International and European Affairs since its foundation. He is Chairman of Sustainable Energy Ireland. A former member of both Houses of the Oireachtas and of the European Parliament he was General Secretary of the Labour Party from 1967 to 1980. He was Adjunct Professor of European Integration, University of Limerick, 1990-2000.

John Handoll is a partner in the Competition and Regulation Unit of William Fry, Solicitors, specialising in European Union law. He is author of *Capital, Payments and Money Laundering in the European Union* (2007, Oxford University Press).

Patrick Keatinge is Emeritus Associate Professor, Department of Political Science, Trinity College Dublin. He is author of books on Irish foreign policy including *European Security: Ireland's Choices* (1996, IEA, Dublin) and edited *Maastricht and Ireland: What the Treaty Means* (1992, IEA, Dublin).

Brigid Laffan is Principal of the College of Human Sciences in University College, Dublin. From 1991 to 2004 she was Jean Monnet Professor of European Politics at UCD. Among her many publications on European issues she edited *Constitution Building in the European Union* (1996, IEA, Dublin).

Peadar ó Broin is Research Officer at the Institute of International and European Affairs. He is editor of the *Consolidated and Annotated Versions of the Treaties as amended by the Treaty of Lisbon* (2008, IIEA, Dublin).

Denis O'Leary was Deputy Permanent Representative of Ireland to the European Communities in the period 1985-1990 and Permanent Representative to the European Union in the period 1995-2001. He is author of *Improving the Functioning of the European Union* (2007, IEA, Dublin).

Andrew O'Rourke was Secretary General of the Department of Foreign Affairs and Permanent Representative of Ireland to the European Communities. He is Chairman of the IIEA Enlargement Project. He was co-editor of the IEA Study *Europe Re-United: A Constitutional Treaty* (2004, IEA, Dublin).

Summary

Reflection
Brigid Laffan

The drafting of the Constitutional Treaty was an attempt to define and shape the European Union as a political order. It was part of a process of treaty change that began in the mid-1980s with the Single Act. It is unsurprising, therefore, that the failure of the Constitutional Treaty should have prompted an intense debate among academics about the implications for the future of the EU. It will become clear that there is considerable contestation among academics concerning the ratification failure. The first reading suggests that the ratification failure is not a problem for the efficiency or legitimacy of the European Union. The second adopts a very different perspective arguing that there is something wrong with the European Union that can only be rectified with a further politicization of the Union. A third reading cautions against politicization.

Andrew Moravcsik has put forward a vision of the EU as a problem-solving system, whose goal is to achieve consensual solutions to common problems that cannot be solved by the nation states acting alone, but whose development path is controlled by national political leaders.

Moravcsik's starting point is that the constitution failure does not represent a crisis for the EU because a "constitutional settlement" already exists in the European Union. A division of competences between the EU and the Member States has been agreed and the balance has stabilised. Because the EU is pre-eminent in areas which correspond more or less with those where citizens say they

3

want to see EU action there is no political will to further deepen integration. In support of this argument, he notes that the Constitutional Treaty – unlike the Single Act, the Treaty on European Union or the Amsterdam Treaty – was notable by its "stunning lack of positive proposals for reform". A constitutional settlement in substantive terms has been reached and Moravcsik concludes that "once we set aside ideal notions of democracy and look to real world standards, we see that the EU is at least as transparent, responsive, accountable and honest as its Member States".

Simon Hix shares Moravcsik's view that the ratification failure does not represent a crisis for the EU, and he agrees that the EU has reached an equilibrium point in terms of its institutional and substantive development. The economic and political architecture is largely complete but an assessment of the ratification failure points to the need for the Union's popular legitimacy to be urgently strengthened in order to ensure long-term effectiveness and stability. More democratisation of EU policy-making is both inevitable and desirable.

His argument begins from the premise that few EU policies actually produce the kind of all-round benefits which Moravscik claims. Rather, EU decision-making produces winners and losers and in many areas the choices made are political and have significant redistributive consequences. Now that the basic constitutional architecture has been established, difficult ideological choices must be made. Politicisation would make policy-makers accountable for the results of their decisions, would allow citizens to debate rival policy agendas and rival candidates for office, and would make policy more responsive to changing preferences

For Hix, without greater citizen engagement in the EU, the system's stability is at risk since, because they have no way of influencing decision-making, citizens who oppose the direction of EU policy have no choice but to oppose EU integration as a whole. This could be observed in the debates surrounding the Constitutional Treaty, which were more concerned with the orientation of the

EU's political economy than with the substance of the document itself. Much opposition to the treaty was founded on the belief that if it were accepted it would hasten the dismantling of the European social model, and the moves to neo-liberal policies throughout Europe. Many of the elements to which the objections were strongest were already contained in the existing treaties and thus unaffected by the rejection of the Constitutional Treaty.

Politicisation would overcome this problem by providing institutional mechanisms to generate debate about politics in the EU and, as a result, the Union's efficiency as a system would no longer be hindered by a lack of popular support.

Stefano Bartolini analyses the restructuring of political order in Europe as a consequence of European integration and challenges the depiction of the EU as a mere problem-solving system. He rejects the view that there is a division of labour between the Union and the nation state with the EU exclusively responsible for the regulation/deregulation of the market and the nation state responsible for introducing the necessary compensatory measures.

Bartolini shares Hix's view that the management of the internal market has political consequences but finds his prescription to remedy this state of affairs by engineering greater politicization at European level highly problematic.

His first objection is that politicization would not be limited to issues of policy and political economy, allowing European politics to be structured along the same lines as national issues. Political battles would be much more likely to focus on issues pertaining to membership, competences and decision-making rules, which he does not believe are yet resolved. He argues further that the areas that most exercise European citizens relate to conflicts over the EU's scope, competences and even its existence.

A further objection is that politicization would inevitably create unrealistic expectations about what could actually be achieved within the existing goals of the EU. Bartolini questions whether in fact the EU has reached a constitutional settlement, given that there is no clear-cut separation of powers and that Union competences

5

are set out in relation to loosely defined goals. The peculiarity of this arrangement is that the treaties actually protect the competences from political contestation and that it is possible to speak of the "constitutionalisation" of economic rights and market making goals, but not of corresponding political or social rights. Consequently, fostering public deliberation over alternative political mandates is doomed to failure.

The three readings sketched here highlight the differing perspectives of the EU as a form of political order in the opening decade of the 21st century. According to Moravcsik, the EU is a constrained but legitimate polity, a creature of its Member States that has reached an equilibrium. Hix would also agree that the EU has reached an equilibrium but argues strongly that it is desirable and feasible to further democratize the Union though politicization. Bartolini is skeptical about the capacity of the system to withstand politicization and wonders what kind of politicization would emerge.

The EU was conceived as an experimental and distinctive form of political order to achieve objectives that could no longer be effectively achieved within the nation states. Its complex system of fluid and differentiated boundaries developed in response to the challenges of interdependence in a changing international order. What would be the point of attempting to transform the EU into an enlarged territorial order that resembled its Member States in all ways but size?

EU integration has succeeded because it has been consensus oriented and has taken place on the basis of a fluid and loosely coupled order. Moreover, the EU has shown ability to live with an open ended process and enduring tensions and inconsistencies, not only in terms of policies but also institutional arrangements. This conceptual and political openness provides the key to understanding how the European Union has managed to marry increasing diversity with the deepening of its policy agenda, the widening of its membership and the strengthening of its institutional capacity.

On the "State of the Union", a multitude of conflicting visions exist among politicians and citizens. Attempting to resolve them has proved neither helpful nor possible. The core question for academics, practitioners and citizens is whether this system of managed internationalization that evolved in Western Europe after the second world war can continue to adapt to intense processes of globalization, competitiveness, security, the challenge of climate change and sustainability in the context of a continent-wide scale and a shifting international system.

The failed Constitutional Treaty has been followed by the Lisbon Reform Treaty.

The period of reflection that followed the ratification failure is characteristic of the EU as is the agreement on the Lisbon Treaty. The Union, in the absence of agreement on its final shape and in the context of the deep diversity that characterizes Europe, evolves in fits and starts in response to the challenges faced by its Member States. The key challenges facing Europe emanate both from the international system and from within the Member States. Intensified globalization, climate change, and shifting geopolitics increase the salience of the EU for its Member States and increase the salience of the Union in the world. The Lisbon Treaty enhances the ability of the Union to meet those challenges as it seeks to become a shaper of a changing world.

The modest changes in Lisbon are likely to make the decision making in the Union smoother. The addition of a President of the European Council will add much needed continuity and coherence to the work of the Council. The addition of the Charter makes more explicit the underlying values of the Union while the enhanced roles of the European parliament and national parliaments deepens the process of democratizing political space above the level of the state. The EU is as relevant to the challenges facing its Member States in 2007 as it was in 1958 when the "inner six" began the experimental process of establishing a common market and an economic community.

Nice to Lisbon
Tony Brown

Agreement on the Lisbon Treaty came at the end of a process which began in 2000 with the signing of the Nice Treaty and the adoption of the Charter of Fundamental Rights. At the time there was a growing debate on the future of the EU, raising fundamental questions.

Ratification of Nice was interrupted by the first Irish referendum in June 2001 which rejected the treaty. With opinion surveys indicating an inadequate understanding of the Treaty, the Taoiseach announced the creation of the National Forum on Europe.

The Laeken Declaration of December 2001, agreed by the Heads of State and Government, addressed the major challenges facing the Union and established the European Convention, representing the governments and parliaments of 28 countries, including the candidate countries, the European Parliament, the Commission and observers from civil society. The Convention met during 2002 and 2003, concluded its work on the basis of consensus and presented the draft Constitutional Treaty in June 2003. Meanwhile, in Ireland, a second referendum of the Nice Treaty resulted in a two-thirds majority in favour of ratification.

The Irish Presidency achieved consensus within the Intergovernmental Conference on the Constitutional Treaty which agreed text, formally signed in Rome in October 2004. Just weeks before the finalisation of the text, on 1st May 2004, the Union welcomed ten new Member States at an historic ceremony in Dublin.

Between 2004 and 2005, eighteen Member States ratified the Constitutional Treaty, two by referendum but two Member States – France and the Netherlands – rejected it in referendums. This shock to the EU system led to the conclusion of the European Council that "citizens have ... expressed concerns and worries which need to be taken into account." A period of reflection began which, in Ireland, centred on the work of the National Forum on

Europe. During the period the EU faced a growing agenda ranging from the integration of twelve new Member States to the need for policy initiatives on Energy and Climate Change and on co-operation in the Justice and Home Affairs area.

In 2007, the German Presidency, under Chancellor Merkel, set out to achieve a consensus on the way forward and engaged in direct negotiations with other leaders which identified a number of key concerns such as the treaty reference to undistorted competition, the double majority voting system, the role of national parliaments and concerns about the Charter of Fundamental Rights and the Justice and Home Affairs area.

In March 2007, on the occasion of the 50th Anniversary of the Treaties of Rome, the EU leaders recalled the Union's history and achievements, outlined its future aspirations and challenges and agreed on the aim of placing the EU on a renewed common basis before the European Parliament elections in 2009.

The European Council of June 2007 reached consensus on a Mandate for an IGC with the purpose of finalising the text of a new treaty. The Constitutional Treaty was abandoned in favour of the traditional form of a revising treaty. The logical and clear presentation, in a single document, disappeared although it was agreed that the new text would incorporate the main innovations of the Convention and the 2004 IGC.

The IGC met in July 2007 and concluded its work within a matter of weeks. The European Council met in an informal session in Lisbon in mid-October and, with the inclusion of a specific reference to policies to deal with Climate Change, reached unanimous agreement on the text which was formally signed by the representaives of the 27 Member States at a ceremony in the historic cloisters of the Mosteiro de Jeronimos outside Lisbon. The Treaty was then submitted to the 27 Member States for ratification in accordance with national procedures.

The Lisbon text has resulted from the initial discussions surrounding the Nice Treaty, including the emergence of the Charter of Fundamental Rights, from the intensive work of the European

Convention and from the period of reflection. There appears to be a general will across the Union's states and its political families to move forward on the basis of what has emerged from the past eight years and to focus attention and action on policy delivery. The European Parliament Report on the Lisbon Treaty, adopted in February 2008, argues that "the agreement to the Treaty of every single national government in the European Union demonstrates that the elected governments of the Member States all consider that this compromise is the basis on which they wish to work together in the future and will require each of them to demonstrate maximum political commitment to ensuring ratification by 1st January 2009."

Overview and Structure
Peadar ó Broin

The content of the Treaty represents the product of nearly twenty years of debate over the nature and shape of the European Union. During the 1980s the European single market began to grow organically, requiring policy initiatives in areas such as as transport, environmental protection or the rights of employeees.

The advent of these policies, created by the Single European Act of 1986, sparked a debate on the political legitimacy of the European Union to take action in such areas, but also led to the development of a complex legal structure. The treaties of Maastricht (1992), Amsterdam (1997) and Nice (2001), while succeeding in achieving specific amendments, failed to achieve a sustainable institutional settlement. Twenty years later, the European Union is still wrangling with this reform.

The Constitutional Treaty of October 2004 proposed to resolve the question of political legitimacy by democratising the institutions and procedures that adopt legislation in the European Union. However, the Constitution went beyond its basic remit by conferring certain "state-like" qualities on the European Union.

In the wake of the rejection of the European Constitution, the governments of the Member States were torn between abandoning a treaty text that benefited from arguably the most democratic legitimacy of any international treaty – the broadly representative European Convention – and the need to give effect to the outcome of the French and Dutch voters.

The resulting document, the Treaty of Lisbon signed by the national governments on 13 December 2007 in Lisbon's historic quarter of Belem, discards the statelike elements of the European Constitution. It does not seek to resolve the political legitimacy debate, although it does attempt to democratise decision-making in the European Union. Instead, it focuses purely on institutional reform by creating a durable, efficient and democratic institutional framework for the European Union.

The Treaty of Lisbon is a traditional amending treaty. It modifies what are collectively referred to as the "founding treaties" of the European Union, namely the Treaty on European Union and the Treaty Establishing the European Community which together constitute the EU's rulebook. The Treaty is intended to reform the institutional architecture of the European Union, hence the original name, "Reform Treaty" which has been retained by the Irish Government.

The current structure of the European Union has been in place since 1993, created by the Treaty of Maastricht and amended at Amsterdam and Nice. Under this structure action takes place in three policy areas, referred to as "pillars": the European Community, where Member States vote by majority on whether to adopt legislation along with the European Parliament and the second and third pillars, respectively foreign and defence and criminal law which remain intergovenmental in character with decisions taken by unanimity with each Member State retaining a veto. The European Parliament and the European Court of Justice play consultative roles, but lack real power or influence in the latter two pillars. The reason for such a complex structure is best explained by reference to national sensitivities in the second and third pillars.

The Treaty of Lisbon abolishes the three pillars referred to above, while respecting national concerns in foreign affairs and defence policy, which remain intergovernmental in character (i.e. each Member State has a veto). On criminal law, however, the threats posed by international criminality have resulted in competences in criminal law moving from intergovernmental co-operation to majority voting among the Member States along with the European Parliament. All laws in this field will also be subject to judicial review by the European Court of Justice. It is made clear that the change in decision-making in this field will not result in the harmonisation of national criminal laws. Nonetheless, Ireland and the United Kingdom have requested specific provisions to be included in the Treaty of Lisbon to enable the governments of those two countries to decide which legislation they will implement in the field of criminal law.

The Treaty of Lisbon provides for the amendment of the two treaties which contain the rules of the present Communities and Union: the Treaty on European Union (TEU), the Maastricht Treaty (1992), as amended and the Treaty Establishing the European Community i.e. the Treaty of Rome (1957) as amended and renamed the Treaty on the Functioning of the European Union (TFEU).

The fundamental amendment is contained in the Preamble and in the first article of the Treaty on European Union which establish a European Union. This will replace and succeed the limited European Union, as established by the Maastricht Treaty in 1992. and the European Community, established by the treaties of the 1950s. The Union will exist and operate insofar as its Member States confer competences upon it "to attain objectives they have in common".

The Treaty on European Union will have a Preamble and six sections: Common Provisions; Democratic Principles; Institutions; Enhanced Co-operation; External Actions and Common Foreign and Security Policy. The Treaty on the Functioning of the European Union will have seven parts: Principles; Non-discrimination and citizenship of the Union; Union Policies and Internal Action;

Overseas Countries and Territories; External Action; Institutional and Budgetary Provisions; General and Final Provisions.

The text of the Charter of Fundamental Rights of the European Union, including the Explanations relating to the Charter, is appended. The Charter is given the same legal value as the treaties in accordance with Article 6 of the Treaty on European Union.

The Treaty of Lisbon affirms the European Union as an international organisation that exists only by the will of its Member States, whose national Constitutions remain above the treaties of the European Union. Policies depend on the choices made by the governments of the Member States, which in turn depend on the political parties that citizens elect into office.

The Treaty of Lisbon will, however, allow for such choices to benefit from greater democratic legitimacy through the creation of an efficient institutional structure for the European Union, where the European Parliament will have increased powers. Council meetings will be held in public; legislation will be susceptible to judicial review by the European Court of Justice and national parliaments will have greater powers of scrutiny of EU legislation. An overarching set of values, principles and objectives seek to govern all policies and action undertaken by the European Union.

Values, Objectives and Competences
Paul Gillespie

The Lisbon Treaty provisions on values, objectives and competences are plain and straightforward and clearly spell out the fundamental features of how the EU functions.

It is possible to identify a logical and political chain connecting values, objectives and competences in the Treaty, which, if ratified, will in turn give rise to agreed policies and the allocation of resources to implement them.

Values are a primary and fundamental part of the Treaty. They are presented at the very beginning and underpin the later Titles and Chapters. They represent a crystallisation of political argument and debate over recent years, drawing fully on more long-standing commitments. In this respect the Treaty is a consolidating rather than an innovating document.

The Preamble draws inspiration "from the cultural, religious and humanist inheritance of Europe, from which have developed the universal values of the inviolable and inalienable rights of the human person, freedom, democracy, equality and the rule of law". Human dignity, freedom, democracy, equality, the rule of law and respect for human rights are affirmed rather than defined. More precise definitions and applications are spelled out in subsequent parts of the treaties and in the Charter of Fundamental Rights.

It is provided that the EU shall observe the principle of the equality of its citizens. Every national of a Member State is to be a citizen of the Union. EU citizenship is, however, additional to national citizenship. The basic principle goes back to the Maastricht Treaty of 1992, which introduced the concept of EU citizenship predicated on national citizenship and which was additional, not substitutive.

National parliaments are recognised as contributing actively to the good functioning of the Union in important areas: by advance sight of draft legislation; applying subsidiarity and proportionality principles to it; evaluating how policies on freedom, security and justice are applied; helping to revise the treaties; dealing with new accessions; and generally cooperating amongst themselves and with the European Parliament.

"The Union's aim is to promote peace, its values and the well-being of its peoples." This simple and well-honed sentence confidently declares the EU's main objectives in Article 3.1 of the TEU. In the remaining paragraphs of that article the objectives are spelled out. Little supplementary commentary is required to understand what is at stake, but it must be borne in mind that most of these objectives were established in previous treaties.

The detailed statement of Objectives covers key areas: freedom, security and justice; an internal market with the goals of sustainable development, price stability and full employment; a high level of environmental protection; social concerns such as combating social exclusion and discrimination; equality and solidarity and respect for Europe's cultural diversity and heritage. The Treaty seeks a balance between a liberal economic agenda and a more social European model, reflecting the political arguments between all the actors involved in drawing it up. These will continue as and when it is implemented.

Objectives related to external policy explicitly link values to interests so that, in its relations with the wider world, the Union is to uphold and promote its values and interests. The Union is to contribute to peace, security, sustainable development, free and fair trade, eradication of poverty and the protection of human rights. The EU is committed to the strict observance and the development of international law, including respect for the principles of the United Nations Charter.

A fundamental constraint on the EU's action is contained in the section on competences which outlines clearly for the first time the distinction between competences that are exclusive to the EU, those that are shared with the Member States and those where the EU takes supportive or supplementary action only.

The outcome is a major political achievement, which should determine the EU's political life for some time to come, after the turbulence and uncertainty of the period following the end of the Cold War, the continent's subsequent reunification and the EU's enlargement. A system of multi-level governance is laid down which looks sustainable and durable, allowing political leaders to concentrate on effective results or outputs, while citizens gradually become aware of the legal constraints on "ever closer union".

The Treaty states baldly that "competences not conferred upon the Union in the treaties remain with the Member States" and recognises national rights, structures and identities.

It is provided that the Union shall respect the equality of Member States before the treaties as well as their national identities, inherent in their fundamental structures, political and constitutional, and shall respect their essential State functions.

Subsidiarity limits Union action only to those objectives which cannot be achieved by Member States at central, regional or local levels, but can better be achieved at Union level. National parliaments are given the task of policing the subsidiarity norm, as set out in a special Protocol, with a separate one on proportionality. The new procedures involving national parliaments are a significant innovation introduced by the Lisbon Treaty. Insofar as the so-called democratic deficit exists as much at domestic as transnational level this addresses one of its most important sources. National parliaments will have to adapt their procedure to deal with EU business in a more transparent manner.

Article 49 of the Treaty on European Union sets out clearly that any European state which respects the values referred to in Article 2 and is committed to promoting them may apply to become a member of the Union. These values are expressed in Articles 2 and 3. Article 50 provides that any Member State of the EU may withdraw from the Union in accordance with its own constitutional requirements. A negotiation will be conducted and concluded by the Council, acting by qualified majority, including timing and particular arrangements. This is the first time an exit option has been included in the treaties.

Values, objectives and competences go to the heart of any political system. They need to be identified clearly if it is to enjoy legitimacy among those bound by it. The Lisbon Treaty is certainly intended to achieve that goal, whatever the peculiarities of its specific origins in the aftermath of the French and Dutch referendum.

The "constitutional" content of the Treaty remains intact and can readily be identified. The referendum campaign necessarily pitches those in favour in opposition to those against the Treaty. It is in several respects an artificial contest, in that it conceals differences of view about the merits of "politicising" the EU, mostly, but not exclusively, on the Yes side of the argument. These arguments will continue whether or not the Treaty is ratified by all Member States. There is plenty to argue about whichever way it goes.

Institutions and Decision-Making
Denis O'Leary

The forms of decision-making developed by the European Union are unique to it as an international organisation. These changes brought about by the Lisbon Treaty confirm existing arrangements in some instances, notably the continued inter-governmental character of the common foreign and security policy, while in other instances anomalies and lacunae are corrected, for example, by the abolition of the system of pillars and the reduction in the number of legal instruments and procedures. The driving political force behind the changes lies in the recognition that rules that worked well for a Union that had grown from six to fifteen members cannot do so for a Union of twenty-seven Member States, a number likely to grow even further.

The Treaty of Lisbon establishes the European Union "on which the Member States confer competences to attain objectives they have in common". The Union replaces and succeeds the European Community. It is founded both on the Treaty on European Union and the Treaty on the Functioning of the European Union, each of which have the same legal value. The new treaty builds on the existing European Union and the treaties that underpin it.

Articles 2 to 6 of the Treaty on the Functioning of the European Union spell out for the first time the "categories and areas of Union competence". This categorisation is a recognition by the Member States of the situation as it stands, the only substantive change being the abolition of the special status of police and judicial cooperation pillar and its inclusion among shared competence under the Area of Freedom, Security and Justice.

The power to implement actions under competences ceded to the Union is subject to democratic representative requirements and a system of checks and balances akin to what would be found in any democratic system, whether unicameral, bicameral or federal. The three institutions, European Parliament, Council of Ministers and Commission, under the overall power of review by the European Court of Justice, each have a role to play.

The Lisbon Treaty changes the institutional structure in a number of important respects, as follows. Firstly, the European Council will become an Institution and will elect its President by qualified majority for a period of 2½ years, renewable once. Secondly, the High Representative of the Union for Foreign Affairs and Security will simultaneously chair the Foreign Affairs Council and be a Vice-President of the Commission. Thirdly, as from 2014, the number of Commissioners will correspond to two-thirds of the Member States chosen "on the basis of a system of strictly equal rotation between the Member States".

There is already widespread recognition that the chairing of the European Council by each succeeding Presidency is unsatisfactory, since the rotating President, as a Head of State or Government, has many other demands on his/her time. The role of the elected President is, in any case, carefully circumscribed.

The "double-hatting" role given to the High Representative is both more substantive and innovative and may prove more problematical, especially in relation to setting up the arrangements for the External Action Service. Again, however, the need for better coordination between all aspects of the conduct of the external action of the Union is already widely recognised.

Fifteen different legal instruments spread across the three pillars are reduced to five: Regulations, Directives, Decisions, Recommendations and Opinions. There is provision for creating a hierarchy of legal norms – distinguishing between legislative and other acts – allowing the Council to delegate certain implementing powers to the Commission.

The current rules setting out the voting arrangements for the Council assign a specific total of weighted votes to each Member State with a threshold set for the establishment of a qualified majority. Each time a new Member State joins, the table of voting weights has to be re-negotiated. This has given rise to major difficulties and diplomatic struggles between Member States, especially the six largest Member States. The negotiations on the Treaty of Lisbon proved no exception.

Agreement was reached that, from November 2014, a qualified majority should be defined "as at least 55% of the members of the Council, comprising at least fifteen of them and representing Member States comprising at least 65% of the population of the Union". A blocking minority must include at least four Council members.

The members of the European Commission, in terms unchanged by the Lisbon Treaty, shall be chosen on the grounds of their general competence and European commitment from persons whose independence is beyond doubt and shall neither seek nor take instructions from any government or other institution, body, office or entity.

However, the Lisbon Treaty changes both the method of appointment of the Commission and its President. As from November 2014, the number of Commissioners will equate to two-thirds of the number of Member States. They are to be chosen on the basis of a system of strict "equal rotation". The European Council will make the necessary decisions by unanimity and may decide to alter the number of Commissioners.

The Treaty makes specific, and extensive, provisions for the role of national parliaments which are set out in a Protocol appended to the Treaties. Under its terms, proposals must be sent by the Commission to them and one-third have the power to object within an eight-week time limit ("yellow card"). If a simple majority continues to object, the Commission must refer the issue to the Council and the Parliament for decision ("orange card").

Furthermore, national parliaments are given a particular role with regard to the Area of Freedom, Security and Justice; they will take part in the revision procedures of the treaties; they are to be notified of applications for accession to the Union and they will take part in inter-parliamentary cooperation between national Parliaments and with the European Parliament. These provisions reinforce the role of national parliaments but, they do not remove from them the existing fundamental requirements of policing the role of national Ministers in the Council and implementing EU legislation when action by national Parliaments is required.

A feature of these changes is their integrated or inter-locking character. They introduce a considerable degree of clarity with regard to the legal instruments that can be used, the procedures to be applied and the role of the institutions in each instance. This avoids needless repetition in individual articles and adds greatly to the ready comprehension of the texts.

The Social Dimension
Tony Brown

The social dimension of the EU has evolved over the years in areas such as equality between men and women, training opportunities and mobility for young workers and labour law, but with important issues remaining the subject of intense political debate across the Union, ranging from the provisions for social protection and workers' rights to measures to combat discrimination and social exclusion.

In the Convention the social dimension became a key issue with the Social Europe Working Group rejecting any artificial division between economic and social objectives and identifying social concerns for inclusion among the Union's values and objectives.

From a social perspective, the Lisbon Treaty builds on the substance and achievements of the previous treaties. It provides a basis for progress towards the stated values and goals of a Social Europe, facilitating increased connection between the Union and its citizens and States but without creating new competences. The Treaty does not endorse a particular economic and social model but rather balances competing options.

Most of the provisions relating to the social dimension of the Union are found in the Treaty on the Functioning of the European Union, yet the social dimension informs the entire text. In particular, the Values and Objectives in the early articles of the Treaty on European Union and the incorporation of the Charter of Fundamental Rights into the treaties and an attached Protocol provide a basis for development of a "Social Europe".

All of the listed Objectives have policy implications and are picked up throughout the text. Of particular significance is the Social Clause – Article 9 of the Treaty on the Functioning of the European Union – which requires the Union in defining and implementing its policies to take account of social concerns linked to employment, adequate social protection, combating social exclusion and achieving high levels of education, training and protection of human health.

The incorporation of the Charter of Fundamental Rights into the Treaty on European Union will give the Union a framework of individual rights covering key economic and social areas. It will ensure that individuals and concerned groups can access effective remedies where the rights and freedoms guaranteed are violated either by the Union's institutions or by Member States implementing EU law. The Treaty also provides authorisation for the EU to accede to the European Convention on Human Rights.

In general, competence is shared between the Union and the Member States in areas of social policy such as employment, living and working conditions, social protection, social dialogue, the development of human resources and the combating of exclusion. Given the sensitivity of some Member States, a combination of QMV and unanimity has been agreed, with unanimity retained in fields such as social security, representation of workers and employment of third country nationals. EU competence does not extend to pay, the right to strike and the right of association. Social policy is an area of activity in which both political and national differences of real substance are obvious.

The Treaty provides that the Union shall give opportunities to citizens and civil society bodies to make known their views on EU action and to maintain open dialogue with representative associations. The Citizens' Initiative establishes that "not less than one million citizens…" may invite the Commission to submit a proposal for EU legislation on a matter they consider should be the subject of a legal act of the Union. There is provision for recognition and promotion of the role of the social partners and of social dialogue, taking into account the diversity of national systems.

The Convention saw a debate on the position of public services. An important article provided a legal basis for regulations establishing and defining the principles and conditions for the provision of public services, "without prejudice to the competence of Member States, in compliance with the Constitution, to provide, to commission and to fund such services". A Protocol on Public Services was added in the latter stages of the IGC to emphasise the importance of such services and containing provisions based on the shared values of the Union.

Questions concerning the relationship between the Common Commercial Policy and Public Services give rise to controversy, in particular in respect of the negotiation of international trade agreements by the European Commission which has done so on behalf of the Member States in GATT/WTO talks since the 1960s. The Common Commercial Policy has since then constituted an exclusive competence of the Union. Council decisions on such negotiating mandates have normally been adopted by QMV but a number of areas are subject to unanimity and the IGC under the Irish Presidency inserted a specific safeguard clause in respect of trade in social, education and health services.

The Social Dimension of the Union is given strong foundations in the Treaty, in particular in terms of its Values and Objectives. The important links between goals and policies are better established than in previous texts. In summary, the concept of a "Social Europe" is clearly defined. However, there remains a real debate on the degree of the Union's ambition in social matters and the European Trade Union Confederation, for example, has called for a broad review of social provisions once the Treaty is ratified to ensure continuing development of policies to help workers and citizens generally to handle change. This may well become a campaign issue across the Member States in the 2009 elections to the European Parliament.

External Action of the Union
Patrick Keatinge

With regard to how the European Union relates to the rest of the world, the Lisbon Treaty does not introduce major new policies. It codifies existing policies, sometimes in a more detailed way and with amendments on specific points. However, this is accompanied by a change in structure which represents one of the Treaty's major innovations – the post of High Representative of the Union for Foreign Affairs and Security Policy. The emphasis is thus not so much on what the EU does in the world as on how its external policies may best be decided and delivered.

All of the varied aspects of the EU's international role, now summarised as "external action", rest on a statement of general principles contained in Article 21 of the Treaty on European Union. That reflects the ideal of an international order resting on the rule of law and peaceful relations between independent states cooperating in multilateral organisations, with particular reference to the United Nations. It promotes human rights, economic integration, sustainable development and concern for the environment.

Much of the content of external action is contained in Part Five of the amended Treaty on the Functioning of the European Union. The first major element is the Common Commercial Policy – in effect the outward face of the internal market. Its provisions are typical of the traditional community approach. Trade is an exclusive competence of the Union, negotiations are conducted by the Commission on the basis of a Council Mandate and QMV is normally used in decision making. However, continuity with previous treaties is not total. The European Parliament has an enhanced co-decision role, and Article 207.4 lists specific fields of trade where unanimous agreement by Member States is required. Furthermore, Article 215 authorises economic sanctions, in the context of decisions made under the Common Foreign and Security Policy.

As is the case with trade policy, the Treaty text on Development Policy covers a long standing and in world terms significant policy programme and provides that policy shall be conducted within the framework of the principles and objectives of the Union's external action. Union policy will have the primary objective of the reduction and, in the long term, the eradication of poverty. The EU and its Member States must comply with commitments made in the context of the United Nations.

The emphasis on the eradication of poverty reflects the Union's overall values and objectives. The Treaty includes for the first time a commitment under the heading of humanitarian aid to provide ad hoc assistance for victims of man-made or natural disasters including the establishment of a European Voluntary Humanitarian Aid Corps.

The final article in this part of the Treaty is the solidarity clause, largely inspired by the large scale terrorist attacks in Madrid in 2004. This provides for a joint response by the Union and its Member States in the event of a terrorist attack or a natural or man-made disaster. While the text refers to the Union mobilising "all the instruments at its disposal, including the military resources made available by the Member States", the obligations are framed in such a way as to give them discretion as to what sort of assistance they actually provide. In particular, military assistance comes under the unanimity rule and the action envisaged is restricted to the territory of the Member States.

The remaining elements of external action are found in Title V of the revised Treaty on European Union including specific provisions for the Common Foreign and Security Policy which maintains the present pattern of structures and procedures. The system of intergovernmental policy making, under unanimity, are not significantly altered.

However, there is a potentially important change in the institutional structure of the CFSP in the new post of High Representative of the Union for Foreign and Security Policy. In effect, this is an extension of role of the High Representative for the Common Foreign and Security Policy, authorised by the Treaty of Amsterdam in 1997 and held today by Dr Javier Solana. The new element in the Lisbon Treaty lies in what is often referred to as "double-hatting". Up to now the High Representative has operated as an agent of the Council on CFSP matters while external relations has been the responsibility of a designated member of the Commission. Now, however, these two posts become one and the same individual has a key position in the Foreign Affairs Council and is a Vice-President in the Commission.

The High Representative is appointed by the European Council by QMV, subject to the agreement of the President of the Commission. He or she "conducts" the Union's foreign and security policy: making proposals to the foreign ministers, chairing the meetings of the Foreign Affairs Council; implementing their agreed policies; in effect operating as the Union's "chief diplomat". In the Commission, the High Representative is responsible for the external relations portfolio and for ensuring consistency in EU external action.

The Lisbon Treaty gives a fuller picture of "security and defence" than previous treaties, contained in Section 2, Chapter 2 of Title V of the amended Treaty on the European Union. Article 42.1 provides an overview of what is described as "an integral part of the common foreign and security policy". Much of this reflects existing practice, but since it is the first time some of it appears in a Treaty it merits further attention.

Both Article 24.1 and Article 42.2 contain an aspiration to a "common defence" that is generally understood to imply a mutual defence clause similar to that of a military alliance like NATO. Though there is a variation in the way this is expressed, the aspiration can only be realised by a unanimous decision of the Member States. Even where Article 42.7 spells such a commitment out more explicitly, it is qualified in such a way as to remain in aspirational form. The key phrase attached to all three articles is that this "shall not prejudice the specific character of the security and defence policy of certain (*neutral or non-aligned*) Member

States" and "shall respect" (i.e. defer to) the mutual defence obligations other Member States have in the context of the NATO alliance. This formula, first seen in the Maastricht Treaty of 1992, has not changed.

Article 20.9 of *Bunreacht na hÉireann* – inserted by the terms of the amendment approved in the second referendum on the Nice Treaty and replicated in the Bill published by the Government as the basis for the referendum on the Lisbon Treaty – provides that the state "shall not adopt a decision taken by the European Council to establish a common defence ... where that common defence would include the State". Thus it is firmly established that should a situation arise in future where it was proposed to establish a common defence it would not involve this country unless it was approved by the Irish people in a referendum.

The purpose of the security and defence policy – "peace-keeping, conflict prevention and strengthening international security in accordance with the principles of the United Nations Charter" – is spelled out more fully in Article 43.1. This reflects the increased complexity of international crisis management as experienced since the scope of crisis management was described in the so-called "Petersberg tasks" in the Maastricht Treaty in 1992.

Since the European Union started to take its security and defence policy more seriously in 1999 there has been an emphasis on ensuring it has the necessary means, in terms of both civilian and military capabilities. Article 42.3 says that Member States "shall make civilian and military capabilities available to the Union", but there is no stated level of contribution and no way in which the Union can enforce sanctions against what might be perceived as a recalcitrant Member State; Member States decide their own contributions.

The critical decision to be made in the security and defence context is whether to deploy a mission in any specific case. Here the Lisbon Treaty makes no change to the existing rule of unanimity, which is emphasised as absolute for decisions with military implications (Article 48.7). Nor is there any change to the Member

State's right to decide whether or not to participate in a particular mission. In Ireland's case this national decision is circumscribed by the "triple lock" provision, formally appended to the Treaty of Nice in the "Seville Declarations", negotiated by the Government and agreed by the other Member States in the context of the second referendum campaign. This requires that any deployment of national forces outside the state must be under UN authorisation, formally approved by the government and endorsed by the Dáil.

The common security and defence provisions in the Lisbon Treaty have been agreed not only on the basis of commitments formulated in previous treaties, but also in the context of the actual operation of EU missions since the beginning of 2003 when the European Union deployed its first missions under the European Security and Defence Policy, a police task force in Bosnia and a military force in the Former Yugoslav Republic of Macedonia. Since then, 21 have been agreed, forming part of the EU's response to a wide variety of demands for peacekeeping and humanitarian assistance in areas of conflict in Europe, Africa and Asia. A striking feature is the greater number of civilian rather than military missions: 15 to 6.

In some cases these operations are on a small scale, involving perhaps just a dozen personnel from EU Member States helping in the reform of police, judicial or administrative systems. In all cases the policy framework is designed to balance civilian and military contributions, and to place them in the broader diplomatic context, involving the United Nations or other regional organisations.

The military missions are usually on a larger scale, being faced with the difficult task of providing political stabilisation. Two operations have taken place in the Balkans – Concordia (Former Yugoslav Republic of Macedonia) and Althea (Bosnia), the latter still in place at a force strength of 2,500. In Africa, Operation Artemis in 2003 consisted of a force of about 2,000 troops sent to the Democratic Republic of the Congo at the behest of the United Nations, pending the much delayed deployment of an agreed UN force.

The Lisbon Treaty makes changes to the way in which the European Union relates to the rest of the world. All of these changes are evolutionary in character. They are pragmatic extensions of the legal base agreed in previous treaties, and do not alter the fact that the Union does not replace the Member States in the international sphere, but rather works with them. This complex arrangement has no historical precedent or parallel in the contemporary world, and for that reason it is often difficult to grasp what changes to a legal text like the Lisbon Treaty really mean. Putting them in the much broader context of a changing world may give us a better perspective to assess their significance.

Area of Freedom, Security and Justice
John Handoll

In the area of freedom, security and justice, the Lisbon Treaty is at the same time innovative and rather conservative, giving Member States concerned about the encroachment of Union powers a level of protection not seen in many other areas of Union activity. Ireland continues to be able to strike the balance it desires between engagement and non-participation in areas threatening the Common Travel Area and its common law tradition particularly in the area of criminal law.

A key achievement of the new Treaty is the abolition of the two-pillar structure for freedom, security and justice. A new Title in the TFEU contains a number of general and specific provisions on (a) policies on border checks, asylum and immigration; (b) judicial cooperation in civil matters; (c) judicial cooperation in criminal matters; and (d) police cooperation.

In some respects, the treaty provisions have simply "caught up" with policy changes since the launch of the 1999 Tampere programme, reflecting the evolving nature of the freedom, security and justice agenda since the signing of the Amsterdam Treaty. This is the case, for example, for immigration and asylum policy.

In other respects, the new provisions are innovative. The criminal justice provisions are broader than before and the increased use of the co-decision procedure should strengthen democratic accountability and reduce blockages. However, in relation to judicial cooperation in criminal matters in particular, there are a number of areas where extension of Union activity to new areas will require not only unanimity in the Council but also the assent of the European Parliament.

Although still constrained in some respects, the Court of Justice will have greater powers of judicial review. This change, welcomed by the Irish Government, augurs well for the observance of the rule of law, and the application of fundamental rights law. At the same time, national sensitivities are taken into account and traces of the intergovernmental approach remain. The frontiers of Union and Member State competence have been better delineated in order to protect areas of retained national power. In relation to judicial cooperation in civil and criminal matters, the central principle of mutual recognition is designed to reassure Member States that their individual legal systems will be respected.

In especially sensitive areas, such as family law, the Council will be the sole legislator acting by unanimity, thus retaining the national veto. In some criminal justice areas, a Member State concerned about the consequences of the ordinary legislative procedure can apply an "emergency brake" by referring the matter to the European Council. If a consensus cannot be achieved, a body of at least nine Member States can then decide to establish enhanced cooperation (referred to colloquially as the "accelerator clause").

Ireland, together with the UK, will continue its policy of semi-detachment from all of the Title V areas. The existing "out/opt-in" protocol will continue in expanded form, as will the Schengen and internal market protocols. However, provided that the key concerns of protecting the Common Travel Area and the Irish legal system (especially in relation to criminal justice) are addressed, the present Government policy is one of constructive engagement.

The existing Protocol on the position of the UK and Ireland, which excludes these two Member States from participating in the adoption of Community measures in relation to visas, asylum and other policies related to free movement of persons until either of them "opts-in" to specific measures has been amended and will now apply to the whole of Title V, including former third pillar areas of judicial cooperation in criminal matters and police cooperation.

The rationale for the exclusion varies between areas of activity. In relation to immigration and asylum, the principal reason is the desire to protect the Common Travel Area. In relation to the area of judicial and police cooperation, Ireland and the UK share concerns about respect for the core elements of their shared common law tradition.

However, the Irish Government has declared that it will participate to the maximum extent it deems possible and that it will, in particular, opt into police cooperation measures. It will review the operation of these arrangement within three years of the Lisbon Treaty's entry into force.

Article 67.2 of the Treaty on the Functioning of the European Union provides that the Union "shall ensure the absence of internal border controls for persons and shall frame a common policy on asylum, immigration and external border control, based on solidarity between Member States, which is fair towards third-country nationals". The Treaty references to a common policy, solidarity and fairness formalises the framework agreed by the European Council at Tampere in 1999.

There is a new provision that the policies of the Union and their implementation are to be governed by the principle of solidarity and fair sharing of responsibility, including its financial implications, between Member States.

In relation to border checks, the Union is to develop a policy: (a) to ensure the absence of internal border controls; (b) to carry out checks on persons crossing, and efficient monitoring of, external borders; and (c) to gradually introduce an integrated management system for external borders. Under the out/opt-in Protocol Ireland will be able to impose frontier controls for as long as the Common Travel Arrangements are maintained.

In relation to asylum, Article 78 provides a clearer legal basis for the developing common policy on asylum, subsidiary protection and temporary protection applying to third-country nationals (and stateless persons). In relation to immigration, there is provision for the development of a common immigration policy "aimed at ensuring, at all stages, the efficient management of migration flows, fair treatment of third-country nationals residing legally in Member States, and the prevention of, and enhanced measures to combat, illegal immigration and trafficking in human beings".

EU powers in relation to the integration of legally-resident third-country nationals are also addressed in a new provision for incentives and support for Member State action. That migrant integration policy is an essentially national preserve is seen in the express exclusion from such measures of any harmonisation of laws and regulations.

The Treaty requires the Union to "develop judicial cooperation in civil matters having cross-border implications, based on the principle of mutual recognition of judgments and of decisions in extrajudicial cases". The overarching principle of mutual recognition is new and is designed to reassure Member States that their individual civil law systems will be respected. However, there is now an explicit recognition that, where there are "cross-border implications", approximation measures may be adopted.

Provisions on judicial cooperation in criminal matters are covered by the shift to a single Treaty framework. The new criminal justice framework contains important protection even for those Member States committed to the common project. Ireland can, of course, choose to stay outside, with the "out/opt-in" Protocol extended to cover this area. As an overarching principle, ensuring respect for national criminal law systems, judicial cooperation in criminal matters shall be based on the principle of mutual recognition.

Directives may set minimum rules to facilitate mutual recognition and judicial cooperation in criminal matters having a cross-border dimension. Such rules shall take account of the different legal traditions and systems of the Member States. There may be approximation of national laws and regulations in areas such as: mutual admissibility of evidence; the rights of individuals in criminal procedure; and, the rights of victims.

Directives may also set minimum rules on the definition of criminal offences and sanctions in areas of particularly serious cross-border crime such as terrorism, human trafficking, sexual exploitation of women and children, illicit drug and arms trafficking, money laundering, and corruption.

Measures are envisaged to promote and support Member State action in the field of crime prevention. Any harmonisation of national laws and regulations is excluded.

Although police cooperation is covered by the "out/opt-in" Protocol, it should be noted that Ireland has declared that it will participate, "to the maximum extent possible", in measures in this area. This reflects its current position and the future debate will doubtless centre on the limits of the possible. Article 87.1 requires the Union to "establish police cooperation involving all the Member States' competent authorities, including police, customs and other specialised law enforcement services in relation to the prevention, detection and investigation of crime".

A number of specific areas of action are identified, ranging from analysis and exchange of information to measures concerning operational cooperation between the national authorities. Regulations will determine the structure and operation of Europol and the coordination and implementation of actions carried out jointly with the Member States or in liaison with Eurojust.

Key Policies: Energy and Environment
Joseph Curtin

Although climate change is a relatively new policy challenge, and despite the fact that it is not mentioned in the present European Union or European Community Treaties, it has become a key policy area for the EU. This may be because the climate change problem is global in nature and necessitates structured cooperation between sovereign states to overcome blockages which can stymie efforts to address the challenge. With its global role and experienced in cultivating cooperation between Member States and with an established institutional framework to develop policy, the EU is well equipped to deal with problems both between individual Member States and on the international stage.

While the EU is responsible for only 10% of global emissions, it has become the global leader on climate change through ground breaking emission reduction commitments, first agreed by the European Council in March 2007, and followed up by the Commission package of implementation proposals, published in January, 2008. These proposals, if agreed, would not only necessitate radical restructuring of Member States' economies but would also profoundly influence the direction of international negotiations on a successor agreement to the Kyoto Protocol, expected in Copenhagen in December 2009.

For these reasons, it is valid to ask whether the Lisbon Treaty will affect or alter the way climate change policy is conceived, decided upon, or implemented in the EU? If so, what are the implications for EU Member States and the international climate change regime? In order to address these issues, it is useful to divide climate change policy making into two separate categories – internal and external policy-making – and assess the implications for these areas in turn.

Directives and regulations relating to climate change policy-making fall under the environment chapter of the present EC Treaty

(Arts 174-176). In general, qualified majority voting in the Council and the co-decision procedure is used for the adoption of legislative acts with the European Parliament playing a co-equal role in legislation with national governments. However, several exceptions to the use of qualified majority voting exist, meaning that decisions taken in these areas must be taken unanimously. Proposals with fiscal implications require unanimity – a proposal on an EU-wide carbon tax in 1992 failed to garner the unanimous support it required. Agreement is needed by a high proportion of participants across the institutions for climate change policy to be adopted.

In the areas of climate change policy where the EU has a role, the Directorate General (DG) Environment of the European Commission is responsible for drafting legislation, with its Climate Change and Air Directorate given the lead. In several areas with implications for climate change, such as education and awareness, policy oversight and coordination, planning, transport and infrastructural development, competences remain largely in the hands of Member States and the Commission's role is marginal.

Overall, though the Lisbon Treaty includes a number of significant revisions it is not anticipated that they will radically alter the way that the EU designs, decides on or implements internal climate change policy. Several aspects of the new Energy Title XXI could have indirect implications for EU climate change policy. Article 194.1 of the Treaty on the Functioning of the European Union, which refers to the establishment of an internal market for energy, points to "the need to preserve and improve the environment" and goes on to commit Union policy to "promote energy efficiency and energy savings and the promotion of new and renewable forms of technology". These articles offer a clear legal basis outside the political agreements at European Councils for policies consistent with the achievement of these objectives.

The EU Energy Efficiency Action Plan, agreed in November 2006, requires of Member States the production of National Energy Efficiency Action Plans to set out how 20% energy efficiency savings are to be achieved by 2020 (Ireland's consultation was launched in October 2007). However, unlike the case with renewables, no legally binding agreements have been or will be entered into by Member States. The Treaty basis for policy might prove significant were the political climate to change and the determination to tackle climate change to recede.

International environmental policy-making is described as an area of "mixed competences". This means that individual Member States have competences to negotiate in international bodies and to conclude international agreements. Positions adopted prior to UN Framework Convention on Climate Change negotiations must therefore be based on consensus. Positions are prepared by a working party on International Environmental Issues (IEI) and the Council of Environment Ministers or the European Council – if necessary – adopts final positions. The Council Presidency has responsibility for drafting EU positions and representing the EU at negotiations. Given the requirement for consensus, the Presidency plays an important role in coordinating positions during negotiations.

The Lisbon Treaty contains provisions which may influence external EU climate change policy making. Article 191.1 commits the EU to: "promoting measures at international level to deal with regional or worldwide environmental problems, *and in particular combating climate change*". For the first time combating climate change is explicitly stated as an EU Treaty objective. Although this reference to combating climate change is limited to the international level, it is possible that a proactive ECJ could take a maximalist approach and use this Article to challenge other EU laws. The Commission could also use this reference to challenge Member States' policy that is incompatible with "combating climate change".

Article 218 outlines how international negotiations would be undertaken and has implications for how the EU would approach international climate change negotiation. It states that: "The Council shall authorise the opening of negotiations, adopt negotiating directives, authorise the signing of agreements and conclude them", and "the Commission.....shall submit recommendations to the Council, which shall adopt a decision authorising the opening of negotiations and, depending on the subject of the agreement envisaged, nominating the Union negotiator or head of the Union's negotiating team". The nominee would replace the Presidency as the lead EU negotiator at climate change negotiations. It would be the Union negotiator who would propose an agreement to the Council for decision.

Although the words "climate change" only appear in the Treaty of Lisbon on one occasion, there are several areas which might influence how internal and external climate change policy is made in the EU. The new Energy Title, XXI, though for the most part a formalisation of policies that the EU had taken on under its internal market and environmental competences, nevertheless solidifies and strengthens the direction the EU has taken. Promotion of renewables and energy efficiency in particular are established in the Treaties for the first time. For international negotiations, the Commission may play an increasing visible role, with the ECJ ensuring outcomes compatible with Art. 191.1.

Key Policies: Economic Governance
David Croughan

Most of the key policy issues relating to economic governance, sectoral and social policies are contained in Part 3 of the Treaty on the Functioning of the European Union which concerns Union Policies and Internal Actions. There are only a small number of changes of substance relating to economic governance contained in the Treaty.

The Treaty on European Union redefines and mainly restates the objectives of the Internal Market: sustainable development; balanced economic growth; price stability; a competitive social market economy; the aim of full employment and social progress; protection and improvement of the quality of the environment.

A reference to "free and undistorted competition" contained in the Constitutional Treaty was deleted, raising some concerns that competition policy might be diluted but, in mitigation of these concerns, the Protocol on the Internal Market and Competition mentions a "system ensuring that competition is not distorted".

Changes to economic governance are limited, given the sensitivity of Member States on their right to run their own economic affairs and many of the amendments apply only to those Member States that have adopted the euro, where there is a modest strengthening of the rules of governance.

The Treaty restates the obligation of Member States to regard their economic policies as a matter of common concern and maintains the power of the Council to formulate and adopt broad economic policy guidelines for the Member States. The Commission is given a new power to address a warning to a Member State which pursues policies inconsistent with the guidelines.

The terms of the Stability and Growth Pact are restated. If a Member State does not fulfil the requirements, the Commission may prepare a report if it is of the opinion that there is a risk of an excessive deficit. The Commission is given a new power to address an opinion to the Member State and to inform the Council. If effective action is not taken the Council can decide to apply the sanctions that already existed in the treaties.

In a new provision the Treaty recognises the informal Euro Group of Finance ministers, enhancing its standing by recognising the desirability of ever closer coordination of economic policies within the Eurozone A significant rewriting of the articles relating to those Member States which are on the way to membership of the Eurozone was required following the 2004 enlargement. At least once every two years the Council will receive a report on progress of such Member States in fulfilling their obligations.

On Social Policy the European Parliament gains some enhanced powers and a new article recognises and promotes the role of the social partners, facilitating dialogue.

The European Parliament and the Council may adopt measures

designed to encourage co-operation in social fields but excluding any harmonisation of the laws and regulations of the Member States.

The Union and Member States must promote the competitiveness of industry with actions to speed up structural change, fostering initiative and the exploitation of innovation, research and technological development. Member States shall coordinate their action through the application of the Open Method of Co-ordination which is characteristic of the Lisbon Strategy.

Nowhere in the treaties, including the Treaty of Lisbon, is there mention of direct taxation and in particular corporation tax. This means that matters relating to direct taxation remain, as they always have remained, within the exclusive competence of each Member State. The European Union can do nothing to compel a change in Irish domestic policy on corporation taxation. This is confirmed in the Treaty of Lisbon which secures the power of the Irish State to set its own corporate tax rate for the foreseeable future. A further treaty revision would be required to alter this position which would undoubtedly require approval of the electorate in a referendum.

The Common Commercial Policy remains an exclusive competence of the Union. The Treaty, in Article 207 brings Foreign Direct Investment (FDI) within the Common Commercial Policy. This change was introduced in the Convention text "in recognition of the fact that financial flows supplement trade in goods and today represent a significant share of commercial exchanges." The Commission requested the change to provide a basis for negotiations on a multilateral investment treaty in the WTO in the longterm as there is no prospect of such a treaty emerging from the present Doha Round.

The Council will continue to act by QMV in most areas but it will act unanimously in the fields of trade in services, the commercial aspects of Intellectual Property and Foreign Direct Investment. The Council shall also act unanimously in the field of cultural and audiovisual services, where agreements risk prejudicing the Union's cultural and linguistic diversity, and in the fields of trade in social, education and health services where agreements risk seriously disturbing the national organisation of such services and prejudicing the responsibility of Member States to deliver them. It is provided that the exercise of the competences conferred by the article in the field of the Common Commercial Policy shall not affect the delimitation of competences between the Union and the Member States, and shall not lead to harmonisation of legislative or regulatory provisions of the Member States.

Enlargement and Europe's Neighbours
Andy O'Rourke

The Lisbon Treaty does not change the existing provision that membership of the Union shall be open to all European States which respect its values and are committed to promoting them. However, the incorporation of the Charter of Fundamental Rights, the accession of the Union to the European Convention on Human Rights and the expansion of the statement of EU values reinforce the obligations of candidate countries to respect the values of the Union.

The bar for acceptance into the Union has thus been raised, in particular by the inclusion of references to minority rights and to equality between men and women which create additional conditions to be met by future new members. Otherwise, the current membership negotiations with Croatia and Turkey will be unaffected by the Lisbon Treaty and will continue on the basis of existing mandates.

The institutional changes made in the Treaty of Nice were essential to allow the enlargement of the Union to proceed in 2004. Subsequent discussion on the future of the Union revealed a consensus that further institutional change was necessary in order to ensure the greater effectiveness of a Union of twenty-seven and more members in dealing with new policy areas and new world-wide challenges.

The amendments contained in the Lisbon Treaty should remove for the foreseeable future any concerns that inadequate structures might be a barrier to the pursuit of the Union's enlargement policy. This policy has been of major importance in expanding an area of peace and prosperity across Europe, in consolidating democracy and in strengthening the transition of the former communist states.

The present enlargement policy of the Union does not extend beyond the countries negotiating for membership and the states of the Western Balkans where the prospect of closer integration provides support for political and economic reforms. These are vital for the long-term stability of that region.

The necessary strengthening of relations with countries in the neighbourhood of the enlarged Union will be enhanced by the changes introduced in the Lisbon Treaty and intended to provide increased coherence for EU action at the international level.

Final Provisions
Gavin Barrett

Some of the most important stipulations of the foundational treaties of the European Union are to be found in their so-called final provisions. This chapter examines briefly the most significant changes which the Treaty of Lisbon effects to these provisions.

The new Art. 47 of the Treaty on European Union provides simply that "the Union shall have legal personality". This is a significant, but not revolutionary step. The Treaty on European Union has in any case for long implicitly conferred legal personality on the European Union. An international organisation can only conclude international agreements if it has legal personality and the existing Treaty on European Union confers power on the Union to conclude international agreements in the fields of common foreign and security policy and police and judicial cooperation in criminal matters.

The Treaty of Lisbon alters the procedures for amending the constitutive Treaties, which are at present set out in Art. 48 of the Treaty on European Union. Under Art. 48 in its present form, an intergovernmental conference is convened for the purpose of determining by common accord amendments to be made to the treaties. The amendments then enter into force after being ratified by all the Member States in accordance with their respective constitutional requirements. In practice, implementing these procedures is a lengthy, drawn-out process, too cumbersome to be used every time a technical provision in the treaties needs to be amended and otherwise lacking both transparency and sufficient democratic input and control.

The amendment procedure set out in a new Art. 48 seeks to address such difficulties. It will replace the old single-lane road for treaty change with a four-track procedure for treaty amendment. There will be an "ordinary revision procedure" – which is to be the main procedure for amending the Treaty. And there will be three separate "simplified revision procedures", each of them constituting an effort to provide an accelerated procedure for technical amendments.

The proposed ordinary revision procedure is an enhanced and extended form of the existing Art. 48 procedure. Under it, the process of revision of the Treaties will take place in four steps: submission of proposals for amendment; European Council decision to proceed by convening a representative Convention; convening a conference of representatives of the governments (IGC) for the purpose of determining by common accord the amendments to be made; ratification by all the Member States in accordance with their respective constitutional requirements.

The first simplified revision procedure will apply only to Part Three of the Treaty on the Functioning of the European Union dealing with Union policies and internal actions. When proposals are made for revising all or part of the provisions of Part Three the European Council – acting by unanimity after consulting the European Parliament, the Commission, and the European Central

41

Bank in the case of institutional changes in the monetary area – will be able to adopt a decision amending all or part of the relevant provisions. This decision will not enter into force until it is approved by the Member States in accordance with their respective constitutional requirements.

Two further simplified revision procedures are laid down by the new Art. 48.7. These procedures, sometimes referred to as general *passerelle* clauses, constitute a route whereby a decision-making procedure stipulated in the Treaties can be switched from unanimity to qualified majority voting or co-decision without going through the ordinary process of Treaty amendment. But, to do so, a unanimous decision by the European Council will be required. The European Parliament is given a power of veto over deployment of these simplified procedures. Any initiative to switch to qualified majority voting or co-decision, as the case may be, is required to be notified to the national parliaments. If any national parliament makes known its opposition within six months of the date of such notification, the decision shall not be adopted thereby giving it a veto. This provision may not be used in relation to decisions with military or defence implications.

The third simplified revision procedure will apply where legislative acts are adopted by the so-called "special legislative procedure", involving the final decision being taken by the Council of Ministers. Art. 48.7 provides that, where this is the case, the European Council may adopt a decision allowing for the adoption of such acts in accordance with the so-called "ordinary legislative procedure" involving co-decision by the Council and the European Parliament. This continues the trend towards co-decision which has prevailed since its introduction by the Treaty of Maastricht and which is regarded as the most democratically acceptable means of lawmaking.

One of the most significant changes is found in the new Art. 50, providing simply that "any Member State may decide to withdraw from the Union in accordance with its own constitutional requirements". The five sections of the article deal with the modalities of such a withdrawal – in essence, what one might call the divorce procedures – in the event of this article ever being invoked by a Member State. What this says about the nature of the European Union should not be underestimated. It has been argued that this right clarifies a basic issue: that the Union is a voluntary association between states which remain sovereign as to the question of whether or not they remain in as members.

The European Court of Justice has played a key role in shaping the nature of the European Community legal order. The Court has been important in terms of regulating relationships between member states. But it has also been important in terms of the protection of the individual under Community law.

The existing Art. 46 of the Treaty on European Union is to be deleted when the Treaty of Lisbon comes into force. The most significant effect of the deletion will be that (subject to one exception) the entire area of justice and home affairs will finally be brought under the jurisdiction of the Court of Justice – a step which seems an appropriate, welcome and long overdue increase in the protection of individual rights.

The Treaty of Lisbon also effects a number of amendments to the General and Final Provisions of the Treaty Establishing the European Community, the most important of which is the generalisation to Union level of the so-called "flexibility clause".

The Treaty of Rome itself, in Article 235, provided that, if action should prove necessary to attain one of the objectives of the Community and the Treaty had not provided the necessary powers, the Council, acting unanimously, could take the appropriate measures. This provision – currently included in Article 308 of the Treaty establishing the European Community – has been a useful instrument in the Community's legislative toolbox but, because of the scope it could give for circumventing treaty restrictions of Community action, it has been subjected to considerable restrictions, notably that it cannot be used to amend the Treaty without following the appropriate procedures.

Under the Treaty of Lisbon, Art. 308 is to be replaced by the new four-paragraph Article 352 which extends the Article to the Union generally and sets out the restrictions to the deployment of the "flexibility clause" which go beyond those which have applied to date.

The article will apply where action by the Union is necessary to attain one of the objectives set out in the treaties. Such action must take place "within the framework of the policies defined in the treaties". A major change is the requirement to obtain the consent of the European Parliament which increases the level of democratic control on the deployment of the "flexibility clause" and provides an additional hurdle to be overcome should use be made of it. The new Article expressly requires the Commission to draw national parliaments' attention to such proposals using the subsidiarity-monitoring procedure.

Europe After Lisbon
Tony Brown

The European Council meeting in December 2007 concluded that "the Lisbon Treaty provides the Union with a stable and lasting institutional framework. We expect no change in the foreseeable future so that the Union will be able to fully concentrate on addressing the concrete challenges ahead, including globalisation and climate change...."

The current agenda of the Union covers many issues of real urgency among which may be listed the institutional efficiency and effectiveness of the EU; subsidiarity and the role of national parliaments; policies to cope with globalisation; energy and the environment; enlargement; justice and home affairs; the rule of law and human rights; social solidarity; foreign policy and security; the democratic deficit, accountability and transparency.

The Treaty provisions for institutional reform and restructuring present challenges to the efficiency and effectiveness of the EU. Each of the institutions will find it necessary to adapt to significant changes: the permanent President of the European Council; the High Representative for Foreign Policy; the new regime for the Council of Ministers; reduction of the size of the Commission and the new status of the Commission President. Issues also arise in respect of voting arrangements and the extension of the co-decision system. The European Parliament has gained in terms of power and influence and must arrange its business to live up to this added responsibility. Provisions on subsidiarity will challenge the political systems in Brussels and the national capitals.

Globalisation is a dominant issue and the Lisbon Treaty is seen to improve consistency in internal and external policies. Priority must be given to economic development, growth and job creation to meet widespead perceptions of economic and social insecurity in a globalised economy.

The sheer scale of the issues arising at global level in relation to Environment and Energy is fully recognised. The EU response is an integrated Energy and Climate Change policy. Internationally, the EU has led the way on the Kyoto Protocol and now seeks to increase global co-operation on the key issues.

Enlargement has been the EU's greatest historic achievement as it has spread stability, security, prosperity and democracy across most of the continent. The most recent expansion has been highly successful but with continuing challenges. It has been decided to open accession talks with Turkey and Croatia, and Macedonia has been given candidate status. While Croatia is likely to become the 28th Member State, the position of Turkey remains highly controversial with no clear indication of the outcome.

Current debate on enlargement is centred on so-called absorption capacity of the EU. However, commitments to the states of the Western Balkans on future EU membership are critical for the stability of that region. Expansion to 27 Member States gives rise to issues of security and of longer-term relationships with new neighbours such as Ukraine and the Caucasus states. Relations with Russia are increasingly significant.

The Justice and Home Affairs area has an agenda of real concern to citizens – human rights, police and judicial co-operation, anti-terrorism policy, external border control, asylum policy, common migration policy and efforts to combat international crime and trafficking. Policy directly reflects the fundamental values set out in the existing treaties and re-emphasised in the Lisbon Treaty. The Tampere and Hague programmes set out a comprehensive programme of joint measures. For Ireland, the implementation of the opt-out/opt-in provisions set out in a Protocol to the Treaty will require sensitive responses to what is likely to be a rapidly evolving EU system.

The Lisbon Agenda brings together key policy concerns: building a knowledge economy, sustainable development, social cohesion and environmental protection. Emphasis is placed on the need for enhanced training and up-skilling provisions and for greater investment in the fields of R&D and innovation. Social cohesion and inclusion policies are important aspects of the Lisbon Agenda. Targeted policy initiatives such as the 2010 European Year for Combating Poverty will be of importance.

The intensity of debate on the nature and future of the European Social Model has been heightened by the recent controversies over the Services Directive and the Laval and Irish Ferries cases. The issue of the competences of the Union and the individual Member States in the social field, which was debated but not finally resolved by the Convention, remains contended. The intense debate in the European Parliament on the Services Directive engaged public opinion and may be a model in the period ahead.

In the fields of foreign, security and defence policy the provisions of the Treaty are of relevance, including the new position of High Representative. The EU is playing an important role in international diplomacy, maintaining peace and security in sensitive areas where relations with the UN are crucial. Among the many issues of current concern are EU-US relations, the Middle East, assisting Africa in the search for answers to its great problems and ensuring that Human Rights remain a clear focus of policy.

The role of the EU in Development Co-operation remains a

priority, emphasising both effectiveness and capacity for co-ordinated response to humanitarian crises. The Lisbon Treaty contains important commitments, notably to the eradication of poverty. It also includes a chapter on Humanitarian Aid. The implementation of these commitments will require clarity and openness in management and co-ordination. The insistence on the need for consistency between key policies is significance and the overall provisions add up to a benchmark for monitoring both policy and performance.

The so-called democratic deficit exists fundamentally at home, in the national political and media systems. Irish political debate is slow to mainstream EU matters while decrying "Brussels" remains a mainstay of political discourse. And, there are serious questions about the role of the media in covering EU matters. The key lies in the areas of education, information and media, requiring the availability of authoritative material as an input to debate. The National Forum on Europe is doing much to close this gap.

The European Union has been through a period of frustration and introspection just as the world environment experienced change at an unparalleled pace and intensity. The agreement on the Lisbon Treaty holds out the hope of a lengthy period without the distraction of institutional wrangling. Attention can be devoted to the day-to-day concerns of Europe's citizens and neighbours. But, there is still a need to find space for reflection on fundamentals. The decision to establish a Reflection Group on Europe's Horizon 2020-2030 shows that there is a recognition of the challenges ahead.

Implications for Ireland
Brendan Halligan

The preamble to the Treaty of Lisbon explains that its express purpose is to enhance the efficiency and democratic legitimacy of the Union and to improve the coherence of its action. If adopted, it would complete the process of reforms initiated by the Single

European Act (1987) and continued by the treaties of Maastricht (1992), Amsterdam (1997) and Nice (2001) in response to new global economic challenges and the imperative of admitting central European states into membership. The Lisbon Treaty is intended to bring this process of reform to an end, at least for a generation according to the Heads of State and Government in their joint statement in December 2007 having agreed the final text.

This particular Treaty has the great merit of combining all existing treaties and the amendments agreed by the 2007 Intergovernmental Conference into two complementary treaties, which are to be of equal value. The result is a more simplified structure in that, for example, the confusing division between the European Community and European Union is to be ended.

In broad terms, the first treaty deals with how the Member States have decided to pool sovereignty with each other, by defining the competences they wish to confer on the Union and those they wish to retain for themselves while the second treaty sets out the policies which the Member States will pursue in common and indicates how they will arrive at decisions.

There are good reasons for believing that the reform of the common institutions has, indeed, come to a natural end. No further change in their composition or role is contemplated. That being the case, a consolidation phase is about to begin as it is generally conceded that a respite from institution building is urgently needed. The Lisbon Treaty is intended to give the Member States and their Union the necessary breathing space to accomplish tasks which are well recognized. Whether it has succeeded in this ambition is the central focus of the analysis following, with particular emphasis on the implications for Ireland.

This analysis follows the logic of the Laeken Declaration which sets out the agenda for the final phase of the reform process and was assigned to the Convention which produced the Constitutional Treaty. By force of circumstances these same tasks were bequeathed to the Intergovernmental Conference convened in the wake of the Constitution's rejection; the Lisbon Treaty is the outcome.

The reference points for the following analysis are democracy and legitimacy, structural simplicity, transparency and efficiency. The implications for Ireland will be assessed in this broad framework, and so too the implications for the Union as a whole. The underlying assumption is that a functioning and successful Union is inherently good for all Member States and that their individual welfare is intrinsically linked with the welfare of the whole.

The first question for consideration is whether the Lisbon Treaty reforms relating to competences would change the scope and purpose of the European Union in any fundamental sense. This was the approach taken by the Supreme Court in the Crotty judgement. The second is whether the contemplated reforms would add new policy competences to the Union which, in turn, would amount to significant change.

From the outset, differences of opinion, first about the European Community and now about the European Union, have depended on how people viewed the rationale and modus operandi of this new and unique international organisation, some recognising it as a novel experiment in sharing sovereignty, for which there was neither an analog nor precedent and others regarding it as a revival of the worst features of Europe's imperialist past, of which there had been too many distressing examples. This explains why, in the same debate, it is sometimes possible for the European Union to be hailed as the greatest peace experiment in history and simultaneously damned as an incipient federalist superstate or, alternatively, to be praised for being the first ever experiment in shared sovereignty based on interdependence while condemned for being a military superpower in the making. These depictions are polar opposites, and self-evidently, cannot both be true.

Looking back at the history of the past fifty years, the evidence points one way: European countries, all of them sovereign and independent, founded on democracy and based on the rule of law, have sought to cooperate in the areas of economic, monetary, political, social and trade policy to their mutual advantage.

Uniquely, they have done so on the basis of jointly making law, while also co-operating in more traditional modes of inter-governmentalism. Observation confirms that the Union they have voluntarily created is something novel, as its founders intended, and that its defining characteristic is the sharing of sovereignty in clearly defined policy areas for specific purposes.

The Treaty on European Union is short, running to fifty-five articles and only twenty-eight pages in the edition published by the Institute. Of these, the first twelve articles spell out the nature of the Union, its role and raison d'être and the democratic principles on which it is based. If words mean anything, then the literal interpretation of these twelve articles is that the Union is in essence democratic, in ambition peaceful and in practice rule-bound.

What comes across from a comparison of the existing treaties and the consolidated text as amended by the Lisbon Treaty is that no changes are contemplated in the fundamental nature of the Union or in the principles on which it is founded. The immediate implication for Ireland and, indeed, for all the other Member States, is that the European Union is to continue in being, unchanged in either the principles on which it is based or objectives it is to pursue. The purpose and nature remain as they were.

The equality of the Member States is to be respected and this is of vital importance to the small members, such as Ireland, for it ensures that the composition of the common institutions is to be based on equity and fairness. This principle is re-endorsed in the Treaty and it is to continue with respect to representation in the European Parliament, although strict equality is to apply to the composition of the Commission and, in some instances, to voting in the Council.

In addition to respecting the equality of Member States, the Lisbon Treaty marks a significant advance in the respect for the fundamental rights of the citizen. Although adopted in 2000 and then appended to the Nice Treaty (2001) the Charter of Fundamental Rights of the European Union was not incorporated into the text of the treaties. This is to be done in Article 6 which states that the

Charter is to have the same legal value as the treaties. Furthermore, the Union, under the article, is to accede to the European Convention for the Protection of Human Rights and Fundamental Freedoms, the full significance of which is spelled out in Chapters Five and Seven. In short, the new Treaty on European Union would greatly enhance individual rights and freedoms within the Union and copperfasten its democratic nature.

The question posed at the start of this section was whether the Lisbon Treaty changed the scope and purpose of the European Union in any fundamental sense. The conclusion reached here is that it does not. It is equally important to examine the changes made to the institutions to see if this element of the reform process has introduced any changes of a fundamental nature.

The European Union is unlike any other international organisation in that it can not only make law, but, in certain circumstances, can do so by a majority vote of its Member States. When presented in these terms it is understandable why the decision-making provisions, including the composition of the common institutions, should be subject to close scrutiny.

The role and power of the three institutions involved in law making (Commission, Council and Parliament) have constantly evolved over the past fifty years in the light of experience. There has been a continuous trend towards transforming the Council of Ministers and the European Parliament into co-legislators which are on equal footing with each other. In this system of co-decision, both bodies act on the basis of majority voting, although the definition of what constitutes a majority can be complex enough. Nevertheless, the principle is clear. On the other hand, the Member States have been resolute in confining certain sensitive policy areas to decision-making by unanimity.

It is proposed that the European Council, consisting of the Heads of State and Government, should become an institution of the Union and have its own Chairman, elected by the Council for a period of two and a half years with the task of chairing its meetings, ensuring continuity in its work and facilitating cohesion and consensus. This catalytic role is important since the main tasks of the European Council are to make policy (it does not make law) and to define the general political direction and priorities of the Union. The significance of this role can be appreciated when looking back, for example, at the major climate change initiatives taken over the past decade. All of them came via the European Council and many went beyond what had been anticipated at the time.

The implications of the proposed change are straightforward enough for this country. Whoever is Taoiseach will, as a matter of course, require a good working relationship with the President of the Council analogous to that with the Presidents of the Commission and the European Parliament.

It has been said above that where decisions are made by majority voting under the co-decision procedure the Member States are sharing sovereignty and that where they use unanimity they are acting intergovernmentally and retain sovereignty. But the logic inherent in the system of creating ever closer unity among the peoples of Europe as set down in the preamble to the Treaty of Rome is that the boundary between the two is periodically shifted in the direction of shared sovereignty. The Lisbon Treaty, it is hoped, will bring this evolutionary process of moving from unanimous to majority voting to an end, at least for a generation ahead.

The rules governing the size of a majority in the Council of Ministers have been altered. The philosophy behind qualified majority voting, as it has been since the beginning of European integration over half a century ago, is that the large Member States cannot dominate the small and the small cannot frustrate the large. Consequently, majorities or blocking minorities require coalitions of both large and small Member States. The Lisbon Treaty continues this principle but it establishes population size as the formula for weighting the vote of each country in place of the mathematical formulae used for the past half century. It seems capable of being extended to a Union of even thirty or more Member States (as is likely to happen).

Self-evidently, small Member States are not disadvantaged in moving towards population as the basis for determining voting strengths in the Council: the new system would still require coalitions of the large and small states to either pass or block legislation and has the merit of objectivity. The practical implications for the future arise not from a change in Ireland's relative voting strength but from the reality that the number of countries in the Council has quadrupled since Ireland's accession in 1973, thereby diminishing the influence of all Member States. This is the political consequence of a mathematical reality. Advancing the national interest in harmony with the general European interest will be more difficult as the Council gets bigger. All other Member States (even the biggest) face a similar challenge, of course, and the outcome clearly depends on the quality of the people chosen to represent the country in the common institutions and the clarity with which they and the government articulate national policy.

The other institutional change ahead, should the new treaty be ratified, is the composition of the Commission. The ever-increasing number of Member States has put irresistible pressure on the principle that each should be able to appoint a Commissioner. That point was conceded, reluctantly it should be said, nearly a decade ago and a pragmatic solution has steadily won acceptance whereby the size of the Commission will correspond to two-thirds of the number of Member States. If this provision comes into force as a result of ratification then from 2014 onwards nine Member States would be without a Commissioner during each period of office, now set at five years. The implications of the loss of a Commissioner for one in every three terms of office would be no different in formal terms for Ireland than for any other Member State.

The periodic loss of a Commissioner is the price the Member States are willing to pay for ensuring that size does not compromise the efficiency of this key institution. It is a truism that an effective Commission is of more importance to small Member States given its role as the guardian of the treaties and the protector of the European interest. If that viewpoint is accepted then the implications of the new rules governing the composition of the Commission would, on balance, be benign for a small country, such as Ireland.

As is always the case with treaty reforms there are innovations which compensate for a perceived or actual loss of national influence elsewhere. On this occasion, the treaties are to be amended by giving national parliaments an explicit voice in what might be called the constitutional acts of the Union, in addition to a new role in the passage of ordinary legislation. Interestingly, the treaty article setting out the overall role for national parliaments is part of the provisions on democratic principles in the amended Treaty on European Union and precedes provisions on the common institutions. This sequence confers a solemn status on the constitutional standing of the national parliaments, one which is spelled out in a protocol appended to the Treaty.

The implications are straightforward. The Oireachtas will have to be equipped with the necessary resources to scrutinize draft legislation emanating from the Commission with the attention it deserves, and needs, if there is to be any substance in the allegation that the Union suffers from a *democratic deficit* then henceforth that charge will have to be laid at the feet of national parliaments should they fail to measure up to the new demands being placed upon them. The full implications of this increased workload on the Oireachtas, will, no doubt, be studied by the government and the political parties.

It would be misleading to view the Treaty as an isolated stand-alone event divorced from what was happening in the Union and the wider world at the time it was being drafted. Since the beginning of the new millennium one of the issues progressively dominating the global agenda has been climate change and the European Union has led the response, set the pace, fashioned the policies, implemented emissions reduction measures, and pioneered new mechanisms, such as the Emissions Trading Scheme.

The principal political implication of the Lisbon Treaty in respect of climate change is that Ireland would be part of the leadership group which is setting the pace for the rest of the world. Self-evidently, this would be an ethical role for this country and would provide opportunities for influencing global policy that would be denied to an EU outsider. If the Lisbon Treaty is ratified then the European Union's leadership role will receive increased momentum within international fora, and Ireland will be placed in the vanguard.

That said, a new concern of the generic variety surfaced upon the publication of the Lisbon Treaty text. It was alleged that the treaties would become self-amending if the Lisbon Treaty was ratified. The basis for this claim allegedly comes from the final provisions of the Treaty on European Union in which Article 48 deals at length with the procedure for revising the treaties.

Two methods can be employed: one styled the ordinary revision procedure and the other the simplified revision procedure. As the name suggests, the ordinary procedure is that conventionally in use for the amendment of the treaties with the outcome subject to ratification by the Member States in accordance with their respective constitutional requirements. The only change introduced by the Lisbon Treaty is an additional layer of democratic legitimation to be provided by the Convention.

The problem arises with the proposed simplified revision procedure. It can only be invoked, however, in respect of the second treaty, that on The Functioning of the European Union, and is confined exclusively to its Part Three, which covers economic, fiscal and social policies, as well as police and judicial co-operation, which are expressed in 171 articles.

The simplified procedure would consist of the Heads of State or Government unanimously agreeing to revise all or any of these articles. The decision would not enter into force until it was approved by the Member States in accordance with their respective constitutional requirements. Such decisions are limited under the procedure to proposals which do *not increase the competences conferred on the Union in the Treaties.*

Procedures to allow for the substitution of qualified majority voting for unanimity specifically exclude *decisions with military implication or those in the area of defence* which remain subject to unanimity. Decisions require unanimity in the European Council and there is a new element requiring national parliaments to be notified before the European Council adopts its decision. If any national parliament makes known its opposition within six months then the European Council cannot adopt a decision. In other words, every national parliament has a veto over the proposed revision.

This is hardly the stuff of conspiracy. The allegation that the Lisbon Treaty would make the treaties self-amending is unfounded and is based on a misreading or misunderstanding of the revision provisions. The new procedure holds no threat whatever to Ireland.

One of the generic fears voiced from the outset was that Irish membership of the then EEC would compromise and even expunge Irish military neutrality. These fears were repeated when a Common Foreign and Security Policy emerged a decade later and are still in vogue today.

Two conclusions follow from an examination of the Treaty text. The first is that the Security and Defence Policy is focused on attempting to prevent or stabilise conflicts in the context of a political approach. Secondly, there will be a common defence only if the European Council unanimously decides so and if the Member States ratify that decision in accordance with their respective constitutional requirements. The policy may not prejudice the specific character of the security and defence policy of certain Member States. This wording in Article 42 protects the Irish position on neutrality, as well as that of Austria, Finland, Sweden, Cyprus and Malta. In short, the status quo is undisturbed. Consequently, the Treaty of Lisbon cannot be invoked as a threat to Irish neutrality.

However analyzed, neither the text nor past experience corroborate the claim that the European Union is either a superstate or a super-power with imperialistic ambitions. Irish military neutrality is not imperilled by the provisions of the Lisbon Treaty.

A reference to corporate taxation is necessary as fears about enforced harmonisation being possible under the Lisbon Treaty surfaced after its publication. The legal situation is that the Lisbon Treaty does not change the status quo. The Union never had and does not have any competence in direct taxation, either personal or corporate. That situation will remain unchanged under the Lisbon Treaty. There is not, nor can there be, any legal basis within the treaties for the harmonization of corporate taxation either in respect of a consolidated tax base or a minimum rate. Furthermore, the simplified revision procedure cannot be used to increase the competences conferred on the Union; that is quite clearly stated in the Lisbon Treaty text. Hence, it cannot be used to bring direct taxation within the ambit of the treaties, even if the Member States wanted to. They would have to use the ordinary revision procedure and proceed by way of an Intergovernmental Conference.

It is true at present, with or without the Lisbon Treaty, that some Member States could seek to use the existing provisions on enhanced cooperation to introduce a harmonised direct tax system applying only to them. In short, Ireland is free to opt out of such a scheme and cannot be coerced into joining. Whether they would succeed in their attempt to avail of the enhanced cooperation mechanism remains to be seen. It is also true that sovereign states can enter into tax treaties with each other and this could lead at any time to new agreements on corporation taxation that would introduce elements of harmonisation. But this is a matter of international law and has no bearing on the Lisbon Treaty.

The implications of the Lisbon Treaty for Ireland naturally depend on the outcome of the referendum. Ratification would give rise to a whole series of changes which have been identified and analyzed in preceding chapters. By and large their implications are predictable since the aims of the negotiators were well known in advance and have been endlessly explained every since. On the other hand, the implications of a rejection lie in the future and are open to conjecture. Nevertheless, it is possible to put various scenarios together on the basis of past experience and our present understanding of how the Member States of the European Union relate to each other and, more importantly, what they expect of each other in terms of mutual solidarity.

As stated at the outset of the chapter, the implications of a rejection of the Lisbon Treaty have to be assessed against a number of objective realities. The first is the prolonged process of negotiation over the past decade. The Lisbon Treaty is regarded as the final instalment of a set of reforms initiated by the Maastrict Treaty in 1992, final in the sense that there are no plans to revisit the make-up of the European Union for a generation.

In these circumstances, the immediate implication of a rejection by this country would be consternation among the other Member States because there is no fall-back position. There would be no plan B – for the good reason that the Lisbon Treaty is plan B following the defeat of the Constitutional Treaty. At least, when the European Constitution was rejected by France and the Netherlands the automatic response was to revert to the traditional form of treaty amendments, as are set out in the Treaty before us. No such strategy is available on this occasion and the future implications for this country would depend on the degree of determination on the part of the other Member States to introduce the reforms agreed in Lisbon.

The core of the Lisbon Treaty is the reform of the common institutions and the simplification of the decision-making processes. Crudely put, there is nothing from which Ireland could derogate, à la Denmark, after it rejected the Maastrict Treaty. It would appear to be all or nothing, as in the case of France and the Netherlands, except that on this occasion there is no obvious fall-back position for the Union. The most likely outcome would be stalemate and the Union would be denied important new competences, like fighting climate change or dealing with trafficking in women and children.

There is no question but that the rejection of the new Treaty would provoke a backlash elsewhere in the Union against Ireland. That was the case after the first Nice referendum and the country's reputation was only salvaged by the skilful management of the situation by the government and through its success in having the Nice Treaty ratified at the second attempt. To argue that there would be no political price to be paid for rejecting the Lisbon Treaty is either disingenuous or consciously misleading. The political consequences would, as common sense suggests, be negative. At their worst they could be deeply wounding, long lasting and self inflicted.

On previous occasions when faced with the implications of rejecting a new treaty the Institute worked out a series of elaborate scenarios as to what might happen. For the purposes of simplicity they can be reduced as follows. Firstly, the other Member States could throw their hats at reform and leave the status quo intact. Secondly, they could offer Ireland some concessions, à la Denmark after Maastrict, and ask for the referendum to be re-run. Thirdly, Ireland could volunteer to hold a second referendum on the basis of clarifications or assurances, as with the Nice Treaty. Fourthly, Ireland could be invited to step aside, develop some uncharted external association with the Union and let the other Member States get on with the reform process. As of now, it is a matter of personal choice as to what scenario seems the more likely.

Ratification of the Lisbon Treaty would not endanger any of the special provisions previously secured by Ireland (neutrality, abortion, common travel, etc.). They all remain intact. Ratification would maintain all the economic advantages (the Internal Market and euro) and the political influence that accrues from membership of the Union. Neither would it open the country to new threats, such as to the corporate tax system or the foreign direct investment regime. There seems no evidence that the European Union is intent on becoming a military super power or an imperialistic super state, or both simultaneously. The actual wording of the Lisbon Treaty is a guarantee against the spectre of a new threat to civilization emanating from Europe. Rather, the Lisbon Treaty offers the prospect that the countries of Europe, united in common endeavour on the principle of democracy, will lead the world in the fight against climate change and world poverty.

As on previous occasions, Ireland has a choice to make, not just for itself, but for the rest of the European Union as well. It is an awesome responsibility.

Reflection: Three Readings of the Failure to Ratify the Constitutional Treaty

Brigid Laffan

Introduction

The drafting of the Constitutional Treaty was an attempt to define and shape the European Union as a political order. It was part of a process of treaty change that began in the mid-1980s with the Single Act. Whether or not the final document matched the ambitions of reformers, the rhetoric surrounding the process cast the Treaty as nothing short of indispensable to ensure efficiency and democracy in a Europe of 25. Romano Prodi, for example, cast the process as a "grand project of creating European Union", needed in order to "take the European project forward".[1] It is unsurprising, therefore, that the failure of the Constitutional Treaty should have prompted an intense debate among academics about the implications for the future of the EU.

This chapter provides a brief overview of the academic debate about the significance or other of the ratification failure. It will become clear that there is considerable contestation among academics concerning the ratification failure. The first reading suggests that the ratification failure is not a problem for the efficiency or legitimacy of the European Union. The second adopts a very different perspective arguing that there is something wrong with the European Union that can only be rectified with a further politicization of the Union. A third reading cautions against politicization.

Reading One: The EU is a problem-solving polity and there is no problem

"For political philosophers engaged in normative analysis of real world constitutional systems, the implication of this episode is to counsel skepticism towards those who recommend politicization, deliberation and mass plebiscitary democracy as panaceas to promote political legitimisation and effectiveness."[2]

Against the multitude of voices searching for a means of legitimizing governance at the supranational level, Andrew Moravcsik has argued trenchantly that the lack of citizen participation and contestation around policy is an *imperative for* rather than a *barrier to* legitimate European Governance. He put forward a vision of the EU as a problem-solving polity, whose goal is to achieve consensual solutions to common problems that cannot be solved by the nation states acting alone, but whose development path is controlled by national political leaders.

In a series of articles, Moravcsik used the failure of the Constitutional Treaty to refute the claims of those who hold that the EU must be democratized in order to combat a perceived democratic deficit. He draws two key lessons from the ratification failure. The first is that the EU as a polity has reached a stable equilibrium point both institutionally and substantively. The second is that this polity is both normatively desirable and fully legitimate.[2]

Moravcsik's starting point is that the constitution failure does not represent a crisis for the EU because a "constitutional settlement" already exists in the European Union. On a substantive level, a division of competences between the EU and the Member States has been agreed and the balance has stabilised. "The EU is now pre-eminent in trade, agriculture, fishing, Eurozone monetary policy and some business regulation and helps coordinate cooperation in foreign policy".[3] According to Moravcsik, these outputs account for little more than 20% of all legislation, and correspond more or less with the areas where citizens say they want to see EU action. They constitute "areas of less concern, or on which there is an administrative, technical or legal consensus".[3]

Moravcsik argues that these are precisely the areas where, even at the nation state level, depoliticised governance is considered normatively legitimate.[2]

Moravcsik maintains that because Member States have already delegated all the competences that constitute such "matters of common interest", there is no political will to further deepen integration. In support of this argument, he notes that the Constitutional Treaty, unlike the Single Act, TEU or Amsterdam, was notable by its "stunning lack of positive proposals for reform".[3] Since supranational institutions only execute the will of the Member States and they have no desire to deepen integration, a constitutional settlement in substantive terms has been reached. For Moravcsik, "once we set aside ideal notions of democracy and look to real world standards, we see that the EU is at least as transparent, responsive, accountable and honest as its Member States."[3]

Reading 2: There is a problem and politicization is the answer

"The challenge now though is not more or less political integration, but rather what to do with the political structure that has already been created .... The only answer for the EU is to gradually allow democratic politics to play a more central role in the way the EU works."[4]

Simon Hix shares Moravcsik's view that the ratification failure does not represent a crisis for the EU, and he agrees that the EU has reached an equilibrium point in terms of its institutional and substantive development. The economic and political architecture is largely complete, comprising "a continental scale market regulated at the European level, taxing and spending at the national level and the coordination of national policies where one Member State's policies affect another".[4] However, for Hix, an assessment of the ratification failure points to the fact that the EU's popular legitimacy must urgently be strengthened in order to ensure long-term effectiveness and stability. Along with other scholars who deride Moravscik for his Panglossian belief that the EU offers "the best of all possible worlds", Hix argues that given the nature and reach of the EU as a political system today, more democratisation of EU policy-making is both inevitable and desirable.[5]

This argument begins from the premise that few EU policies actually produce the kind of outcomes in which there are benefits for all, on which Moravscik bases his claims. Rather, EU decision-making produces winners and losers. Even in the regulation of the internal market, Follesdal and Hix maintain that choices made are political and have significant redistributive consequences. For example through the removal of national protective barriers, liberalization has had negative consequences for domestic producers.[6] Now that the basic constitutional architecture has been established, difficult ideological choices must be taken over how to use this policy apparatus: "should the EU single market be more liberal or regulated? Should macro-economic and monetary policies be more orthodox or Keynesian? Should the EU have a more liberal or more restricted immigration policy?".[4]

Consequently, greater politicization of policy-making is inevitable. According to those who believe the EU should be a democratic polity, however, it is also indispensable, in order to enhance the system's popular legitimacy. Politicisation, it is argued, would have a number of desirable impacts in this respect. First, it would make policy-makers accountable for their policy outputs. Political battles in democracies enable citizens to deliberate rival policy agendas and rival candidates for office, and to kick out those who do not use their power as mandated.[4] Second, the process of deliberation would make policy more responsive to changing preference.

For Hix, the ratification failure served to highlight the thesis that without greater citizen engagement in the EU, the system's stability is at risk. Under the current system, because they have no way of influencing decision-making, citizens who oppose the direction of EU policy have no choice but to oppose EU integration as a whole. Many scholars have noted, for example, that this could be observed in the debates surrounding the Constitutional Treaty, which were more concerned with the orientation of the EU's political economy than with the substance of the document itself:

> In the debate on the Constitutional Treaty in several Member States it became clear that much opposition to the Treaty was founded on the belief that if the Treaty were accepted it would hasten the dismantling of the European social model, and the return to neo-liberal policies throughout Europe. However, since many of the neo-liberal elements to which the objections were strongest were already contained in the existing treaties, they were unaffected by the rejection of the Constitutional Treaty.[7]

Politicisation would overcome this problem by providing institutional mechanisms to generate "debate and contestation about politics *in*, not only *of*, the EU".[6] As a result, the EU's efficiency as a system would no longer be hindered by a lack of popular support. The growing body of work on political contestation led by Hix has produced substantial empirical evidence that politics within the European institutions is increasingly dominated by an ideological cleavage alongside the traditional territorial cleavage.[8, 9, 10]

Reading 3: There is a problem but politicization is risky

Stefano Bartolini, building on Stein Rokkan's analysis of the emergence of the modern nation state, analyses the restructuring of political order in Europe as a consequence of European integration.[11] His conceptualization of integration challenges the depiction of the EU as a mere "problem-solving polity". He views the clear separation of responsibilities between nation state and EU "levels", described by Moravcsik, with Member States retaining complete control over governance as a fallacy:

What cannot be maintained is the thesis of a division of labour between the EU and the nation state according to which the EU should be exclusively responsible for the regulation/ deregulation of the market (in a way that is as independent as possible from political pressures) while the nation state should retain responsibility for introducing the necessary compensatory measures.[11]

Bartolini shares Hix's view that the management of the internal market has political consequences. Both positive and negative types of integration inevitably undermine national mechanisms of political representation and legitimation, leading to "national political destructuring". However, Bartolini finds Hix's prescription to remedy this state of affairs by engineering greater politicization at European level highly problematic.

His first objection is that politicization would not be limited to issues of policy and political economy, allowing European politics to be structured along the same lines as national issues. Political battles would be much more likely to focus on "constitutive issues", i.e. those pertaining to membership, competences and decision-making rules, which unlike both Moravcsik and Hix he does not believe are yet resolved.[11] What reason is there to believe that contestation will simply concern left-right issues, he asks, when the areas that most exercise European citizens relate to conflicts over the EU's scope, competences and even its existence?

Second, Bartolini is skeptical about Hix's optimism regarding the potential for Euro-parties to act as channels to link voter preferences with political behaviour within the European institutions. He attributes their voting cohesiveness to a lack of partisan constraints, low visibility and electoral costs rather than to actual ideological cohesion. This leads him to conclude that politicization would in fact break down internal cohesion in party groups instead of strengthening them.[11]

His third objection is that politicization would inevitably create unrealistic expectations about what could actually be achieved within the existing "pre-defined goals" of the EU. Bartolini questions whether in fact the EU has reached a "constitutional" settlement, given that there is no clear-cut separation of powers and that Union competences are set out in relation to a list of substantive and loosely defined goals. The peculiarity of this arrangement is that, instead of simply setting out "the procedures for selecting those who are allowed to take decisions and the procedures for taking those decisions", the treaties actually protect the competences to be decided from political contestation. It is therefore possible to speak of the "constitutionalisation" of economic rights and market making goals, but not of corresponding political or social rights.[11] Consequently, fostering public deliberation over alternative political mandates is doomed to failure.

He considers the example of a political mandate involving "expansionary monetary policies, European social welfare minima, active occupational or fiscal policies, or a radical alteration of agricultural policy". If such a mandate were to gain public backing, could it help to overcome institutional gridlock as Hix suggests? "The answer is NO. Such a political mandate would be frustrated by the autonomy of the European Central Bank, by the case law of the ECJ, by the blocking vetoes in the Council."[12] Bartolini argues, therefore, that the Union's institutional arrangement militates against the emergence of political structuring mechanisms at the enlarged territorial level to compensate for political de-structuring at the national level. However, simply changing this institutional arrangement from above is not a plausible solution – in fact this prescription could be worse than the disease: "Any institutional democratization without political structuring would be potentially catastrophic."[12] Political structuring implies that the "scattered elements of identities, interests and institutions" in the EU are brought together into a new coherent order.[12]

Conclusions

The three readings sketched in this short overview highlight the differing scholarly perspectives of the EU as a form of political order in the opening decade of the 21st century. According to Moravcsik, the EU is a constrained but legitimate polity, a creature of its Member States that has reached an equilibrium. Hix would also agree that the EU has reached an equilibrium. However, he argues strongly that it is desirable and feasible to further democratize the Union through politicization. Bartolini, on the other hand, is skeptical about the capacity of the system to withstand politicization and wonders just what kind of politicization would emerge. Yet he argues for greater coherence between economic, political and cultural boundaries. The existing EU is far too messy with its "fuzzy borders" and complex institutional architecture. Could or should the EU attempt to replicate the closed borders and political structuring that developed in the national context?

The EU was conceived as an experimental and distinctive form of political order to achieve objectives which could no longer be effectively achieved within the nation states. Its complex system of fluid and differentiated boundaries developed in response to the challenges of interdependence in a changing international order. What would be the point of attempting to transform the EU into an enlarged territorial order that resembled its Member States in all ways but size? A key to understanding the complex, messy, inchoate character of the European Union lies in the need to manage "deep diversity" and to go with the grain of the national. A political community has evolved in the EU precisely because "there has been no agreed-upon political philosophy; no clear, consistent and stable purposes and strategies. Integration has succeeded because it has been consensus oriented and has taken place on the basis of a fluid and loosely coupled order …".[13]

Moreover, "the European Union has shown ability to live with an open ended process and enduring tensions and inconsistencies, not only in terms of policies but also institutional arrangements."[13] In fact, it is probable that this conceptual and political openness provides the key to understanding how the EU has managed to marry increasing diversity with the deepening of its policy agenda, the widening of its membership and the strengthening of its institutional capacity.

The plurality of academic readings concerning the "state of the Union", reflects a multitude of conflicting visions that exist among politicians and citizens. Attempting to resolve these underlying political tensions and visions has proved neither helpful nor possible. The core question for academics, practitioners and citizens is whether this system of managed internationalization that evolved in Western Europe after the Second World War can continue to adapt to intense processes of globalization, competitiveness, security, the challenge of climate change and sustainability in the context of a continent-wide scale and a shifting international system.

The failed Constitutional Treaty was followed by the Reform Treaty, commonly known as the Lisbon Treaty, the subject of this volume. The period of reflection that followed the ratification failure is characteristic of the EU as is the agreement on the Lisbon Treaty. The Union, in the absence of agreement on its final shape and in the context of the deep diversity that characterizes Europe, evolves in fits and starts in response to the challenges faced by its Member States. The key challenges facing Europe emanate both from the international system and from within the Member States. Intensified globalisation, climate change, and shifting geopolitics increase the salience of the EU for its Member States and increase the salience of the Union in the world. The Lisbon Treaty enhances the ability of the Union to meet those challenges as it seeks to become a shaper of a changing world.

Its provisions on foreign policy, the High Representative, climate change, justice and home affairs and trade are an improvement on the status quo. Internally, the Member States are challenged by demography, emigration, and economic and social reform. The modest changes in Lisbon are likely to make the decision-making in the Union smoother. The addition of a President of the European Council will add much needed continuity and coherence to the work of the Council. The addition of the Charter makes more explicit the underlying value of the Union while the enhanced roles of the European Parliament and national parliaments deepen the process of democratizing political space above the level of the state. The EU is as relevant to the challenges facing its Member States in 2008 as it was in 1958 when the "inner six" began the experimental process of establishing a common market and an economic community.

References

1. Olsen, J.P. (2002), Reforming European Institutions of Governance, *JMCS* Vol. 40.
2. Moravcsik, A. (2006) "What Can we Learn from the Collapse of the European Constitutional Project?", *Politische Vierteljahresschrift*, 47, Jg, Heft 2
3. Moravscik, A. (2005) "Europe without Illusions", *Prospects*, Issue 112, July 2005
4. Hix, S. (2006) "Why the EU needs left-right politics" in Politics: the right or the wrong sort of medicine for the EU? Notre Europe Policy Paper no. 19
5. Siedentop, L. (2005) "A Crisis of Legitimacy", *Prospect*, Issue 112, July 2005
6. Follesdal, A. and Hix, S. (2005) "Why there is a democratic deficit in the EU: a response to Majone and Moravcsik", European Governance Papers No. C05 02
7. Gamble, A. (2006) "The European Disunion", *British Journal of Politics and International Relations* Vol. 8, 34-49, No. 3
8. Hix, S. (2001) "Legislative Behaviour and Party Competition in the European Parliament: an Application of Nominate to the EU" *JCMS* 39: 663-688
9. Hix, S. and Kreppel, A. (2003) From Grand Coalition to Left-Right Confrontation: Explaining the Shifting Structure of Party Competition in the European Parliament", *Comparative Political Studies*, 36:75-96
10. Zimmer, C., Schneider, G. and Dobbins, M. (2005), "The Contested Council: Conflict Dimensions of an Intergovernmental EU Institution", *Political Studies* Vol 53, 403-42

11. Bartolini, S. (2005), R*estructuring Europe: Centre Formation, System Building, and Political Structuring Between the Nation State and the European Union*, Oxford: Oxford University Press

12. Bartolini, S. (2006) "Should the Union be politicised? Prospects and Risks" in "Politics: The right or the wrong sort of medicine for the EU?" Notre Europe Policy Paper no. 19

13. Olsen, J.P. (2005), "The Political Organization of Europe: Differentiation and Unification", Arena Working Paper No. 23, 2005

1

From Nice to Lisbon

Tony Brown

Speaking at the University of Ghent in January 2008, the President of the European Commission, Jose Manuel Barroso, referred to developments in the EU and in Belgium in the closing weeks of 2007 and remarked that:

> There was also another important event, which was, of course, the signing in December of the Lisbon Treaty. That signing was the culmination of a protracted institutional debate. But above all it brought to an end two years of deadlock. Europe was in a deadlock but … it was able to find the will to bounce back, thanks to its pragmatism, which drives the search for the best possible compromise.[1]

That compromise, in fact, came at the end of a saga which began eight years ago on the French Riviera with the conclusion of the protracted, and often acrimonious, negotiations on the Treaty of Nice. Three days and nights of tough bargaining within the European Council produced an outcome which, Brigid Laffan argued, tackled the outstanding institutional issues on its agenda and enabled the Union to enlarge. "The political link between the IGC and enlargement was such that agreement at Nice was a political imperative."[2]

Nice: Treaty and Charter

The Treaty of Nice made provision for important changes in the composition of the European Commission, weighted voting in the Council and the application of QMV. The weighting of votes became the main issue of contention, and of eventual compromise, as the leaders of the fifteen Member States sought to find a balance between the need to compensate the larger states for the reduction in their relative weighting because of past enlargements and for their acceptance of the loss of their second Commissioner as the Union prepared for the coming major enlargement. Agreement was achieved on the future size and shape of the Commission with the provision that, when the membership of the Union reached 27, a decision would be made on the composition of a smaller college.

The same European Council (conjointly with the European Commission and the European Parliament) adopted, by way of solemn proclamation, the European Union Charter of Fundamental Rights. The Charter was drafted by a Convention made up of representatives of national governments, national parliaments, the European Parliament and the European Commission. The text was approved by the European Parliament and proclaimed as a political statement of the Union's values. The proclamation, however, did not give the Charter legally binding force.

The Nice European Council, reflecting on the issues which had arisen in the debates within the Intergovernmental Conference and on a growing debate among political leaders and within civil society across Europe on the implications of a greatly enlarged body, reached the general conclusion that there was a real need to look in depth at the future of the European Union as it moved towards an eastward expansion which would give rise to new challenges in terms of geography, economics, energy, migration and new borders.

A Declaration was attached to the Treaty of Nice calling for "a deeper and wider debate about the future of the European Union".[3] During 2001, the Swedish and Belgian Presidencies were asked to conduct wide-ranging discussions across European society with a report to be presented to the European Council in December 2001 when decisions would be taken on the appropriate initiatives for the continuation of the process.

The Declaration listed four issues for in-depth attention: more precise delimitation of powers between the EU and the Member States, reflecting the principle of subsidiarity; the status of the Charter of Fundamental Rights; simplification of the Treaties with a view to making them clearer and better understood without changing their meaning; and, the role of national parliaments in the EU system.[3]

The European Council further underlined the need to improve the democratic legitimacy of the Union, decided that the Nice compromise was likely to be of only temporary utility and agreed that a new IGC was needed to commence work in 2004 to carry out further work on the treaties.

The First Nice Referendum

The process of ratification of the Treaty of Nice was dramatically interrupted on 7th June 2001 when the Irish electorate voted by 54% to 46%, on a turnout of only 35%, to reject the required Constitutional Amendment.

Opinion surveys indicated that the key issue was the remarkable level of abstention, the main reasons for which were summed up by Professor Richard Sinnott, in a research project for the European Commission, in terms which struck an immediate chord:

> ...it appears ... that more than two-thirds of people had an inadequate understanding of what the Treaty was all about, one-third didn't know what it was all about, at all. When you do a detailed analysis of the data you find that people's own understanding of what was going on – or rather their lack of understanding and lack of information – was a major cause of abstention ...

... the basic message that we would want to convey ... is that a lot more persuasion and a lot more information, basically a lot more debate and argument needs to go on so that people arrive at an understanding of European issues and of the Treaty that they themselves have confidence in.[4]

The National Forum on Europe

Prior to the first Nice referendum, the Irish Labour Party had proposed the establishment of a representative forum to facilitate the "deeper and wider debate on the future of the European Union" called for in the Nice Declaration on the Future of Europe. That proposal was initially dismissed but was accorded new respect as the shock referendum result was assessed. In June 2001, the Taoiseach, Bertie Ahern, announced the creation of a National Forum on Europe "to allow for a more systematic and extensive debate on the European Union and its future direction than has ever before proved possible". The Terms of Reference of the Forum located its work in the framework of Ireland's experience of membership and its evolving relationship with the Union, including the context of enlargement.

The composition of the Forum limited membership to members of the Oireachtas and those nominated by parties represented in the Oireachtas. Each party with parliamentary representation was allocated seats on the basis of the outcome of the 1997 General Election and there was provision for representation of the independent members in the two Houses. To involve the broader community it was agreed to constitute a Special Observer Pillar with rights of participation. Senator Maurice Hayes, a non-party member of the Senate was nominated as the Forum's chairman. The inaugural meeting of the National Forum on Europe took place on 18th October 2001 in Dublin Castle.

Laeken

The Irish referendum result came half way through the consultation process initiated at Nice and added a new dimension to its work. The European Council, meeting at Goteborg in June 2001 under the Swedish Presidency, noted the Irish situation and indicated the willingness of Ireland's partners in the Union "to contribute in every possible way to helping the Irish government find a way forward."[5]

While politicians in Ireland turned their thoughts to a second referendum as the only way out of the impasse created by the "no" vote, discussions in Brussels and elsewhere across the current and prospective members turned to fulfilling the prescriptions of the Nice Declaration. The Goteborg Council noted "the many encouraging initiatives which have been undertaken since then" and called for an intensification of efforts up to the planned Laeken European Council in December.

Then an even more dramatic event changed the political world, perhaps forever. On 11th September 2001 New York was attacked by the terrorists of al-Qaeda. I recall that I was in the Head Office of the Labour Party for a meeting on setting up the party's group in the National Forum on Europe when the terrible, initially unbelievable, images appeared on TV screens. Debate on the Future of Europe took on a new and disturbing dimension not least in terms of security and relations with Islam.

The Laeken European Council, on 14th and 15th December 2001, under the Belgian Presidency, adopted a Declaration on the Future of the European Union[6] which addressed the many issues facing the European Union at a time of world crisis and of major internal changes – the introduction of the Euro coins and notes, the impending expansion to the East and South and the emergence of the globalisation phenomenon.

It was decided to establish a European Convention under the chairmanship of former French President Valery Giscard d'Estaing and with two former Prime Ministers, Giuliano Amato and Jean-Luc Dehaene, as vice chairmen. The Declaration set the Convention a number of questions under the headings of: the democratic challenge facing Europe; Europe's new role in a globalised world; the expectations of Europe's citizens; a better division and definition of competence in the EU; simplification of the Union's instruments; more democracy, transparency and efficiency in the EU; a possible Constitution for European citizens.

The detailed questions ranged from assessing the practical meaning of subsidiarity to the redefinition of the Petersberg Tasks and from the role of national parliaments to the six-monthly rotation of the Council Presidency. The central theme was that of better connecting the Union and its institutions with the citizens of the individual Member States. It concluded that "....citizens are calling for a clear, open, effective, democratically controlled Community approach developing a Europe which points the way ahead for the world ... there can be no doubt that this will require Europe to undergo renewal and reform."[6]

The Convention was designed to be widely representative of the Governments and Parliaments of 28 countries – including the twelve candidate countries and Turkey – and with both government and opposition MPs, representatives of the European Parliament, the European Commission and observers from Civil Society, including the European Ombudsman and the Social Partners.

The Irish Delegation was composed of Europe Minister Dick Roche TD (Fianna Fáil), former Taoiseach John Bruton TD (Fine Gael), Proinsias de Rossa MEP (Labour), Pat Carey TD (Fianna Fáil) and John Gormley TD (Green Party), with strong Civil Service backup. John Bruton was elected by parliamentarians to the Convention Praesidium.

Between February 2002 and June 2003 the Convention met in public on 52 plenary days at which there were 1,800 speeches and more than 1,000 formal written contributions. 6,000 text amendments were submitted. The Convention established eleven Working Groups on issues from simplification of EU instruments and procedures to the future of Social Europe. It concluded its work on the basis of consensus with only a handful of dissenting voices and presented the text of a draft Constitutional Treaty to the European Council at Thessaloniki on 19th June 2003.

The Second Nice Referendum

2002 in Ireland saw a General Election on 17th May which returned the Fianna Fail- Progressive Democrat coalition under the leadership of Taoiseach Bertie Ahern for a second five-year term. The government set about preparing for the second Nice referendum by placing EU enlargement at the centre of the "yes" campaign and by moving decisively to remove the emotional issue of neutrality from the debate.

This was achieved in two ways. First, by obtaining the agreement of the other Member States to the so-called Seville Declarations[7] in which Ireland reaffirmed its position outside any mutual defence commitment and set out the tems of the "triple lock" provisions in respect of the deployment of Irish troops in EU missions. The European Council set out its recognition of the Irish position and of its compatibilty with the treaty provisions for European Security and Defence. And, second, by inserting into Article 29 of *Bunreacht na hÉireann* a specific prohibition on Irish participation in a possible EU Common Defence arrangement, thus requiring a referendum in Ireland should such an arrangement be proposed.

The second Nice referendum took place on 19th October 2002 and resulted in a 63% to 37% majority – on a 49.5% turnout – for the "yes" side thus allowing ratification of the treaty to proceed. The European Council meeting in Copenhagen on 12th and 13th December 2002 celebrated the fact that accession negotiations with the ten candidate countries had been successfully concluded and called for immediate action to draft and finalise the terms of the Accession Treaty so that it would be ratified in time for the entry of the new Member States in May 2004.

2003 saw the continuation of the work of the Convention which reached a consensus that its final output should be in the form of a draft Constitutional Treaty, taking up an option in the last paragraph of the Laeken Declaration: "The question ultimately arises as to whether this simplification and reorganisation might not lead in the long run to the adoption of a constitutional text in the Union."[6] A number of members, including Irish delegates, questioned the use of the term "constitution" which, in the context of a referendum campaign, could lead to misunderstanding and misrepresentation.

In April 2003 the Convention President reported to an Informal European Council meeting in Athens. His generally positive summing-up of the Convention's progress was briefly overshadowed by an evident division between the larger and smaller Member States on aspects of the institutional arangements under discussion. This was a repeat of difficulties experienced in the latter stages of the Nice IGC.

The Convention largely succeeded in bridging the "big/small" divide – with the only remaining difficulties involving Spain and Poland – and reached a final compromise in early June. The text was signed in the European Parliament hemicycle on the morning of Friday 13th June 2003 where Giscard d'Estaing made an emotional farewell speech in which he said that

> These proposals constitute a coherent whole and without options. The necessary balance between the demands – often contradictory – of federalists and non-federalists, between bigger and smaller Member States, between the roles of the different institutions has already been achieved within the convention. Many felt that such a result would be very difficult to attain. If we have arrived at such a result it is because everyone accepted that his or her preferred outcome was not necessarily favoured by others…[8]

The Convention text, together with a Minority Report signed by four members, was delivered to the European Council, meeting at Thessaloniki on 19th and 20th June 2003 under the Greek Presidency. The Council stated that "this presentation marks a historic step in the direction of furthering the objectives of European integration."[9] It went on to describe the text as a good basis for starting the Intergovernmental Conference which would be initiated by the Italian Presidency in the second half of the year. The IGC was given a year to complete its work so that the final text would be available before the June 2004 elections for the European Parliament. It was provided that the Constitutional Treaty would be signed by the Member States of the enlarged Union as soon as possible after 1st May 2004.

The IGC began work in October 2003. As it proceeded a number of issues of contention were identified and addressed. A Presidency paper, dated 9th December 2003, listed no less than 44 such questions. Many of these were of minimal significance and the Presidency succeeded in proposing amendments or clarifications which satisfied the Member States which had raised concerns. For Ireland, issues existed in the areas of Defence, Justice and Home Affairs, QMV in the taxation field, the composition of the Commission and the reference to God and/or Christianity in the Preamble.

Considerable progress was made on Social Policy issues with the inclusion of a Social Clause providing that key social considerations must be taken into account in all Union policies. A proposal on the issue of social exclusion from the European Anti Poverty Network at a plenary session of the National Forum on Europe was included in the treaty text at the insistence of the Irish delegation.

When the IGC met in Brussels on 12 December 2003 several issues remained subject to discussion among the participants from both present and future Member States: the minimum threshold of seats in the European Parliament; the scope of QMV, notably in CFSP; the composition of the Commission; the determination of QMV (weighted or double majority); reference to God and/or Christianity in the Preamble.

On 12 December 2003 the Italian Presidency of the IGC stated that it was not possible for the IGC to reach an overall agreement on the draft constitutional treaty. The incoming Irish Presidency was requested on the basis of consultations to make an assessment of the prospect for progress and to report to the European Council in March 2004. The main cause of the breakdown was an impasse on the issue of QMV where the proposed switch to a double majority system was opposed by Spain and Poland which had negotiated a particularly favourable allocation of votes in the complex system agreed at Nice.

In January 2004, the Irish Presidency inherited the unfinished IGC and set out cautiously to achieve a satisfactory outcome, undertaking an intensive series of consultations at political and official levels with the broad membership of the IGC, including all 25 states. The Taoiseach himself visited all 24 capitals for face-to-face consultations with his colleagues in the European Council.

On 18th June 2004 the IGC was successfully concluded when the Irish Presidency brought the negotiations on the Constitutional Treaty to an end with agreement on a text which was formally signed in Rome in October 2004 where the Taoiseach, Bertie Ahern, spoke of the work of the IGC and, reflecting the historic nature of the project, argued that

> Once again Europe proved that it could function effectively. The agreement on the Constitution provides convincing and irrefutable evidence that the EU of 25 can take important decisions for the future of our people....Instead of the feared gridlock and political paralysis, we found within ourselves the political will to achieve an honourable and balanced compromise.[10]

The words "gridlock and political paralysis" were shortly to come back to haunt him and other EU leaders.

Enlargement

Just weeks before the finalisation of the Constitutional Treaty text, on 1st May 2004 the European Union welcomed ten new Member States at an historic ceremony in Dublin – Cyprus, Czech Republic, Estonia, Hungary, Latvia, Lithuania, Malta, Poland, Slovakia and Slovenia. The Union's membership thus expanded from 15 to 25 (with Bulgaria and Romania to follow, on 1st January 2007, bringing the figure to 27).

The Irish President of the European Parliament, Pat Cox, speaking at the ceremony described the new continent-wide Europe as "a witness to the success of the new Member States which had undergone a radical transformation over 15 years. It was also the result of the determined and consistent efforts by successive Presidencies, Member States and the European institutions who have overcome obstacles on the road and provided sustained leadership for the earliest possible enlargement."[11]

And, Nobel Laureate Seamus Heaney read a poetic tribute to the historic event:

So on a day when newcomers appear
Let it be a homecoming and let us speak
The unstrange word as it behoves us here.[12]

The Ratification Process:
France and the Netherlands

As with any EU Treaty ratification of the Constitutional Treaty was a matter for each of the 25 Member States, under their individual constitutional arrangements and with the fundamental requirement of unanimity. It was agreed that the ratification process should be carried out within two years, at which stage any problems would be addressed by the European Council.

It emerged that ten referenda would be held on the Treaty – in Spain, Portugal, France, Denmark, Netherlands, Poland, Czech Republic, Luxembourg, UK and Ireland. In the other fifteen Member States, and in Bulgaria and Romania, the decision would be made by national parliaments.

In the event, eighteen Member States ratified the text: two by referendum (Spain and Luxembourg) and sixteen by parliamentary decision (Austria, Belgium, Bulgaria, Cyprus, Estonia, Finland, Germany, Greece, Hungary, Italy, Latvia, Lithuania, Malta, Romania, Slovakia, Slovenia). Two Member States rejected the treaty by referendum: in France the margin was 55% to 45% and in the Netherlands 62% to 38%. Seven Member States, including

Ireland, postponed or suspended the ratification process in the aftermath of the French and Netherlands results.

The French and Dutch rejections were a shock to the entire EU system. A Federal Trust analysis discussed some of the key issues:

> Research after the French and Dutch referendums suggested that only rarely had voters considerd the specifically new proposals of the Constitutional Treaty and used them as a basis for voting against the Treaty. Considerations of purely domestic politics played some role in both the French and Dutch referendum campaigns and insofar as European issues were decisive for voters they either related to matters unaffected by the the new treaty such as the Stability Pact and Enlargement or stemmed from a general unease with the perceived current direction of the European Union under the existing European treaties.[13]

The leaders of the EU states met in Brussels on 16th and 17th June 2005 in the immediate aftermath of the two negative votes. They described the Constitutional Treaty as "the fruit of a collective process, designed to provide the appropriate response to ensure that an enlarged European Union functions more democratically, more transparently and more effectively."[14] Noting the French and Dutch results they concluded that they did not call into question the fundamental attachment of citizens to the European project but admitted that "citizens have…expressed concerns and worries which need to be taken into account. Hence the need for us to reflect together…"[14]

Period of Reflection

They called for a "period of reflection" to enable a broad debate to take place in each Member State, involving "citizens, civil society, social partners, national parliaments and political parties". It was agreed that the leaders would return to the matter early in 2006 to assess the national debates and to agree on how to proceed. And it was admitted that the process of ratification of the Constitutional Treaty would be altered in response to these developments.

In Ireland the National Forum on Europe was charged by the Government to lead the debate during the period of reflection and this is reflected in the sixth and seventh reports of the Forum's activities. These show a change of emphasis from dealing with the details of, and divergent views on, the Constitutional Treaty to discussion of issues of importance and concern as identified by individuals and groups themselves.

It was decided to work increasingly in partnership with a range of national organisations representative, for example, of women, young people and the media. Youth Fora and Conferences for Women were organised with the National Youth Council, the National Women's Council and the Irish Countrywomen's Association. Publications on the working of the EU institutions, on the Union's policies and main activities and on its relevance to women were widely circulated.

Plenary sessions were devoted to subjects including the key political issues arising in the period of reflection, the Common Agricultural Policy, the Doha Development Round in the WTO, the Media and European Identity, Global Competitive Challenges, Europe and the Wider World and aspects of European Security and Defence including the issue of Battlegroups. Among the individual speakers invited to reflect on the questions facing Europe were the Taoiseach, the Minister for Foreign Affairs, Mr Jens-Peter Bonde MEP, Dr Hans Blix, Ms Catherine Day, Archbishop Diarmuid Martin and the Leaders of the Fine Gael, Labour, Progressive Democrat and Green Parties.[15]

The Commission President, Jose Manuel Barroso, told the National Forum on Europe at a plenary session on 30th June 2005 that the aim of this period of debate and consultation was to set out "clear ideas for the next stage of European development and the areas where Europe should be adding value...we hope to offer answers to the question of what Europe will look like in 10 or 20 years."[16]

A Growing EU Agenda

During this period the European Union was confronted with a growing agenda of major policy and administrative issues, not least of which was the integration of the twelve new Member States as Bulgaria and Romania joined the ten which had entered in 2004. The European Council reached agreement to open enlargement negotiations with Croatia and Turkey and, after much intensive negotiation, agreed on both the budgetary arrangements for the period 2007–2013 and a mid-term review of the budget, including the always controversial question of expenditure on the Common Agricultural Policy.

There were important policy initiatives on Energy and Climate Change together with a review of the Lisbon Strategy on sustainable development and social cohesion. The need for concerted action on terrorism, international crime and trafficking and migration led to advances in co-operation in the Justice and Home Affairs area.

The Austrian and Finnish Presidencies during 2006 carried out intensive consultations with the Member States on their approaches to the future status of the Constitutional Treaty in the light of the French and Netherlands results. The European Council of December 2006 received a report from the Finnish Presidency on these consultations and this was passed to the incoming German Presidency as part of its preparations for the report to be presented in the first half of 2007.

2007

Two important political developments in the early months of 2007 proved critical in the evolution of the EU's search for a way out of the Constitutional treaty impasse. In February a new Government was formed in the Netherlands, following the General Election of November 2006. While Prime Minister Jan Peter Balkenende retained his position at the head of affairs, a new coalition had been formed bringing together his Christian Democrats and the Dutch Labour Party. And, in May, Nicolas Sarkozy succeeded Jacques

Chirac as President of the French Republic, defeating his socialist opponent Segolene Royale in the second round of voting. These changes, in the countries which had rejected the Constitutional Treaty, opened the way for Chancellor Merkel to move to a new phase of high level consultation and negotiation.

The German Presidency set out to achieve a consensus on the way forward and engaged in direct negotiation with the various EU leaders and, in particular, with the newly elected French and Dutch administrations and with the Polish and UK governments. Changes were underway in the latter two countries with a General Election in Poland and the handover from Tony Blair to Gordon Brown in the UK. Key issues causing difficulties for these, and other national leaders, were identified and solutions suggested. Among the main issues so identified were the emphasis on undistorted competition (a reference to a phrase in the statement of Objectives directly taken from the Treaty of Rome); the proposed double majority voting system, the role of national parliaments and a number of concerns in relation to the Charter of Fundamental Rights and the Justice and Home Affairs area.

A Celebration in Berlin

On 24th and 25th March 2007 the Heads of State and Government of the European Union met in Berlin for celebrations on the occasion of the Fiftieth Anniversary of the Signature of the Treaties of Rome. The Declaration issued by the leaders addressed the Union's history and achievements and its future aspirations and challenges. It concluded in the following terms:

> With European unification a dream of earlier generations has become a reality. Our history reminds us that we must protect this for the good of future generations. For that reason we must always renew the political shape of Europe in keeping with the times. That is why, 50 years after the signing of the Treaties of Rome, we are united in our aim of placing the

European Union on a renewed common basis before the European Parliament elections in 2009. For we know, Europe is our common future.[17]

Mandate for an IGC

The outcome of these efforts resulted in the European Council meeting of 21–23 June 2007 which reached consensus on a Mandate for an Intergovernmental Conference (IGC) to be convened by the Portuguese Presidency with the purpose of finalising the text of a new Treaty by the end of 2007 so as to allow sufficient time for ratification by the 27 Member States before the European Parliament elections in June 2009.[18]

Under the terms of the Mandate the form of the Constitutional Treaty was abandoned and there was to be a return to the traditional form of a revising treaty, detailing changes and additions to the existing treaty texts. Thus the logical and clear presentation, within a single document, achieved in the Constitutional Treaty was consigned to history in favour of a text of the kind correctly described by British Prime Minister Tony Blair as "complex and confusing."

On a proposal by Ireland, the new treaty was to be called the Reform Treaty and the Conclusions of the Brussels meeting indicated that the constitutional concept – repealing all existing treaties and replacing them with a single text – had been abandoned. The new treaty would introduce into the existing Treaties, which remain in force, the main innovations resulting from the 2004 IGC.

The IGC met for the first time in July 2007 and concluded its work within a matter of weeks. The Mandate from the European Council was clear and left little room for serious problems. A draft text was published on 5th October and the European Council met in an informal session in Lisbon on 18-19 October to consider the outcome. With a decision to include a specific reference to policies to deal with Climate Change in the Environment Chapter and once a handful of minor "political" points (such as the spelling of "Euro" in Bulgarian) had been cleared up there was unanimous agreement on the text.

On 12th December 2007, the Charter of Fundamental Rights was formally proclaimed at a ceremony in the European Parliament in Strasbourg. The Presidents of the threee EU institutions, Portuguese Prime Minister Jose Socrates, Commission President Jose Manual Barroso and European Parliament President Hans-Gert Pottering signed the definitive version of the Charter.

On the following day, 13th December 2007, the Treaty of Lisbon was signed by the representaives of the 27 Member States at a solemn ceremony in the historic cloisters of the Mosteiro de Jeronimos outside Lisbon. The European Council then met in Brussels, on 14th December 2007 and welcomed the outcome of the IGC, commenting that "the Lisbon Treaty provides the Union with a stable and lasting institutional framework. We expect no change in the foreseeable future, so that the Union will be able to fully concentrate on addressing the concrete challenges ahead, including globalisation and climate change."[19] The Treaty was then submitted to the 27 Member States for ratification in accordance with national procedures, including the Irish referendum.

The European Council decided to follow up a proposal from French President, Nicolas Sarkozy, to establish an independent Reflection Group to identify the key issues and developments which the Union is likely to face and to analyse how these might be addressed. The Group will not deal with institutional matters which form the substance of the Lisbon Treaty. The emphasis will be on the long term, covering a range of issues from the European "model" to global stability. The Group will be chaired by the former Spanish Prime Minister, Felipe Gonzalez, assisted by the former President of Latvia, Vaira Vike-Freiberga, and the Chairman of the Nokia Corporation, Jorma Ollila. Six more members of the Group are to be selected from across the Union on the basis of merit. A report is to be presented to the European Council in June 2010.

Conclusion

The road to Lisbon was long and never easy. Preparing for, and adjusting to, a major enlargement of the Union presented challenges to Member States, old and new. Moving on to address the institutional needs of the enlarged Union in the context of globalisation and climate change added to the range of questions to be addressed. And, in the light of the French and Dutch referendum campaigns, issues surrounding the relations between the Union and the citizen remained at both Brussels and national level.

The Lisbon text has resulted from the initial discussions surrounding the Nice Treaty, including the emergence of the Charter of Fundamental Rights, from the intensive work of the European Convention and from the period of reflection. As a participant in the Convention I recognise the essential compromise involved in its outcome, a compromise involving democratically elected parliamentarians – national and European – from across the political spectrum. Many of the most influential members of the Convention have moved on to key positions at home and in the EU institutions – four members of the present European Commission were Conventionel(le)s.

It seems inconceivable that any further negotiation – for instance after a rejection of the Lisbon Treaty in this ratification phase – could produce significant changes in the treaty text. The long and introspective crisis following the French and Dutch "no" votes proved how difficult it is to find consensus and unanimity among 27 Member States on complex institutional issues and that where such agreement is achieved it must be grasped firmly, as Chancellor Merkel clearly appreciated. Many seasoned observers of the European scene have concluded that reopening debates on the consensus on the EU institutions could lead to serious reversals at a moment when forward momentum is seen to be necessary to meet the imperatives of 21st century Europe.

There appears to be a general will across the Union's states and its political families to move forward on the basis of what has emerged from the past eight years and to focus attention and action on policy delivery, leaving institutional arguments to the historians.

The European Parliament Report on the Lisbon Treaty, adopted in February 2008, argues that "the agreement to the Treaty of every single national government in the European Union demonstrates that the elected governments of the Member States all consider that this compromise is the basis on which they wish to work together in the future and will require each of them to demonstrate maximum political commitment to ensuring ratification by 1st January 2009."[20]

References

1. Barroso, Jose Manuel (2008) Address to the University of Ghent, January 2008.
2. Laffan, Brigid (2001) "Amsterdam to Nice" in Dooge and Keatinge eds *What the Treaty of Nice Means* Dublin, Institute of European Affairs.
3. Treaty of Nice (2000) Declaration 23 on the Future of the Union.
4. Sinnott, Richard (2002) Presentation to the National Forum on Europe, January 2002.
5. European Council (2001) Presidency Conclusions of the Goteborg European Council.
6. European Council (2001) Laeken Declaration on the Future of the European Union.
7. Seville Declarations, June 2002.
8. Giscard d'Estaing, Valery (2003) Address to the Final Session of the European Convention, Brussels, June 2003.
9. European Council (2003) Presidency Conclusions of the Thessaloniki European Council.
10. Ahern, Bertie (2004) Address to Constitutional Treaty Signing Ceremony, Rome.
11. Cox, Pat (2004) Remarks at Accession Day Conference, Dublin, 1st May 2004.

12. Heaney, Seamus (2004) *Beacons at Bealtaine*, Phoenix Park, May Day 2004.
13. The Federal Trust (2008) Constitutionalism Without a Constitution, Policy Commentary, January 2008.
14. Declaration by the Heads of State or Government of the Member States of the European Union, Brussels, 16th and 17th June 2005.
15. National Forum on Europe, Sixth and Seventh Reports.
16. Barroso, Jose Manuel (2005) Address to the National Forum on Europe, June 2005.
17. Declaration by the Heads of State or Government of the Member States of the European Union, Berlin, 24th and 25th March 2007.
18. European Council (2007) Presidency Conclusions of the June European Council.
19. European Council (2007) Presidency Conclusions of the December European Council.
20. European Parliament (2008) Report on the Treaty of Lisbon.

2

Overview and Structure of the Treaty

Peadar ó Broin

Opinion polls taken since the signing of the Lisbon Reform Treaty indicate that for the vast majority of voters there is both a lack of information and perhaps some confusion as to why the European Union needs yet another treaty and what it aims to achieve.

The Road to Lisbon

The Treaty of Lisbon has been somewhat pejoratively referred to as a clandestine marriage between hope and necessity. Although the form of the Treaty was decided by national leaders during a two-year "reflection period' following the rejection of the European Constitution in 2005, the content represents the product of nearly twenty years of debate over the nature and shape of the European Union.

The European Union traces its roots back to the European Economic Community, an international organisation intended to integrate the economies of its Member States into a single market. During the 1980s, however, the single market began to grow, organically, to include policies that were not strictly grounded in an economic bedrock (such as transport, environmental protection or the rights of employees).

The advent of these policies, created by the Single European Act of 1986, sparked a debate on the political legitimacy of the European Union to take action in such areas, but also led to the development of a complex legal structure. The treaties of Maastricht (1992), Amsterdam (1997) and Nice (2001),while succeeding in achieving specific amendments, failed to achieve a sustainable institutional settlement. Twenty years later, the European Union is still wrangling with this reform.

The European Constitution of October 2004 proposed to resolve the question of political legitimacy by democratising the institutions and procedures that adopt legislation in the European Union. However, the European Constitution went beyond this remit and conferred certain "State-like" qualities on the European Union, such as a common flag, anthem, motto and the replacement of the complex treaties with a single European Union rulebook described as a "Constitution".

Following the rejection of the European Constitution by the French and Dutch electorates in 2005, the leaders of the Member States instigated a "period of reflection" during which the future course for reform was to be decided by the national governments, meeting in secret. This process was in stark contrast to the openness of the Convention, the assembly responsible for drafting the European Constitution. The Convention represented an innovative format, involving not merely national governments, but also members of national parliaments, of the institutions of the European Union, and even representatives of civil society. In the wake of the rejection of the European Constitution, the governments of the Member States were torn between abandoning a treaty text that benefited from arguably the most democratic legitimacy of any international treaty and the need to give effect to the outcome of the French and Dutch voters.

The resulting document, the Treaty of Lisbon, drafted under the formidable leadership of German Federal Chancellor, Angela Merkel, and signed by the national governments on 13 December 2007 in Lisbon's historic quarter of Belem, discards the "stateliness" of the European Constitution. Although the "downgrading" of the European Constitution has been dismissed as mere window dressing as opposed to substantive alterations, it would be almost impossible for a court of law to interpret a document that calls itself a "Constitution" and which contains a clear statement of the primacy of EU law as being no more significant than previous treaties.

Perhaps most significantly, the Treaty of Lisbon does not seek to resolve the political legitimacy debate, although it does attempt to democratise decision-making in the European Union. Instead, the Treaty of Lisbon focuses purely on institutional reform by creating a durable, efficient and democratic institutional framework for the European Union.

What the Treaty of Lisbon aims to achieve

The Treaty of Lisbon is a traditional amending treaty, in the same vein as the treaties of Amsterdam (that gave the European Union competences in justice and security policies) and Nice (that allowed the European Union to bring in more Member States). In other words it does not aim to replace what currently exists with entirely new provisions. It modifies what are collectively referred to as the "founding treaties" of the European Union, namely the Treaty on European Union and the Treaty Establishing the European Community (which will be renamed the Treaty on the Functioning of the European Union) which together constitute the EU's rulebook. The Treaty is intended to reform the institutional architecture of the European Union (hence the original name, "Reform Treaty" which has been retained by the Irish Government).

The current treaties on which the European Union is founded are rather like a completed jigsaw puzzle. The Treaty of Lisbon is a box that contains new pieces that will be inserted into the picture. To understand this process, it is necessary to comprehend how the European Union is organised at present.

The current structure of the European Union has been in place since 1993, created by the Treaty of Maastricht and amended by the treaties of Amsterdam and Nice. This structure established the European Union as an umbrella organisation under which action would be taken in three policy areas, referred to as "pillars". The first is the European Community, where Member States vote by majority on whether to adopt legislation along with the European Parliament. All legislation adopted in this field is subject to review by the European Court of Justice. The second and third pillars of this organisation, respectively foreign and defence and criminal law, remain purely intergovenmental in character, which meant that decisions are taken by unanimity with each Member State retaining a veto. The European Parliament and the European Court of Justice play consultative roles, but lack real power or influence in the latter two pillars.

The reason for such a complex structure is best explained by reference to national sensitivities in the second and third pillars. Foreign affairs and defence are considered wholly national competences, as each Member State, in the light of its history and interests, will conduct its foreign policy in a different manner to that of its neighbours. Similarly, on the issue of defence policy, certain Member States – such as Ireland, Austria, Finland, Sweden, Malta and Cyprus, have a strong commitment to neutrality or non-alignment, which prevents the creation of a harmonized European defence policy.

The same is true of criminal law, where some Member States fear that harmonization of national laws and the emergence of a European criminal court system may seriously undermine the role of the national judiciary and national legal procedure.

Global challenges, however, such as multilateral negotiations on international trade; the fight against climate change; energy security and supply; dealing with conflicts in the developing world through peacekeeping operations; the need to combat poverty; the fight against human trafficking; are examples of areas in which the individual Member States of the European Union can work more efficiently if they present a united approach to negotiations on the international level. There is an argument that such co-operation increases the clout of economically and demographically smaller nations, such as Ireland, as otherwise there is a fear that larger states will dominate and manipulate the rules of international law to suit their own objectives.

The Treaty of Lisbon abolishes the three pillars referred to above, while respecting national concerns in foreign affairs and defence policy, which remain intergovernmental in character (i.e. each Member State has a veto). On criminal law, however, the threats posed by international criminality, including money laundering, human trafficking, terrorism, have resulted in competences in criminal law moving from intergovernmental co-operation to majority voting among the Member States along with the European Parliament. All laws in this field will also be subject to judicial review by the European Court of Justice. The Treaty of Lisbon, however, is clear that the change in decision-making in this field will not result in the harmonisation of national criminal laws. Nonetheless, Ireland and the United Kingdom have requested specific provisions be included in the Treaty of Lisbon that enable the governments of those two countries to decide which legislation they shall implement in the field of criminal law.

Structure of the Treaty

The Treaty of Lisbon provides for the amendment of the two treaties which contain the rules of the present Communities and Union. These are:

- the Treaty on European Union (TEU), the Maastricht Treaty (1992), as amended;

- the Treaty Establishing the European Community i.e. the Treaty of Rome (1957) as amended, now renamed the Treaty on the Functioning of the European Union (TFEU).

The fundamental amendment is contained in the Preamble and in the first article of the Treaty on European Union which establish a European Union. This will replace and succeed the limited European Union, as established by the Maastricht Treaty in 1992, and the European Community, established by the treaties of the 1950s. The Union will exist and operate insofar as its Member

States confer competences upon it "to attain objectives they have in common".

The format of both treaties will be changed.

The Treaty on European Union will have a Preamble and six sections or Titles:

PREAMBLE

Title I: Common Provisions (Values; Objectives)

Title II: Democratic Principles

Title III: Institutions

Title IV: Enhanced Co-operation

TitleV: External Actions and Common Foreign and Security Policy

The layout of the Treaty on the Functioning of the European Union will be:

Part One: Principles

Part Two: Non-discrimination and citizenship of the Union

Part Three: Union Policies and Internal Action

Part Four: Overseas Countries and Territories

Part Five: External Action by the Union

Part Six: Institutional and Budgetary Provision

Part Seven: General and Final Provisions

As many as thirty-five binding Protocols are appended to the treaties, together with a number of Declarations intended to clarify the treaty provisions.

The Protocols include some which are of direct relevance to this country, including those on the movement of persons between Ireland and the UK (Common Travel Area) and on the position of the UK and Ireland in respect of the Area of Freedom, Security and Justice (opt-out / opt-in provisions). The Protocol relating to Article 40.3.3 of *Bunreacht na hÉireann*, dealing with abortion, is retained.

The text of the Charter of Fundamental Rights of the European Union, including the Explanations relating to the Charter, is appended. The Charter is given the same legal value as the treaties in accordance with Article 6 of the Treaty on European Union.

Conclusion

The Treaty of Lisbon represents a compromise between those who sought greater political independence for the European Union and those who preferred an organisation that remained the product of its component states. The European Constitution would have conceivably increased the political autonomy of the European Union, whereas the Treaty of Lisbon affirms the European Union as an international organisation that exists only by the will of its Member States, whose national Constitutions remain above the treaties of the European Union.

Despite statements to the contrary, the Treaty of Lisbon does not provide a blueprint for future reforms of policy implementation in the European Union. Policies depend on the choices made by the govenments of the Member States, which in turn depends on the political parties that citizens elect into office.

The Treaty of Lisbon will, however, allow for such choices to benefit from greater democratic legitimacy through the creation of an efficient institutional structure for the European Union, where the European Parliament will have increased powers; Council meetings will be held in public; legislation will be susceptible to judicial review by the European Court of Justice; national parliaments will have greater powers of scrutiny of EU legislation; and citizens of the European Union will be consulted via representative organisations, such as trade unions, and will even be afforded the opportunity to directly influence legislative initiatives through the "citizens' initiative". An overarching set of values, principles and objectives seek to govern all policies and action undertaken by the European Union.

Individual opinions on jigsaw puzzles aside, one that is twenty years in the making must be finished and new projects begun. Only once the European Union has ended its process of introspective navel-gazing will it be able to turn its attention to playing the game, rather than writing and rewriting the rules.

3

Values, Objectives and Competences

Paul Gillespie

Introduction

This chapter concentrates on the introductory sections of the Lisbon Treaty dealing with the European Union's values, objectives, democratic principles, competences, membership criteria and legal personality. They are described and analysed by looking at how this treaty amends the Treaty on European Union and the newly entitled Treaty on the Functioning of the European Union.

When they are read in a consolidated way these articles are plain and straightforward, not at all as complex as first appears from the legal form taken by the Lisbon Treaty. The articles spell out these fundamental features of the EU's functioning clearly. It is possible to identify a logical and political chain connecting values, objectives and competences in the Treaty, which will in turn give rise to agreed policies and the allocation of resources to implement them if it is ratified.

While there is much scope for continuing normative and functional argument about the balance achieved between different values, interests and political orientations it should not be assumed they are unintelligible for the ordinary citizen. Normative debate focuses mainly on whether the values and objectives identified are appropriate and have democratic credentials, whereas functional debate primarily concerns the effectiveness of what is proposed.

Values

Values are a primary and fundamental part of the Treaty. They are presented at the very beginning and underpin the later Titles and Chapters. They represent a crystallisation of political argument and debate over recent years, drawing fully on more long-standing commitments. They are presented accessibly, belying talk of the Treaty's complexity. The Lisbon Treaty presents a summation of the values incorporated in successive treaties, adding some elements and with some redrafting. But in this respect it is a consolidating rather than an innovating document.

In the Preamble the second paragraph/indent draws inspiration "from the cultural, religious and humanist inheritance of Europe, from which have developed the universal values of the inviolable and inalienable rights of the human person, freedom, democracy, equality and the rule of law". This is a clear and balanced statement of Europe's historical role in developing these values, affirming their significance for the whole of humanity. Other indents in the Preamble confirm its signatories' attachment to "the principles of liberty, democracy and respect for human rights and fundamental freedoms and the rule of law", to fundamental social rights and to "deepening the solidarity between their peoples while respecting their history, their culture and their traditions." They resolve "to continue the process of creating an ever closer union among the peoples of Europe, in which decisions are taken as closely as possible to the citizen in accordance with the principle of subsidiarity".

The principal substantive values and their associated political mechanisms are then affirmed and catalogued as follows in Article 2 of the Treaty on European Union:

> The Union is founded on the values of respect for human dignity, freedom, democracy, equality, the rule of law and respect for human rights, including the rights of persons belonging to minorities. These values are common to the

Member States in a society in which pluralism, non-discrimination, tolerance, justice, solidarity and equality between women and men prevail.

Human dignity, freedom, democracy, equality, the rule of law and respect for human rights (including of minorities) are here affirmed rather than defined. That is the normal procedure in documents of this kind which pronounce such fundamental values. Their more precise definition and application are spelled out in subsequent parts of both treaties, in the Charter of Fundamental Rights of the European Union appended to it and given legal effect by the Lisbon Treaty as well as in the European Convention for the Protection of Human Rights and Fundamental Freedoms to which the Union will accede.

It should naturally be remembered when considering these values that the treaty represents a series of compromises between contending political forces. But it is based on an extended deliberative process in the Convention which prepared the EU's Charter of Fundamental Rights (1998-2000), in the Convention on the Future of Europe (2002-3) and then in the treaty negotiations proper – first on the 2004 Treaty Establishing a Constitution for Europe and then on this Lisbon Treaty agreed in 2007 which followed on from that after it failed to be ratified. This book spells out how different sections of the treaty were further amended between the two treaties, but there is a fundamental continuity between them and the political processes involved. Had that not been the case the actual outcome in the consolidated text would have been much more incoherent than it actually is.

The legal reasoning involved is elaborated on in the set of Explanations Relating to the Charter of Fundamental Rights appended to the Charter, which although it does not have the force of law is a useful tool for interpreting these values. Thus human dignity is there explained to be "not only a fundamental right in itself but constitutes the real basis of fundamental rights", as in the

1948 Universal Declaration of Human Rights. It is pointed out that the European Court of Justice confirmed in a 2001 case that a fundamental right to human dignity is part of EU law.

This subject is dealt with substantively in Title I of the Charter under the heading Dignity, which affirms that "[e]veryone has the right to life" and that "[n]o one shall be condemned to the death penalty, or executed". Title II of the Charter deals similarly with Freedoms, Title III with Equality, Title IV with Solidarity, Title V with Citizens' Rights, Title VI with Justice and the rule of law. So readers of the Lisbon Treaty must be aware of these deeper legal and ethical/normative underpinnings as they contemplate the values it affirms.

As and when the treaty becomes applied in European Court of Justice case law the implications could be far-reaching. This is acknowledged in Article 6.3 of the Treaty on Eurpean Union stating that fundamental rights, as guaranteed by the European Convention and the constitutional traditions common to the Member States, "shall constitute general principles of the Union's law". The combination of foundational texts, judicial review and political practice over the course of the EU's history has built up a body of constitutional law with general application in cases where European law applies. The Lisbon Treaty adds to this process, but neither originates nor concludes it.

Scholarly work on this subject uses the term "constitutionalisation" to describe this legal/political process, irrespective of whether the treaties are formally referred to as constitutional documents.[1,2] "Constitutionalisation" is an inherent aspect of such political systems. Its novelty in the EU is that the process is now being applied beyond the nation-state, where such practices originally began. It is a major political and scholarly challenge to find a vocabulary adequate to this task, since it must not be assumed that what applies in the context of the nation-state automatically applies beyond it.

Democratic Principles

Reference in Article 2 of the Treaty on European Union to "a society in which pluralism, non-discrimination, tolerance, justice and solidarity and equality between women and men prevail" deals with political mechanisms to achieve values, as well as their inherent substance. These mechanisms and institutions are similarly based on deliberative processes, constitutional conventions and legal reasoning within the EU and beyond it. They are elaborated on in Title II – Provisions on Democratic Principles – dealing especially with citizenship, political parties, institutions and parliaments.

A covering Article 9 spells out the basic parameters:

> In all its activities, the Union shall observe the principle of the equality of its citizens, who shall receive equal attention from its institutions, bodies, offices and agencies. Every national of a Member State shall be a citizen of the Union. Citizenship of the Union shall be additional to national citizenship and shall not replace it.

Thus a complementary dual affiliation is affirmed, to national and Union citizenship. The basic principle goes back to the Maastricht Treaty of 1992, which first introduced the concept of European citizenship. This is predicated on national citizenship and is additional, not substitutive.

Representative democracy is declared to be the foundational principle – of Member States through their heads of state and governments and of citizens through their national parliaments, or directly at Union level through the European Parliament. Every citizen is entitled to such representation and decisions "shall be taken as closely as possible" to them. Political parties at the European level are recognized "to contribute to forming political awareness and to expressing the will of citizens of the Union". Its institutions must give them and their representatives the means and opportunity to "make known and publicly exchange their views in all areas of Union action", through an "open transparent and regular dialogue" with civil society.

Article 12 declares that "[n]ational parliaments contribute actively to the good functioning of the Union" in the following ways: by advance sight of draft legislation; applying subsidiarity and proportionality principles to it; evaluating how policies on freedom, security and justice are applied; helping to revise the treaties; dealing with new accessions; and generally cooperating amongst themselves and with the European Parliament. This treaty definitely advances the democratic role of national parliaments by spelling out these functions.

These democratic principles are elaborated in subsequent provisions of the Treaty on the Functioning of the European Union, which spells out how they are to be implemented in practical legislation and administration. Part Two of that treaty deals with Non-Discrimination and Citizenship of the Union. It says, for example, that the Council of Ministers, within the limits of its powers, may "take appropriate action to combat discrimination based on sex, racial or ethnic origin, religion or belief, disability, age or sexual orientation". EU citizens have such rights as to: move and reside freely within the territory of the Member States; vote and stand as candidates in European Parliament elections and in municipal elections on the same basis as national citizens; and to diplomatic representation by other Member States where their own state is not represented – rights substantively established in earlier treaties.

Finally, both treaties provide – in Article 11 and Article 24 respectively – for citizens' initiatives involving a request by at least one million signatures from a minimum number of Member States yet to be determined. This could be the germ of a greater direct citizen involvement in EU affairs.

Objectives

"The Union's aim is to promote peace, its values and the well-being of its peoples." This simple and well-honed sentence confidently declares the EU's main objectives in Article 3.1 of the Treaty on European Union. In the remaining paragraphs of that article these are spelled out. Little supplementary commentary is required to understand what is at stake, but it must be borne in mind that most of these objectives were established in previous treaties. Citizens are offered an area of freedom, security and justice without internal frontiers. An internal market shall be established to "work for the sustainable development of Europe based on balanced economic growth and price stability, a highly competitive social market economy, aiming at full employment and social progress, and a high level of protection and improvement of the quality of the environment. It shall promote scientific and technological advance."

The EU "shall combat social exclusion and discrimination, and shall promote social justice and protection, equality between women and men, solidarity between generations and protection of the rights of the child."

The Union "shall promote economic, social and territorial cohesion, and solidarity among Member States". Finally, "[i]t shall respect its rich cultural and linguistic diversity, and shall ensure that Europe's cultural heritage is safeguarded and enhanced".

Article 4 commits the Union to "establish an economic and monetary union whose currency is the euro". It can be seen that the treaty seeks a balance between a liberal individualistic economic agenda and a more social European model, reflecting the political arguments between all the actors involved in drawing it up. These will continue as and when it is implemented.

Article 5 deals with external policy, explicitly linking values to interests. "In its relations with the wider world, the Union shall uphold and promote its values and interests. It shall contribute to peace, security, the sustainable development of the Earth, solidarity and mutual respect among peoples, free and fair trade, eradication of poverty and the protection of human rights, in particular the rights of the child, as well as to the strict observance and the development of international law, including respect for the principles of the United Nations Charter."

These objectives are referred to elsewhere – not least in the Preamble – where they are invoked as guiding principles. Their operation and constraints are spelled out in the Treaty on the Functioning of the European Union. By accepting the Lisbon Treaty voters are agreeing to make these values and interests the determining ones in the EU's emerging foreign policy, capable of being invoked when there is dispute about its objectives. As is normal in such cases, they are pitched sufficiently abstractly to allow substantial room for argument about their substance and the appropriate balance between different political orientations.

Competences

A fundamental constraint on the EU's action is contained in the section on competences in Articles 4 and 5 of the Treaty on European Union and in Title I of the Treaty on the Functioning of the European Union. These state clearly for the first time the distinction between competences that are exclusive to the EU, those that are shared with the Member States and those where the EU takes supportive or supplementary action only. General principles are set out to determine how this will work in the Treaty on European Union, while the other treaty lists the relevant policy domains. It is a good example of how this treaty clarifies and consolidates contentious issues in the political division of labour, reflecting political leaderships' awareness of how sensitive a matter it is for citizens. One commentator concludes that "if there are losers and winners in institutional terms, the most significant factor is the increase in the power of national institutions vis-à-vis the EU institutions – a trend exemplified by the new role given to national parliaments".[3]

The outcome is a major political achievement, which should determine the EU's political life for some time to come, after the turbulence and uncertainty of the period following the end of the Cold War, the continent's subsequent reunification and the EU's enlargement. A pattern of multi-level governance is laid down which looks sustainable and durable, allowing political leaders to concentrate on effective results or outputs, while citizens gradually become aware of the legal constraints on "ever closer union". This does not resolve arguments about the risks or opportunities attending politicisation of EU affairs, or how to create a transnational politics and public sphere, but it can put them on a more stable plane. The scholarly literature on the EU echoes mainstream political debate among its leaders and citizens on this subject as described in Brigid Laffan's chapter above.

Article 4.1 of the Treaty on European Union states baldly that "competences not conferred upon the Union in the Treaties remain with the Member States". Article 4.2 strongly acknowledges national rights, structures and identities:

> The Union shall respect the equality of Member States before the Treaties as well as their national identities, inherent in their fundamental structures, political and constitutional, inclusive of regional and local self-government. It shall respect their essential State functions, including ensuring the territorial integrity of the State, maintaining law and order and safeguarding national security. In particular, national security remains the sole responsibility of each Member State.

This is balanced by a commitment of the Member States and the Union to assist each other, facilitate achievement of the Union's tasks and refrain from any measure that could jeopardise attainment of the Union's objectives.

Union competences are limited by the principle of *conferral* from the Member States, and their use by those of *subsidiarity* and *proportionality*. Competences not conferred on the EU by the treaties remain with the Member States. This is a fundamental principle, agreement on which looks like determining the EU's operation for a long time to come. Subsidiarity limits Union action only to those objectives which cannot be achieved by Member States at central, regional or local levels, but can better be achieved, "by reasons of the scale or effects of the proposed action," at Union level. National parliaments are given the task of policing the subsidiarity norm, as set out in a special Protocol on that subject and a separate one on proportionality. This latter norm specifies that "the content and form of Union action shall not exceed what is necessary to achieve the objectives of the Treaties". Draft legislation must henceforward be justified on this basis by the Commission, dealing with financial impact, quantitative and qualitative indicators.

TREATY ON THE FUNCTIONING OF THE EUROPEAN UNION

TITLE I – CATEGORIES AND AREAS OF UNION COMPETENCE

Article 2
1. When the Treaties confer on the Union exclusive competence in a specific area, only the Union may legislate and adopt legally binding acts, the Member States being able to do so themselves only if so empowered by the Union or for the implementation of Unions acts.
2. When the Treaties confer on the Union a competence shared with the Member States in a specific area, the Union and the Member States may legislate and adopt legally binding acts in that area. The Member States shall exercise their competence to the extent that the Union has not exercised its competence. The Member States shall again exercise their competence to the extent that the Union has decided to cease exercising its competence.

3. The Member States shall coordinate their economic and employment policies within arrangements as determined by this Treaty, which the Union shall have competence to provide.
4. The Union shall have competence, in accordance with the provisions of the Treaty on European Union, to define and implement a common foreign and security policy, including the progressive framing of a common defence policy.
5. In certain areas and under the conditions laid down in the Treaties, the Union shall have competence to carry out actions to support, coordinate or supplement the actions of the Member States, without thereby superseding their competence in these areas.
6. The scope of and arrangements for exercising the Union's competences shall be determined by the provisions of the Treaties relating to each area.

Article 3
1. The Union shall have exclusive competence in the following areas:
   (*a*) customs union;
   (*b*) the establishing of the competition rules necessary for the functioning of the internal market;
   (*c*) monetary policy for the Member States whose currency is the euro;
   (*d*) the conservation of marine biological resources under the common fisheries policy;
   (*e*) the common commercial policy.
2. The Union shall also have exclusive competence for the conclusion of an internal agreement when its conclusion is provided for in a legislative act of the Union or is necessary to enable the Union to exercise its internal competence, or insofar as its conclusion may affect common rules or alter their scope.

Article 4

1. The Union shall share competence with the Member States where the Treaties confer on it a competence which does not relate to the areas referred to in Articles 3 and 6.
2. Shared competence between the Union and the Member States applies in the following principal areas:
   (*a*) internal market;
   (*b*) social policy, for the aspects defined in this Treaty;
   (*c*) economic, social and territorial cohesion;
   (*d*) agriculture and fisheries, excluding the conservation of marine biological resources;
   (*e*) environment;
   (*f*) consumer protection;
   (*g*) transport;
   (*h*) trans-European networks;
   (*i*) energy;
   (*j*) area of freedom, security and justice;
   (*k*) common safety concerns in public health matters, for the aspects defined in this Treaty.
3. In the areas of research, technological development and space, the Union shall have competence to carry out activities, in particular to define and implement programmes; however, the exercise of that competence shall not result in Member States being prevented from exercising theirs.
4. In the areas of development cooperation and humanitarian aid, the Union shall have competence to carry out activities and conduct a common policy; however, the exercise of that competence shall not result in Member States being prevented from exercising theirs.

Article 5

1. The Member States shall coordinate their economic policies within the Union. To this end, the Council shall adopt measures, in particular broad guidelines, for these policies. Specific provisions shall apply to those Member States whose currency is the euro.
2. The Union shall take measures to ensure coordination of the employment policies of the Member States, in particular by defining guidelines for these policies.
3. The Union may take initiatives to ensure coordination of Member States' social policies.

Article 6

The Union shall have competence to carry out actions to support, coordinate or supplement the actions of the Member States. The areas of such action shall, at European level, be:

(*a*)   protection and improvement of human health;
(*b*)   industry;
(*c*)   culture;
(*d*)   tourism;
(*e*)   education, vocational training, youth and sport;
(*f*)   civil protection;
(*g*)   administrative cooperation.

These new procedures involving national parliaments are a significant innovation of the Lisbon Treaty. The parliaments will have eight weeks in which to provide a reasoned argument objecting to EU legislation on the grounds of subsidiarity – a kind of "yellow card" procedure. The two protocols spell out procedures for voting, review and judicial action. Insofar as the Union's democratic deficit exists as much at domestic as transnational level this addresses one of its most important sources. It is one response to the defeat of the constitutional treaty in France and the Netherlands, and could be especially effective in dealing with justice and home affairs issues.

Membership Criteria

Article 49 of the Treaty on European Union sets out clearly and concisely how states may apply for membership. It says "[a]ny European State which respects the values referred to in Article 2 [dealt with in section II of this chapter] and is committed to promoting them may apply to become a member of the Union". No definition of European is given, whether geographical or cultural, in keeping with the tradition of leaving that open to political decision by the European Council over successive enlargements of the EU.

The article goes on to lay down a procedure for application, which is addressed to the Council. The European Parliament and national parliaments shall be notified. The Council "shall act unanimously after consulting the Commission and after seeking the consent of the European Parliament, which shall act by a majority of its component members". The conditions of eligibility agreed upon by the Council are to be taken into account in the negotiations (normally conducted by the Commission) with the applicant state. When they are concluded an agreement is reached with Member States and "submitted for ratification by all the contracting States in accordance with their respective constitutional requirements". In the negotiations with Bulgaria and Romania there were 31 chapters in the accession treaty, whereas those currently under way with Croatia and Turkey have 36.

Criteria for membership include for the first time those laid down at the 1993 Copenhagen Council, whose Conclusions read as follows:

Membership requires that the candidate country has achieved stability of institutions guaranteeing democracy, the rule of law, human rights and respect for and protection of minorities, the existence of a functioning market economy as well as the capacity to cope with competitive pressure and market forces within the Union. Membership presupposes the candidate's ability to take on the obligations of membership including adherence to the aims of political, economic and monetary union.

These values are now expressed in Articles 2 and 3.

Membership may be suspended according to a procedure laid down in Article 7. It provides that on a reasoned proposal by one third of the Member States, by the European Parliament or by the Commission, the Council, acting by a four fifths majority and with the European Parliament's assent, may determine there is a clear risk of a breach by a Member State of the values referred to in Article 2. The Member State must be heard and can be given recommendations, using the same procedure and subject to regular verification that the grounds for complaint continue to apply. If a breach is confirmed the Council can suspend certain membership rights, with the legal obligations of the Treaties continuing to apply. The article does not deal explicitly with expulsion.

Article 50 of the TEU provides that any Member State of the EU may withdraw from it in accordance with its own constitutional requirements. A negotiation will be conducted and concluded by the Council, acting by qualified majority, including on timing and particular arrangements. Any application to rejoin would be subject to the accession criteria. This is the first time an exit option has been included in the treaties.

Finally, Article 8 provides that the EU "shall develop a special relationship with neighbouring countries, aiming to establish an area of prosperity and good neighbourliness, founded on the values of the Union and characterized by close and peaceful relations based on cooperation". Specific agreements may be so concluded, containing reciprocal rights and obligations and the possibility of joint activities. This gives legal force to the European Neighbourhood Policy, which has now been extended to include the EuroMed countries of North Africa and the Middle East, eastern European states such as Ukraine, Belarus and Moldova, and certain Caucasian states. Neighbourhood status and prospective EU membership are hereby distinguished more systematically.

Legal Personality

Article 47 of the Treaty on European Union reads: "The Union shall have legal personality." This will allow the Union itself to take legal action, become a member of international organisations, become a party to an international convention such as the European Convention on Human Rights (ECHR) and to conclude international treaties and agreements. It will make the EU's external role more effective, transparent and legally certain. But it does not alter the existing balance of competences between the Union and the Member States, nor the procedures for concluding international agreements. But agreements concluded by the Union are binding on its institutions and members.

Conclusion

Values, objectives and competences go to the heart of any political system. They need to be identified clearly if such a system is to be comprehensible and legitimate among those bound by it. The Lisbon Treaty is certainly intended to achieve that goal, whatever the peculiarities of its specific origins in the aftermath of the French and Dutch referendum votes in 2005 against its predecessor, the Treaty Establishing a Constitution for Europe. Symbolic, state-like constitutional language has been stripped from that document in the Lisbon Treaty, but its institutional content remains mostly intact in the new text.[4]

In moving from one text to the other there has been a definite change of political emphasis. The constitutional treaty was intended to address a crisis of legitimacy as well as of effectiveness in the EU's governing structures and values. Its point of departure was expressed inquisitorially in the 2001 Laeken Declaration as follows: "How to bring citizens, and primarily the young, closer to the European design and the European institutions, how to organise politics and the European political area in an enlarged Union, and how to develop the Union into a stabilising factor and a model in the new, multipolar world?"

The resulting Convention on the Future of Europe which bargained the major draft of the Constitutional Treaty in 2002-3 was drawn from a much wider circle of political actors than the usual diplomatic and governmental ones in the four successive treaties from 1987 onwards. This, it was hoped, would enhance the EU's public legitimacy, in the sense that the exercise of power and collective decisions are accepted voluntarily even by those who dislike or disagree with them. The accumulation of change since the 1980s was widely assumed to have transformed European integration from a mainly elite-driven endeavour to one requiring the consent and participation of mass publics.[5]

If that is so the interval following the Dutch and French results can be seen as a retreat in terms of political process from public engagement back to diplomatic inter-governmentalism. The governments are still convinced of the need for more effective institutions and decision-making as they use the EU to deal with a more interdependent world, and they know that effective outputs will determine their legitimacy; but they have cast aside the effort to seek symbolic legitimation, many fearing that populist nationalism would overtake their capacity to sell such an outcome to domestic publics in referendums. In the event Ireland is probably the only Member State having a referendum on the Lisbon Treaty and bears the burden and the opportunity for public deliberation and decision about it.

The analysis in this chapter shows that despite the shift of political emphasis the "constitutional" content of the treaty remains intact and can readily be identified. The referendum campaign necessarily pitches those in favour in opposition to those against the treaty. It is in several respects an artificial contest, in that it conceals differences of view about the merits of "politicising" the EU, mostly, but not exclusively, on the Yes side of the argument. At least three readings of this issue are current in the scholarly literature and in wider political debate, as discussed in Brigid Laffan's introductory chapter. A liberal inter-governmental view holds that irrespective of whether the treaty is passed the EU has reached an effective political settlement depending on useful policy outputs and not requiring further political inputs.[6] A quasi-federal argument in favour of politicising says that is required to make its political system more democratically accountable and competitive on left-right lines.[7,8] And thirdly is the view that holds the EU does not have sufficient political glue to hold together if politicisation proceeds too rapidly or extensively, which could rebound on those who favour that course.[9,10]

These arguments will continue irrespective of whether the treaty is ratified by all Member States. This chapter has shown there is plenty to argue about whichever way it goes.

References

1. Weiler, J.H.H. (1999) *The Constitution of Europe*, Cambridge University Press.
2. Rittberger, Berthold and Frank Schimmelfennig eds (2006), The Constitutionalisation of the European Union, special issue *Journal of European Public Policy* 18 (8).
3. Lequesne, Christian 2007, "Towards a new institutional balance?" pp 13-21 in *Challenge Europe* 17, special issue, "The people's project, the new EU Treaty and the prospects for future integration", Brussels: European Policy Centre.
4. Gillespie, Paul (2007), "EU must combine National and European Politics", *The Irish Times*, 6 October.
5. Follesdal, Andreas and Simon Hix (2006) "Why There is a Democratic Deficit in the EU: A Response to Majone and Moravcsik", *Journal of Common Market Studies* 44(3), 533-562.
6. Moravcsik, Andrew (2005), "The European Constitutional Compromise and the Neofunctionalist Legacy", *Journal of European Public Policy* 12.2: 349-386.
7. Hix, Simon 2005, Why the EU Needs (Left-Right) Politics: Policy Reform and Accountability are Impossible Without It, Paris: Notre Europe Policy Paper No.13.

8. Hix, Simon (2008), What's Wrong With the European Union and How to Fix It, Cambridge Polity Press.

9. Bartolini, Stefano (2005) Should the Union be "Politicised"? Prospects and Risks, Paris: Notre Europe, Policy Paper No.19.

10. Bartolini, Stefano (2005a) *Restructuring Europe*, Oxford: Oxford University Press.

4

Institutions and Decision-making

Denis O'Leary

*Editor's Note: In this chapter the two treaties are designated as:
TEU (Treaty on European Union) and TFEU (Treaty on the
Functioning of the European Union)*

Introduction

The forms of decision-making developed by the European Union
are unique to it as an international organisation. This chapter
concentrates on the main changes that will be brought about by the
Lisbon Treaty. The changes confirm existing arrangements in some
instances, notably the continued inter-governmental character of
the common foreign and security policy, while in other instances
anomalies and lacunae are corrected, for example, by the abolition
of the system of pillars and the reduction in the number of legal
instruments and procedures.

The driving political force behind the changes lies in the
recognition that rules that worked well for a Union that had grown
from six to fifteen members cannot do so for a Union of twenty-
seven Member States (a number that is likely to grow even
further).

The present situation

The work of the European Union is at present divided between three different legal orders and methods of decision-making, the so-called three pillars. The first pillar encompasses the work of the European Community, the second the common foreign and security policy and the third police and judicial cooperation. However, action under all three takes place in the context of a single institutional framework as stipulated by Article 3 of the existing Treaty on European Union. These arrangements have proved to be unsatisfactory. There is a lack of clarity between the pillars and this has given rise to both political and legal dispute between Member States and the institutions and between the institutions themselves.

Abolition of the three pillars with the European Union becoming successor to the European Community

The Treaty of Lisbon adds to the opening paragraph of Article 1 of the existing Treaty on European Union that reads – "By this Treaty, the HIGH CONTRACTING PARTIES establish among themselves a EUROPEAN UNION, hereinafter called 'the Union'" – the words "on which the Member States confer competences to attain objectives they have in common".

Also added to Article 1 is the provision that "The Union shall be founded on the present Treaty and on the Treaty on the Functioning of the European Union (hereinafter referred to as 'the Treaties'). These two Treaties shall have the same legal value. The Union shall replace and succeed the European Community". (Article 2 of the Lisbon Treaty changes the title of the "Treaty establishing the European Community" to "Treaty on the Functioning of the European Union").

In other words, the new Treaty builds on the existing European Union and the treaties that underpin it. The failed Constitutional Treaty would have abolished all existing treaties and re-founded the Union.

Division of competences between the Union and the Member States

Underlying many of the disputes relating to the use of the three pillars, and the reason why they came into existence in the first instance, was the concern of Member States not to cede inadvertently to the European Union competences that they wished to retain. In this context, a distinction has to be drawn between competences that are ceded between governments and the rules in respect of which cession bind them only i.e. have an inter-governmental character and those ceded to the European Community which bind not only governments but their peoples i.e. have a supra-national character.

The European Court of Justice, in a landmark judgement (1963 *Van Gend en Loos*) stated, in terms easily accessible to the layman, that "the European Economic Community constitutes a new legal order of international law for the benefit of which the [Member] States have limited their sovereign rights, albeit within limited fields, and the subjects of which comprise not only the Member States but also their nationals". In other words, the Court established that the EEC was not only a "union" of governments but of peoples and that individuals could seek to have their rights protected under EC law before their national courts and that these national courts had a duty to guarantee them. The Court also underlined that "these rights arise not only where they are expressly granted by the Treaty but also by reason of the obligations which the Treaty imposes in a clearly defined way".

It is, therefore, not easy to draw a dividing line between national and EC competences and, indeed, no such absolute dividing line is possible as obligations, such as that of non-discrimination, can arise in any area of activity. But this does not mean that the Union is encroaching on national competences in an uncontrolled way. Member States have "limited their sovereign rights" in only "limited fields". A simple measure is the balance between EU expenditure and that of the governments of the Member States. The EU budget accounts for only 2% of the Member States' public expenditure.

Articles 2 to 6 TFEU spell out for the first time the "categories and areas of Union competence".

SUMMARY OF CATEGORIES AND AREAS OF UNION COMPETENCE

EXCLUSIVE [Article 3 TFEU]	SHARED [Article 4 TFEU]	SUPPORT, COORDINATION, etc. [Article 6 TFEU]	COORDINATION [Article 3 TFEU]	COMPETENCE TO DEFINE & IMPLEMENT [Article 2/4 TFEU]
Customs Union	Internal Market	Human Health	Economic policy	CFSP/CSDP
Competition Rules	Social Policy	Industry	Employment policies	
Monetary Policy	Cohesion	Culture	Social policies	
(Euro Area)	Agriculture and	Tourism		
Marine Conservation	Fisheries	Education, Vocational		
Common Commercial	Environment	Training, Youth and		
Policy	Consumer Protection	Sport		
Conclusion Certain	Transport	Civil Protection		
International	Trans-European	Administrative		
Agreements	Networks	Cooperation		
	Energy			
	Area of Freedom, Security and Justice			
	Public Health (Safety)			
	Research, Technology and Space	"parallel" [Article 4.3 TFEU]		
	Development	competences		
	Cooperation and	[Article 4.4 TFEU]		
	Humanitarian Aid			

This categorisation builds on the case-law of the European Court of Justice and is a recognition by the Member States of the situation as it stands, the only substantive change being the abolition of the special status of police and judicial cooperation under the third pillar and its inclusion among shared competence under the Area of Freedom, Security and Justice.

As far as the common foreign and security policy is concerned, the competence is one "to define and implement", the situation as it exists at present. There is no jurisdiction for the European Court of Justice (except in some limited cases). The continuing inter-governmental character of actions by the Union is underlined by the fact that the present right of proposal by the Commission and/or to convene a meeting of the Council, set out in Article 22 of the existing Treaty on European Union is removed. These powers are, instead, assigned to the High Representative. The Council, i.e. the representatives of national governments, acts alone although it must have regard to the opinion of the European Parliament, the role of which is carefully circumscribed in Article 36 of the Treaty on European Union.

However, there is provision, in Article 288 TFEU, for the Council to use only one form of legal instrument, that of a "decision". In terms, therefore, of the legal instruments used, the distinction between the pillars will cease to exist.

The Community Method

The essential characteristic of the system of decision-making governing the first pillar, and known as the Community method, is that the European Commission is not simply a secretariat in the normal sense but a political or supra-national body that makes proposals and participates in the decision-making procedure with Member States.

Its weight in the negotiating process is guaranteed by three equally essential elements:

(i) Ministers (i.e. the Council) can only make decisions (usually in adopting legislation) on the basis of a Commission proposal and after consulting the European Parliament

(ii) Decisions are usually taken by qualified majority vote (QMV)

(iii) Ministers can only overrule the Commission by unanimity (Article 293.1 TFEU). Furthermore, the Commission "may alter its proposal at any time during the procedures leading to the adoption of a Union act" (Article 293.2 TFEU), an option that is often an essential tool in the Commission's negotiating strategy to "promote the general interest of the Union", this being its core Treaty task (Article 17.1 TEU).

The Commission's role and power has been diluted somewhat by the introduction of the co-decision procedure (Article 294

TFEU) under which the Council and the European Parliament now act jointly as the legislature. Unless both these bodies agree, a proposal cannot be adopted.

If the procedure reaches the conciliation stage, they can agree a proposal with which the Commission may not be in agreement (cf. Article 293.1 reference to Articles 294.10 and 294.13 TFEU).

The institutional balance

The power to implement actions under competences ceded to the Union (or, rather the European Community, until the Union becomes its successor) is subject to democratic representative requirements and a system of checks and balances akin to what would be found in any democratic system, whether unicameral, bicameral or federal. The three institutions, European Parliament, Council of Ministers and Commission, under the overall power of review of their actions by the European Court of Justice, each have a role to play.

The system is also referred to as the institutional triangle. The institutions enjoy prerogatives in their own right. Their role in decision-making varies depending on the relevant provisions of the Treaties. The Council of Ministers, as seen above, acts alone in relation to the common foreign and security policy (and will continue to do so). The European Council is not currently an institution and is not part of the formal decision-making structure.

The Lisbon Treaty changes the institutional structure in a number of important respects:

(i) The European Council becomes an Institution (Article 13 TEU)

(ii) It elects its President by qualified majority for a period of 2½ years, renewable once (Article 15.5 TEU)

(iii) The ECJ will be able to review the legality of its acts "intended to produce legal effects vis-à-vis third parties" (Article 263 TFEU)

(iv) The High Representative of the Union for Foreign Affairs and Security Policy will simultaneously (*a*) chair the

Foreign Affairs configuration of the Council (Article 1.3 TEU) and (*b*) be a Vice-President of the Commission (Article 18.4 TEU)

(v) The common foreign and security policy "shall be put into effect by the High Representative and by the Member States, using national and Union resources" (Article 26.3 TEU).

(vi) As from 2014, the number of Commissioners shall correspond to two-thirds of the Member States chosen "on the basis of a system of strictly equal rotation between the Member States" (Article 17.5 TEU).

The major question raised is whether the changes will contribute to improving the functioning of the Union without disturbing the existing institutional balance. There are a number of considerations that suggest that this will be the case. There is no major change to the legal prerogatives of either the Commission acting as a college or the European Parliament. The institutional role of the European Council is strengthened but it is specifically precluded from exercising "legislative functions". (Article 15.1 TEU).

There is already widespread recognition that the chairing of the European Council by each succeeding Presidency is unsatisfactory, the rotating President, as a Head of State or Government, having many other demands on his/her time. The role of the elected President is, in any case, carefully circumscribed (Article 15.6 TEU).

The "double-hatting" role given to the High Representative is both more substantive and innovative and may prove more problematical, especially in relation to setting up the arrangements for the External Action Service. Again, however, the need for better coordination between all aspects of the conduct of the external action of the Union is already widely recognised. The detailed system for the nomination of Commissioners to apply from 2014 has yet to be worked out.

Legal personality of the Union, simplification of legal instruments and creation of a hierarchy of legal norms

A new provision (Article 47 TEU) states explicitly that "The Union shall have legal personality". This confirms its existing implicit legal personality (flowing from its capacity to sign international agreements under the terms of Articles 24 and 38 of the existing Treaty on European Union) and its role as successor to the European Community that, of course, always enjoyed an explicit legal personality.

Fifteen different legal instruments spread across the three pillars are reduced to the existing five instruments contained in Article 249 of the Treaty establishing the European Community viz. Regulations, Directives, Decisions, Recommendations and Opinions (Article 288 TFEU). The only substantive change is to make the definition of a decision somewhat wider to include the circumstances in which it may not have an addressee (correcting a lacuna in the existing treaty text).

The Lisbon Treaty also introduces a major innovation in that it creates a hierarchy of legal norms i.e. it distinguishes between legislative and other acts, the distinctive characteristic of the former being that they are adopted under the ordinary legislative procedure (the existing co-decision procedure) or a special legislative procedure where the Council is usually acting alone (Article 289 TFEU).

The major impact of the change is that it enables the legislature (under either procedure) to create new forms of either a "delegated act" that allows the Commission to "adopt non-legislative acts of general application to supplement certain non-essential elements of a legislative act" (Article 290 TFEU] or an "implementing act" that allows for the conferral of implementing powers on the Commission (Article 291 TFEU).

These new forms of subordinate legal instrument will provide an essential element of flexibility in an enlarged European Union that is presently missing. Legislation is often too detailed and prescriptive and incapable of amendment other than by re-starting lengthy legislative procedures. The powers delegated to the Commission are, however, carefully circumscribed. Delegated powers may be revoked by either the Council or the European Parliament or may blocked by them. With regard to implementing powers, the Council and the European Parliament may decide, by way of regulations and under the ordinary legislative procedure, to establish committees of national Member State representatives to monitor and control the actions of the Commission ("comitology" procedures).

The Treaty of Lisbon extends the coverage of the ordinary legislative procedure to the extent that it can be viewed as the default procedure, as its title suggest, for most of the business of the European Union involving the adoption of legislation.

The Lisbon Treaty also provides that the Council shall act by qualified majority except where the Treaties provide otherwise (Article 16.3 TEU). The previous rule in this area was that of simple majority. This change requires that the rule of simple majority be stated explicitly at various points in the new treaty texts for the adoption of procedural decisions.

Changes in voting rules

The current rules setting out the voting arrangements for the Council are contained in Article 205 of the Treaty Establishing the European Community. They assign a specific total of weighted votes to each Member State with a threshold set for the establishment of a qualified majority. Each time a new Member State joins, the table of voting weights has to be re-negotiated. This has given rise to major difficulties and diplomatic struggles between Member States, especially the six largest Member States which now account for 75% of the populations (and economic activity) of the Union. The negotiations on the Treaty of Lisbon proved no exception. Agreement was reached, in extremis, that, as from 1 November 2014, a qualified majority should be defined "as at least 55% of the members of the Council, comprising at least fifteen of them and representing Member States comprising at least 65% of the population of the Union". A blocking minority must include at least four Council members.

However, in the Protocol on Transitional Provisions attached to the Lisbon Treaty, it is stipulated that between 1 November 2014 and 31 March 2017 a member of the Council may demand that a decision be taken under the existing mechanism. In other words, during this period Member States must have regard to which of the two systems would prove most advantageous to them and act accordingly.

Furthermore, Declaration No. 7 sets out the terms of a draft Decision of the Council that allows percentages of population and Member States "necessary to constitute a blocking minority", varying between the period 1 November 2014 and 31 March 2017 and "as from 1 April 2017" i.e. open-ended, to block the Council from proceeding by qualified majority and to have the matter referred to the European Council. The latter is to "do all in its power to reach within a reasonable time and without prejudicing obligatory times limits laid down by Union law, a satisfactory solution to address concerns raised".

In other words, the so-called Ionnina compromise (after the Greek town where it was first agreed) is to continue in another form. It allows Member States who are close to achieving a blocking minority to delay a voting decision but not indefinitely.

Changes in the composition of the Commission

The "members of the Commission shall be chosen on the ground of their general competence and European commitment from persons whose independence is beyond doubt"; "shall neither seek nor take instructions from any government or other institution, body, office or entity" i.e. texts left unchanged by the Lisbon Treaty (Article 17 TEU).

However, the Lisbon Treaty changes both the method of appointment of the Commission and its President. (As from 1 November 2014, the number of Commissioners "will correspond to two-thirds of the number of Member States". They are to be chosen on the basis of a system of strict "equal rotation". The European Council must decide unanimously throughout the procedures and "may alter this number".)

The procedure for appointment, in summary, is as follows. The European Council, acting by a qualified majority, will propose a candidate for President of the Commission to the European Parliament "taking into account the elections to the European Parliament" i.e. when the outcome of the elections is known. The Parliament must approve by a majority of its component members. If the Parliament does not agree, the procedure can be repeated. The Council [of Ministers] "by common accord" with the President-elect of the Commission, adopts the list of persons proposed "on the basis of suggestions made by Member States" for appointment as members of the Commission. All members of the Commission (i.e. including President and High Representative) shall be subject "as a body" (i.e. individuals cannot be rejected) to a "vote of consent" by the European Parliament i.e. a majority of Members actually voting.

There has been a deal of criticism of the fact that the number of members of the Commission is to be reduced and that Member States may only make "suggestions" rather than nominate a Commissioner as is presently the case. However, the criticism has been that the Commission lacks democratic legitimacy and the changes are intended to meet, at least to some extent, this criticism by giving a larger role to the directly-elected European Parliament.

As the changes will take place in different timeframes, the nomination of the next Commission being for a "full" Commission i.e. a member from each Member State, there will be experience of the new system of nomination before the knottier problem of agreeing the system of strict "equal rotation" for a Commission reduced in numbers is tackled. The Commission as a body remains "responsible to the European Parliament" (Article 17.8 TEU).

Representative democracy

Article 9 TEU repeats Article 8 of the existing Treaty. "Every national of a Member State shall be a citizen of the Union. Citizenship of the Union shall be additional to national citizenship and shall not replace it."

Article 10.2 TEU adds a very useful clarification. "Citizens are directly represented at Union level in the European Parliament. Member States are represented in the European Council by the Heads of State and Government and in the Council by their governments, themselves democratically accountable either to their national Parliaments, or to their citizens".

Article 11 TEU states that the Institutions must maintain "an open, transparent and regular dialogue" with representative associations and civil society. Not less than one million citizens, who are nationals of a "significant" number of Member States, may invite the Commission to submit proposals.

The Powers of National Parliaments

The Lisbon Treaty makes specific, and extensive, provisions for the role of national parliaments.

(a) A Protocol on the Application of the Principles of Subsidiarity and Proportionality spelling out the role of national Parliaments in the European Union is appended to the Treaties. All draft legislative proposals must be sent by the Commission to them and one-third have the power to object within an eight-week time limit ("yellow card"). If a simple majority continues to object, the Commission must refer the issue to the Council and the Parliament for decision ("orange card").

(b) National Parliaments are given a particular role with regard to the Area of Freedom, Security and Justice (Article 70 TFEU).

(*c*) They now take part in the revision procedures of the Treaties [Article 48 TEU].

(*d*) They are to be notified of applications for accession to the Union.

(*e*) They take part in inter-parliamentary cooperation between national Parliaments and with the European Parliament.

These provisions reinforce the treaty-based role of national Parliaments. However, they do not remove from them the existing fundamental requirements of (*a*) policing the role of national Ministers in the Council and (*b*) implementing EU legislation when action by national Parliaments is required.

Conclusion

The foregoing spells out the main changes to what may be described as the institutional architecture of the European Union. (There are a number of overlapping and residual issues that are dealt with elsewhere in this publication e.g. relating to protection of data, sanctions against individual etc.).

A feature of the changes is their integrated or inter-locking character. They introduce a considerable degree of clarity with regard to the legal instruments that can be used, the procedures to be applied and the role of the institutions in each instance. This avoids needless repetition in individual articles and adds greatly to the ready comprehension of the texts.

5

The Social Dimension

Tony Brown

Background

In 1957, the Treaty of Rome was signed by the six founding members of the European Economic Community and set the objectives of economic and social progress, to be achieved by common action to eliminate the barriers which divided Europe.

In 2007, the twenty-seven members of the European Union signed the Berlin Declaration celebrating the ending of that division by the enlargement of the Union and restating the ideal of a European model combining economic success and social cohesion.

The economic dimension of European integration has been developed and expanded by the achievement of the Single Market – with its emphasis on free movement of persons, goods, services and capital – the impact of Cohesion Policy and the Structural Funds, and the introduction of the Single Currency. More recently, a key initiative saw the adoption of the Lisbon Agenda with its emphasis on growth, competitiveness and social cohesion.

The social dimension of European Union policy has evolved over the years with solid achievements in areas such as equality between men and women, training opportunities and mobility for young workers and labour law, but with important issues remaining the subject of intense political debate across the Union, ranging from the provisions for social protection and workers' rights to measures to combat discrimination and social exclusion.

The signing of the Lisbon Treaty in December 2007 saw the culmination of a prolonged process of debate and negotiation which centred on the reform of the EU's institutional framework but which also addressed the relative competences of the Union and its Member States and the balance between the economic and social aspects of integration.

Convention on the Future of Europe

The text of the Lisbon Treaty is based on the outcome of the representative Convention which completed its work in the summer of 2003. The social dimension of the Union was a key issue in its deliberations with the Working Groups on Economic Governance and Social Europe exciting deep and, at times, spirited debate. There was a strong Irish input to these groups with all Irish Convention members participating fully and with the Irish Secretary General of the Commission playing a key role.

The report of the Social Europe Working Group which represented a notable compromise between political and social forces and argued that social considerations constitute an essential part of European integration, rejecting any artificial division between economic and social objectives. It identified a range of social concerns for inclusion in the formal statement of the Union's values and objectives. The current competences of the Union in the social field were considered adequate.[1] This approach was sustained in the final Convention text and in the eventual outcome of the Intergovernmental Conference which produced the draft Constitutional Treaty.

The Constitutional Treaty was ratified by eighteen Member States between 2004 and 2005 but was rejected by French and Dutch voters in referendums held in 2005. This led to the so-called "period of reflection" during which EU leaders consulted on the options for progress on the agenda of reform which had led to the formation of the Convention and which was linked to the historic enlargement of the Union from fifteen to twenty-five Member States in May 2004 and eventually to twenty-seven in January 2007. This process resulted in the adoption of the text of the Lisbon Treaty, abandoning the form and some of the content of the Constitutional Treaty for that of a traditional reform treaty.

The Social Dimension in the Lisbon Treaty

From a social perspective, the Lisbon Treaty builds on the substance and achievements of the previous Treaties. It provides a basis for progress towards the stated values and goals of a Social Europe, facilitating increased connection between the Union and its citizens and States but without creating new competences. The Treaty does not endorse a particular economic and social model but rather balances competing options.

The Lisbon Treaty provides a framework for economic and social development in line with the emerging needs of the enlarged Union and on the basis of policy choices by the Member States across a whole spectrum of issues. While fundamental principles are established and the social policy *acquis* is fully protected the future direction of social policy is not settled definitively and many important issues remain properly the subject of normal political debate and decision at both national and EU levels.

A Union of Values and Rights

Most of the treaty articles relating to the social dimension of the Union are found in Part Three of the Treaty on the Functioning of the European Union. Yet the social dimension informs the entire text, which should be assessed as a whole. In particular, the Values and Objectives, in the early articles of the Treaty on European Union and the incorporation of the Charter of Fundamental Rights through an article and an attached Protocol provide a basis for development of a more "social" Europe which takes into account the working and social lives of EU citizens.

The Preamble and the early articles of the Treaty on European Union establish the EU as a Union of Values and Rights. In Article 2, the Union's Values are set out in terms which give positive expression to social concepts: human dignity, equality, respect for human rights, respect for minorities, non-discrimination, tolerance, justice, solidarity and equality between women and men.

The statement of the Union's Objectives in Article 3 reflects the outcome of the Convention Working Group on Social Europe, and gives extensive expression to social considerations: sustainable development; the Social Market Economy; the linked goals of full employment and social progress; combating social exclusion and discrimination; promotion of social justice and social protection; equality between men and women; solidarity between generations; promotion of children's rights and economic, social and territorial cohesion.

The argument has been advanced that other elements of the stated Objectives, such as references to competitiveness amount to a contradiction of the social goals listed above. And while the Treaty of Rome reference to undistorted competition has been removed, at the demand of France following the referendum debate in that country, a Protocol has been agreed to ensure continuity of existing internal market rules.

It must be pointed out that each provision of the Treaty is to be read in the context of the total document. The single market is not yet complete but it has already provided this country with economic opportunities which have been translated into growth and jobs. Remaining distortions of competition in this market constitute barriers to Irish enterprises and constraints to Irish job creation. At the same time, EU social provisions in areas such as gender equality, non-discrimination and labour law provide necessary checks and balances.

Policy Implications

All of the listed Objectives have policy implications. Specific statements in Article 3 of the Treaty on European Union are picked up throughout the texts of both treaties. For example, the general commitments to combat inequality and discrimination is given force in Articles 8 and 10 of the Treaty on the Functioning of the European Union which provide that the Union shall have regard to these overall objectives in defining and implementing all of its policies. There is an agreed Declaration on Article 8, to the effect that the Union should aim in its different policies to combat all kinds of domestic violence and to prevent and punish such criminal acts and to support and protect victims.

Of particular significance is the so-called Social Clause – Article 9 – which requires the EU, in defining and implementing all of its policies to "take into account requirements linked to the promotion of a high level of employment, the guarantee of adequate social protection, the fight against social exclusion and a high level of education, training and protection of human health".

This article was included during the IGC which agreed the text of the Constitutional Treaty on the proposal of Belgium and France.[2] It had been identified as a desirable element of the treaty by a substantial number of members of the Social Europe Working Group of the Convention who argued for a "horizontal clause on social values" but who failed to achieve full consensus on the issue. The specific reference to social exclusion was, however, included as a result of a proposal made by the Irish section of the European Anti Poverty Network in the course of a debate with the Taoiseach at the National Forum on Europe.

It is argued that the goals of full employment and price stability both have implications for the stated objectives and role of the European Central Bank as well as for the development and co-ordination of monetary and economic policies. Added attention has been given in this text than in earlier treaties to workers' rights and employment policy co-ordination though precise implications will need to be teased out in practice.

The advance towards a Union of Values is not restricted to the regional level. Europe's social values are put at the heart of its relations with the wider world under the terms of the Treaty on European Union. Article 3.5 refers to the goals of solidarity and mutual respect among peoples, eradicating poverty, protecting human rights and, in particular, the protection of children's rights. Moreover, Article 21 commits the Union to advancing in the wider world "the principles which have inspired its own creation, development and enlargement" and reiterates the social values, thus ensuring continuity and coherence between the two treaties. This is picked up in Article 205 of the second treaty. Closing the gap between rhetoric and action will be critical, especially as regards development co-operation.

Charter of Fundamental Rights

The incorporation of the Charter of Fundamental Rights into the treaties through the terms of Article 6 of the Treaty on European Union gives the Union a framework of individual rights which includes key economic and social issues. It will ensure that individuals and concerned groups can access effective remedies where rights and freedoms guaranteed by EU law are violated either by the Union's institutions or by Member States when implementing EU law. The Charter does not establish any new power or task for the Union and it is made clear that full account must be taken of national laws and practices. Fundamental rights in the national constitutions are not supplanted but rather complemented by the Charter.

The Charter was originally drafted by the first EU Convention which was set up following the Koln European Council in June 1999, with the former German President Roman Herzog as chairman, and reported to the French Presidency of the Council in

September 2000. It was "proclaimed" by the Institutions of the Union – Council, Parliament and Commission – in Nice in December 2000. It had no more than a declaratory status at that time but the question of its status was listed as one of the issues to be dealt with in the 2004 IGC provided for in the Nice Declaration on the Future of the European Union.

The status question was addressed by the European Convention which established a Working Group on the Incorporation of the Charter under the chairmanship of European Commissioner Antonio Vitorino. The Working Group recommended that the Charter should be made legally binding and given constitutional status, either by insertion of the text in the body of the Constitutional Treaty or by insertion of an appropriate reference combined with the attaching of the Charter in a Protocol. This recommendation was accepted by the Convention. The first of the options was followed in the Constitutional Treaty but the second was favoured in drafting the Lisbon Treaty. The Working Group accepted that the content of the Charter represented a consensus reached by the previous Convention and endorsed by the Nice European Council. The whole Charter should then be respected and not be re-opened.[3]

The Convention also recommended that the Constitutional Treaty should create an authorisation for the European Union as a body to accede to the European Convention on Human Rights. This "would give a strong political signal of the coherence between the Union and the 'greater Europe' reflected in the Council of Europe and its pan-European human rights system." Accession to the ECHR would give citizens an analogous protection vis-à-vis acts of the Union as they currently enjoy vis-à-vis all the Member States which are individual signatories.

The purpose of the Charter is to ensure that the same high standards of rights protection apply to the Union's institutions as are currently applicable to the Member States with better opportunities for citizens to vindicate their rights when affected by the Union.

The Charter of Fundamental Rights is divided into six titles: dignity, freedoms, equality, solidarity, citizens' rights and justice. More than fifty articles cover these subjects. It reaffirms rights already contained in the ECHR and in other relevant documents, including national constitutions. It gives greater visibility to rights deriving from the jurisprudence of the ECJ and includes important social rights, such as workplace rights, side by side with more traditional civil, political and citizens' rights.

PREAMBLE

Title I: Dignity

Title II: Freedoms

Title III: Equality

Title IV: Solidarity

TitleV: Citizens' Rights

Title VI: Justice

Title VII: General Provision

The Charter will take effect under the terms of a number of general provisions which specify its field of application and the modalities for implementation. The treaty text provides that the Union recognises the rights, freedoms and principles set out in the Charter and gives them the same legal value as the Treaties themselves.

The Charter will be legally binding on the Union's institutions, bodies, offices and agencies where they have the power to act, with due regard to the principle of subsidiarity. It thus applies to the Council, Commission and Parliament but also to bodies such as the European Environment Agency and the Agency for Health and Safety at Work. It will be binding on the individual Member States when they are transposing, implementing or interpreting EU Directives or Regulations. It will not apply to the internal legislation or administration of the Member States, for instance in the field of direct taxation.

The incorporation of the Charter is significant in moving towards a more citizen friendly Europe. Its Preamble states that the European Union "places the individual at the heart of its activities, by establishing the citizenship of the Union and by creating an area of freedom, security and justice. It consolidates in one document the rights already expressly recognised in the existing treaties, international agreements and conventions.

The Charter includes certain economic and social rights or principles which are drawn from the Council of Europe Social Charter and the European Community Charter of the Fundamental Rights of Workers. It recognises such rights as the worker's right to information and consultation within the undertaking, the right of collective bargaining and action and protects workers against unjustified dismissal. The Charter does not create any new economic and social rights and it is limited to areas within the conferred competence of the Union.

The Charter provides that "everyone whose rights and freedoms guaranteed by the law of the Union are violated has the right to an effective remedy before a tribunal...." There is an obligation on all Member States to provide appropriate judicial means to ensure effective protection of rights.

The United Kingdom and Poland have indicated that they do not want the Charter to apply to their citizens. A Protocol has been attached to the Treaty which provides that the Charter shall only apply in those Member States "to the extent that the rights or principles that it contains are recognised in the law or practices of Poland and the United Kingdom." In the UK case this approach is controversial since it is based on objections by employers' organisations to the social and economic provisions of the Charter.

The incorporation of the Charter strengthens the provisions of the Treaty which oblige those wishing to accede to the Union to respect the values of the Union and provide for suspension of Union membership rights in the event of a failure to do so.

The Charter thus provides an additional benchmark against which the protection of fundamental rights by future applicants, new accession states and existing Member States may be assessed.

Competences of the Union

Under the terms of Article 5 of the Treaty on European Union the EU acts only with the limits of the competences conferred upon it by the Member States, subject to the important principles of subsidiarity and proportionality. Competences not conferred upon the Union remain with the Member States.

In general, competences are shared between the Union and the Member States in the areas of social policy, economic, social and territorial cohesion, consumer protection and common concerns in public health matters. Competence in importance areas such as health and education remains with the Member States. Social policy is an area of EU activity in which both political and national differences of real substance are obvious. In the Convention debates, many government representatives insisted on the importance of national culture, traditions and systems in sensitive social areas, including labour markets and social protection and these national systems are often jealously guarded.

Article 4 of the Treaty on the Functioning of the European Union sets out the main fields of shared competence in social policy, ranging from workers' health and safety to the combating of social exclusion. Details are set out in Title X and are summarised by Jean-Claude Piris, Director General of the Legal Service of the Council in the following terms:

> ...provisions on social policy will remain identical to the present ones. Article 153 on social policy is identical to the present Article 137 of the EC Treaty.

> As now, the European Parliament and the Council will still be empowered to adopt in codecision, the Council using QMV,

minimum requirements for certain matters. QMV will thus continue to apply for adopting measures on the protection of workers' health and safety, working conditions, information and consultation of workers, integration of persons excluded from the labour market and equality between men and women with regard to labour market opportunities and treatment at work;

As now, unanimity will be kept for the adoption of minimum requirements in the most sensitive matters such as social security and social protection. Unanimity will thus continue to apply for adopting measures on social security and social protection for workers, protection of workers where their employment contract is terminated, the representation and collective defence of the interests of workers and employers and conditions of employment of third-country nationals;

As now, such minimum requirements "shall not affect the right of Member States to define the fundamental principles of their social security systems and must not significantly affect the financial equilibrium of such systems" and "shall not prevent the Member State from maintaining or introducing more stringent protective measures compatible with the Treaties."[4]

The right to pay, the right of association, the right to strike and the use of lockout remain excluded from Union competence under Article 153.

Provision is made, in the treaty articles on competence, for the EU to take complementary or supporting action, in the areas of public health, education, vocational training, youth and sport.

Co-ordination of Economic, Employment and Social Policies

The co-ordination of the economic and employment policies of the Member States are treated separately in Article 5 of the Treaty on

European Union. The IGC adapted the Convention text to make it clear that the Member States have the primary responsibility for co-ordination of economic and employment policies. Article 5.3 provides, however, that the Union may, in future, take initiatives to ensure co-ordination of Member States' social policies.

To ensure fulfilment of the principles of subsidiarity and proportionality which are seen as particularly important in the social field there will be an enhanced role for national parliaments under the terms of Protocols attached to the Treaty. This provision could contribute to reducing the perceived democratic deficit arising from shortcomings in national political and parliamentary systems which have tended to marginalise EU issues but will make significant demands on these systems in terms of attention and resources.

Participatory Democracy and Social Dialogue

Title II of the Treaty on European Union – on the Democratic Life of the Union – arises from the discussions within the Conventioin and is designed to enhance the social dimension as well as to increase the democratic legitimacy of the Union.

Article 10 provides that every citizen shall have the right to participate in the democratic life of the Union. Article 11 provides that the Union shall give opportunities to citizens and civil society bodies to make known their views on areas of Union action and to maintain open dialogue with representative associations.

The Citizens' Initiative, in Article 11 establishes that "not less than one million citizens who are nationals of a significant number of Member States" may invite the Commission to submit a proposal for EU legislation on a matter they consider should be the subject of a legal act of the Union. It is further provided that the European Parliament and the Council shall set out the detailed arrangements for carrying out this initiative.

Addressing the National Forum on Europe, Commission Vice President Margot Wallstrom refuted claims that this provision was no more than "window dressing" by describing it as a political commitment which the Commission could not ignore. The treaty did not lay down that requests made in this way must be accepted since it retains the Commission's right of legislative initiative.[5]

Article 152 of the Treaty on the Functioning of the European Union provides that the Union shall recognise and promote the role of the social partners at Union level – employers, trade unions and representatives of public services – and facilitate social dialogue, taking into account the diversity of national systems. A further clause establishes that the Tripartite Social Summit for Growth and Employment shall contribute to social dialogue. Articles 154 and 155 set out the conditions for consultation of the social partners on Commission proposals while the European trade union movement has expressed disappointment with the fact that these references to social dialogue appear to be confined to the Social Policy field.[6]

Article 301 provides that the Economic and Social Committee, which exercises an advisory function, shall consist of representatives of the social partners and of civil society. Article 12 provides that consumer protection requirements shall be taken into account in defining and implementing other Union policies and activities.

Enhanced Co-operation

Article 20 of the Treaty on EuropeanUnion provides the framework for the establishment of Enhanced Co-operation which may take place, as a last resort, in policy areas including social affairs. It must be established that the objectives of such co-operation cannot be attained within a reasonable period under existing provisions. Co-operation must aim to further the objectives of the Union, protect its interests and reinforce its integration process. At least nine Member States must participate and co-operation must be open at any time to all Member States. Detailed provisions for implementation of the procedure are set out in the second treaty.

Decision-Making Procedures

Qualified Majority Voting has become the normal voting procedure in the Union under the Treaty. However, in relation to social matters, given the sensitivity of some Member States, a combination of QMV and unanimity has been agreed, with unanimity retained, by way of derogation, in certain aspects, notably in the areas outlined above. There was considerable demand during the Convention for the extension of QMV to decisions related to action to combat discrimination, but this was not agreed and the Treaty provides for unanimity, with the consent of the European Parliament, for adoption of regulations or directives which may establish the necessary measures.

QMV has been extended to measures relating to social security for migrant workers, but subject to an "emergency brake". Article 48 of the Treaty on the Functioning of the European Union provides that "where a member of the Council considers that a draft European law or framework law...would affect fundamental aspects of its social security system, including its scope, cost or financial structure, or would affect the financial balance of that system, it may request that the matter be referred to the European Council" for consideration and decision by unanimity.

The so-called Passerelle Clause in Article 48.7 of the Treaty on European Union will apply in the social field. The Clause provides that the European Council, acting by unanimity, may decide to move from decision-making by unanimity to decision-making by QMV in a given area. However, any proposal to utilise this provision must be notified to the parliaments of the Member States and if a single national parliament makes known its opposition within six months the proposal shall not be adopted.

Balancing Economic and Social Europe

The treaty revisions seek to strike a balance between economic and social policies. Of importance in this respect is Article 7 of the Treaty on the Functioning of the European Union, the so-called consistency clause which obliges the Union to "ensure consistency between its policies and activities, taking all of its objectives into account and in accordance with the principle of conferral of powers". This article provides an important link between the stated values and objectives and the practical policies and activities of the Union. Its inclusion was to meet the concerns of those in the Convention who advocated the inclusion of "social" values and objectives but who needed reassurance that they would be reflected in policies and programmes.

Specific Articles in the Treaty on the Functioning of the European Union carry forward the *acquis communautaire* in key social fields: equal pay for male and female workers; paid holidays; the annual report on the achievement of social policy objectives; the work of the Social Protection Committee; the annual Commission report to the European Parliament on Social Developments within the Union; and, the legal basis for the continuing work of the European Social Fund.

Public Health

Significant changes are made in respect of cross-border health threats. The scope of EU action on Public Health is broadened to include "monitoring, early warning of and combating serious cross-border threats to health". It is further provided that the Union shall encourage co-operation between the Member States to improve the complementarity of their health services in cross-border areas. Article 168.5 includes provision for Union measures to protect public health regarding tobacco and the abuse of alcohol.

Article 168.7 further clarifies the competence of the Member States in the health field, including the definition of their health policy, organisation and delivery of health services and medical care and the allocation of the resources assigned to them.

Public Services (Services of General Economic Interest)

The Convention saw a debate on the position of public services (services of general economic interest) which focused on the means by which social inclusion might be achieved through protecting those services from the application of EU competition policy (and thus liberalisation), through increased competition or through a mixture of the two.

The outcome of the Convention discussions, and of further debate within the IGC, was the inclusion of an amended Article 14 in the Treaty on the Functioning of the European Union – building on the previous Article 16 of the Treaty Establishing the European Community) – which makes provision for a legal basis for regulations establishing and defining the principles and conditions for the provision of public services. QMV and co-decision will apply to such decisions. An important addition to the article was inserted by the IGC providing that such laws shall be adopted "without prejudice to the competence of Member States, in compliance with the Constitution, to provide, to commission and to fund such services".

The European Trade Union Confederation and other groups had lobbied intensely in favour of the inclusion of a strong commitment to public services and of a specific provision to protect them from the strict application of competition policy. In the "end game" of the Convention and IGC it was accepted that the introduction of EU regulation and to the Member States' general competence provided a basis for political debate and decision at both national and Union level where the principle of subsidiarity would have relevance.

A Protocol on Services of General Economic Interest was added to the treaty text in the latter stages of the IGC which emphasises the importance of services of general interest and contains a number of interpretative provisions based on the shared values of the Union in respect of services of general economic interest.

The Protocol makes reference to "the essential role and the wide discretion of national, regional and local authorities in providing, commissioning and organising services of general economic interest as closely as possible to the needs of the users". It underlines the diversity of such services and the differences in the needs and preferences of users, arising from geographical, social or cultural situations. It emphasises the importance of ensuring a high level of quality, safety and affordability, equal treatment, universal access and user rights. Critically, the Protocol states that " the provisions of the Treaties do not affect in any way the competence of Member States to provide, commission and organise non-economic services of general interest."

The inclusion of these elements in the treaty text has been welcomed by a broad alliance of bodies, ranging from the Committee of the Regions to the ETUC. A joint statement by the ETUC and the public employers' organisation CEEP declared that "high performance services of general interest are a key factor for sustainable growth in Europe"[7] and welcomed the availability of "legal clarity for public service providers and users, thereby contributing to sustainable economic, social and environmental development in Europe".

Questions concerning the relationship between the Common Commercial Policy and Services of General Economic Interest continue to give rise to controversy. They refer, in particular, to the arrangements for negotiation of international trade agreements conducted by the European Commission on the basis of a mandate from the Council.

The Commission has negotiated on behalf of the Member States in world trade talks since the 1960s. The Common Commercial Policy has since then, and remains, an exclusive competence of the Union.

Negotiations of international agreements under the Common Commercial Policy are conducted by the Commission on the basis of a mandate from the Council and in consultation with a special committee approved by the Council. The Commission must report regularly to that committee and to the European Parliament on the progress of negotiations. The Council's decisions, in relation to the negotiation and conclusion of such international agreements are normally adopted by QMV. However, in certain exceptional cases the Council must continue to act by unanimity. These are set out in Article 207:

- aspects of intellectual property and foreign direct investment, where such agreements include provisions for which unanimity is required for the adoption of internal rules;
- agreements in the field of trade in cutural and audiovisual services which risk prejudicing the Union's cultural and linguistic diversity;
- agreements on trade in the field of social, education and health services, which risk seriously disturbing the national organisation of such services and prejudicing the responsibility of Member States to deliver them.

Concerns that the general application of QMV might facilitate the liberalisation and eventual privatisation of trade in sensitive public services, by removing the power of an individual Member States to veto a proposal with which it strongly disagrees, were taken into account by the IGC, under the Irish Presidency, which inserted a specific safeguard clause – now in Article 207.4 of the Treaty on the Functioning of the European Union – in respect of trade in social, education and health services. These provisions ensure that decisions will be the subject of normal political interaction.

It is specifically stated in Article 207.6 that "the exercise of the competences conferred by this article in the field of the common commercial policy shall not affect the delimitation of competences between the Union and the Member States." This ensures that in the areas referred to above where the Member States and not the Union have responsibility the Union cannot extend its competence through the application of this article. These provisions, together with the special recognition given to services elewhere in the treaties, ensure that the Common Commercial Policy will not affect how Member States choose to organize and fund their public services.

The Open Method of Co-ordination

The Open Method of Co-ordination is aimed at encouraging Member States to co-ordinate their actions in a number of policy areas on a voluntary basis without resort to EU legislation. It is primarily achieved by the establishment of guidelines, indicators or benchmarks, the exchange of best practice and the use of peer review and evaluation.

It is associated primarily with the Lisbon Strategy – the Union's economic strategy to transform the economy of the Union by 2010 into "the most competitive and dynamic knowledge-based economy in the world capable of sustainable economic growth with more and better jobs and greater social cohesion". However, the method has been used with benefit in developing policies and programmes in areas such as combating poverty.

The Convention debate concerned primarily the issue of whether or not there should be an explicit reference to the Open Method. On the one hand it was argued that the inclusion would make the method more transparent while, on the other, it was claimed that it would reduce the flexibility inherent in this approach.

The treaty provides for the use of the Open Method of Co-ordination in a number of areas, without recognising the method as a general principle: Employment; Social Policy; Research and Development; Public Health and Industrial Policy.

Conclusion

The Social Dimension of the Union is given strong foundations in the treaty, in particular in terms of its Values and Objectives. The competences of the Union and of the Member States in social matters are more clearly defined. A range of common policies and programmes are provided for in the Treaty on the Functioning of the European Union. The important links between goals and policies are better established than in previous texts. In summary, the concept of a "Social Europe" is clearly defined.

However, no international political system as far-reaching as the European Union can exist for fifty years without an element of controversy and divergence in attitudes. The debates within the European Parliament in Brussels and Strasbourg increasingly demonstrate classic left-right policy differences and national standpoints.

An area in which there is obvious room for disagreement on the Union's policy direction is that of Social Europe. The EEC/EU has achieved much in this field, notably in the equality agenda and in respect of the health and safety of workers. The first Irish Presidency, in 1975, saw the adoption of landmark equality legislation under the leadership of the then Commission Vice President, Dr Patrick Hillery, and with a strong Irish input from figures such as the late Frank Cluskey. However, the limited competence of the Union in a number of areas of importance to workers and trade unions remains an irritant for many concerned individuals and organisations as do the perceived constraints of social legislation on the flexibilty of the labour market.

The ETUC, for example, while supporting the Lisbon Treaty's provisions on fundamental rights and public services, has commented in strong terms on its lack of ambition in other areas and has called for a Commission review of social provisions once the treaty is ratified to ensure the development of policies to help workers handle change. This may well become a campaign issue across the Member States in next year's elections to the European Parliament.[7]

BUSINESSEUROPE, the employers' body has argued that the Lisbon Treaty introduces reforms which are necessary to ensure that the EU has "the institutional framework, decision-making process and legal bases for policies it needs in order to meet its objectives".[8]

The conclusions of the European Parliament on the Treaty of Lisbon are relevant.

The Corbett/Mendez de Vigo Report on the Treaty, adopted overwhelmingly by the Parliament, welcomes the treaty provisions for social dialogue and the citizens' initiative and goes on to recognise that:

...there is a better focus on policies that visibly benefit citizens: there are new provisions of general application concerning the promotion of a high level of employment, the guarantee of adequate social protection, the fight against social exclusion, a high level of education, training and health, the elimination of all kinds of discrimination and the promotion of equality between women and men; new provisions enhance the promotion of sustainable development and protection of the environment including fighting climate change and the respect of services of general interest; economic, social and territorial cohesion is reaffirmed as an objective of the Union."[9]

References

1. European Convention (2003) Report of Working Group on Social Europe, CONV 516/1/03.
2. Milton G. and Keller-Noellet, J. (2005) The European Constitution, London, John Harper Publishing.
3. European Convention (2002) Report of Working Group on Incorporation of the Charter, CONV 354/02.
4. Piris, Jean-Claude. (2006) The Constitution for Europe: A Legal Analysis, Cambridge University Press.
5. Wallstrom, Margot (2008) Address to the National Forum on Europe, Dublin, 28th February 2008.
6. ETUC (2007) Statement on the Lisbon Reform Treaty.
7. ETUC and CEEP (2007) Joint Statement on draft EU Treaty, Brussels, July 2007.
8. BUSINESSEUROPE (2007) Statement on the Signature of the Lisbon Treaty, Brussels, December 2007.
9. European Parliament (2008) Report on the Lisbon Treaty.

6

The External Action of The European Union

Patrick Keatinge

The Lisbon Treaty and External Action

With regard to how the European Union relates to the rest of the world, the Lisbon Treaty does not introduce major new policies. Under the official label of "external action" it codifies existing policies, sometimes in a more detailed way and with amendments on specific points, but in terms which are generally familiar from previous treaties.

However, this consolidation of existing policy content is accompanied by a change in institutional structures and procedures which represents one of the treaty's major innovations – the post of High Representative of the Union for Foreign Affairs and Security Policy. The emphasis is thus not so much on what the EU does in the world (though that is often more important than is generally realised) as on how its external policies may best be decided and delivered.

The scope of external action is broad and varied, and the relevant treaty provisions are found in both the previous treaties reformed by the agreement at Lisbon. Title V of the Treaty on European Union contains general provisions on external action, followed by specific provisions on the Common Foreign and Security Policy and its sub-set the Common Security and Defence Policy. In the Treaty on the Functioning of the European Union the remaining major elements of external action, Commercial Policy and Development Policy, are contained in Part Five.

Adaptation to a Volatile World

The multifaceted nature of this sprawling collection of policies is largely explained by the broad historical circumstances in which the EU's world role has evolved, and this in turn underpins the argument for reforming the institutional structures to provide consistency and coherence in how the Union conducts its external relations. It may be helpful, therefore, to recall the origins of the main strands of external action.

The European Economic Community established by the Rome Treaty in 1958 adopted a common external tariff which led to a Common Commercial Policy, in which the EEC (and later the EU) both negotiated major trade agreements and the general rules of the multilateral trade system. The broadly parallel process of decolonisation and the creation of new but impoverished states provided the incentive for a second strand, Development Cooperation, in which the EU and its Member States' national development policies now account for over half of the world total of development funding (some Euro 46 billion annually). Both commercial and development policies are decided under the original supranational or "community method" where proposals are made by the Commission and adopted by the Council of Ministers under the rules of quality majority voting.

However, more overtly "political" action was more tentative so long as the main focus of world politics was the Cold War. Through the 1970s and 1980s a form of intensive but low-profile diplomatic consultation (European Political Cooperation) was developed, but this lay outside the community method of decision making, and precluded any form of military cooperation which was seen as NATO business. It was not until the end of the Cold War that the Member States agreed (in the Maastricht Treaty on European Union 1992) to create what is now a further important major strand of external action, the "Common Foreign and Security Policy" (CFSP). The sensitive nature of this commitment was – and still is – hedged around with qualifications. Decisions are made by the "intergovernmental method", that is as a general rule by unanimity of the foreign ministers of the Member States, and the CFSP was described as the "second pillar" of the EU's institutional structure.

The European Union had little impact on the Balkan wars of the 1990s, and with a view to strengthening its capacity to influence international crises the European Security and Defence Policy, described as an "integral part" of the CFSP, was further developed in the treaties of Amsterdam and Nice. On that legal basis new institutions were created and from 2003 Member States committed both military forces and civilian personnel to missions providing political stabilisation in conflict areas outside the EU. These developments in what is now called the Common Security and Defence Policy are reflected more fully in the Lisbon Treaty than was previously the case.

Basic Principles

All of these varied aspects of the EU's international role, now summarised as "external action", rest on a statement of general principles contained in Article 21 of the Treaty on European Union. That reflects the ideal of an international order resting on the rule of law and peaceful relations between independent states cooperating in multilateral organisations, with particular reference to the United Nations. It promotes human rights, economic integration, sustainable development and concern for the environment.

Article 21, Treaty on European Union

Recognising the wide scope of these broad aims and the consequent difficulty of policy coordination, paragraph 3 of this article makes the Commission and Council, assisted by the High Representative of the Union for Foreign and Security Policy (hereafter "High Representative"), responsible for ensuring "consistency between the different areas of ... external action". Article 22 then requires the European Council, acting on the basis of unanimity, to identify "strategic interests and objectives of the Union" with regard to these principles. In pulling the disparate elements of external action together in this way the Lisbon Treaty could be said to lean more in the direction of intergovernmental decision making than of the community method.

Article 21 (Treaty on European Union)
"The Union's action on the international scene shall be guided by the principles which have inspired its own creation, development and enlargement, and which it seeks to advance in the wider world: democracy, the rule of law, the universality and indivisibility of human rights and fundamental freedoms, respect for human dignity, the principles of equality and solidarity, and respect for the principles of the United Nations Charter and international law."

From External Relations to External Action

Much of the content of external action is contained in Part Five of the amended Treaty on the Functioning of the European Union.

This covers in the main the policies which up to the Lisbon Treaty have come under the heading of "external relations", located in the "first pillar" of the European Union structure. The first major element is the Common Commercial Policy - in effect the outward face of the internal market. Its provisions are typical of the traditional community approach. Trade is an exclusive competence of the Union, negotiations are conducted by the Commission on the basis of a Council Mandate and QMV is normally used in decision-making. However, continuity with previous treaties is not total. The scope of the policy is clarified, and extended by the inclusion of foreign direct investment. The European Parliament has an enhanced co-decision role, and Article 207.4 of the Treaty on the Functioning of the European Union lists specific fields of trade where unanimous agreement by Member States is required. Furthermore, Article 215 authorises restrictive measures (economic sanctions), in the context of decisions made under the Common Foreign and Security Policy.

As is the case with trade policy, the treaty text on development policy covers a long standing and in world terms significant policy programme. Article 208 TFEU provides that policy in this field shall be conducted within the framework of the principles and objectives of the Union's external action. "Union development cooperation policy shall have as its primary objective the reduction and, in the long term, the eradication of poverty. The Union shall take account of the objectives of development cooperation in the policies that it implements which are likely to affect developing countries. The Union and the Member States shall comply with the commitments and take account of the objectives they have approved in the context of the United Nations and other competent international organisations."

The emphasis on the eradication of poverty reflects the Union's overall values and objectives. Priority is accorded to the coordination of Member State and EU policies. Economic, financial and technical cooperation with countries other than developing countries has to be consistent with development policy (Article 212, Treaty on the Functioning of the European Union). The treaty includes for the first time a commitment under the heading of humanitarian aid to provide ad hoc assistance for victims of man-made or natural disasters (Article 214, Treaty on the Functioning of the European Union). This includes the establishment of a European Voluntary Humanitarian Aid Corps.

The modalities of EU international agreements and the Union's relations with international organisations and Union delegations are also covered in Part Five of the Treaty on the Functioning of the European Union, fleshing out the picture of what in previous treaties was referred to as "external relations". However, the final article in this part of the treaty, Article 222, is a new commitment, and in some ways sits outside the prevailing pattern of "external" policies, whether designated as "relations" or "actions". This is the solidarity clause, inspired by the large scale terrorist attacks in Madrid in 2004. This provides for a joint response by the Union and its Member States in the event of a terrorist attack or a natural or man-made disaster. While the text refers to the Union mobilising "all the instruments at its disposal, including the military resources made available by the Member States", the obligations faced by the latter are framed in such a way as to give them discretion as to what sort of assistance they actually provide. In particular, military assistance comes under the unanimity rule (paragraph 3) and the action envisaged is restricted to the territory of the Member States (paragraph 1).

The Common Foreign and Security Policy

The remaining elements of external action are found in Title V of the revised Treaty on European Union. Chapter 2 outlines the Specific provisions of the Common Foreign and Security Policy.

Much of this follows a pattern of institutional structures and procedures which has been familiar since the Maastricht Treaty was signed in 1992. In the "second pillar" the main institution has been the Council of Ministers and decisions are taken as a rule on the basis of unanimity. The very limited exceptions to this rule are defined clearly, as is the procedure whereby a Member State government can in effect appeal such a decision to the European Council, where its veto power applies. The CFSP does not come under the jurisdiction of the European Court of Justice, and the concept of co-decision with the European Parliament simply does not arise. These characteristics of intergovernmental policy making are not significantly altered by the Treaty of Lisbon; two declarations (13 and 14) attached to the treaty reiterate the general point in plainer language.

However, there is a potentially important change in the institutional structure of the Common Foreign and Security Policy, in the new post of High Representative of the Union for Foreign and Security Policy. In effect, this is an extension of role of the High Representative for the Common Foreign and Security Policy, authorised by the Treaty of Amsterdam in 1997 and implemented by the appointment of Dr Javier Solana two years later. The new element in the Lisbon Treaty lies in what is often referred to as "double-hatting".

Up to now the High Representative has operated as an agent of the Council on Common Foreign and Security Policy matters, within a strictly intergovernmental mode of policy making; the "external relations" has been the responsibility of a designated member of the Commission. Now, however, these two posts become one and the same individual has a key position in the Foreign Affairs Council and is a Vice-President in the Commission.

This innovation is covered by Article 18, Treaty on the Functioning of the European Union.

Article 18

1. The European Council, acting by a qualified majority, with the agreement of the President of the Commission, shall appoint the High Representative of the Union for Foreign Affairs and Security Policy. The European Council may end his term of office by the same procedure.
2. The High Representative shall conduct the Union's Common Foreign and Security policy. He shall contribute by his proposals to the development of that policy, which he shall carry out as mandated by the Council. The same shall apply to the common security and defence policy.
3. The High Representative shall preside over the Foreign Affairs Council.
4. The High Representative shall be one of the Vice-Presidents of the Commission. He shall ensure the consistency of the Union's external action. He shall be responsible within the Commission for responsibilities incumbent on it in external relations and for coordinating other aspects of the Union's external action. In exercising these responsibilities within the Commission, and only for those responsibilities, the High Representative shall be bound by Commission procedures to the extent that this is consistent with paragraphs 2 and 3.

The High Representative is appointed by the European Council by QMV, subject to the agreement of the President of the Commission. He or she "conducts" the Union's foreign and security policy (including the Common Foreign and Security Policy) – that involves making proposals to the foreign ministers, chairing the meetings of the foreign affairs Council and implementing their agreed policies, in effect operating as the Union's "chief diplomat" (his/her external role is contained in Article 27, Treaty on European Union, paragraph 2). As a member of the Commission, the High Representative has responsibility for the external relations portfolio and is required to "ensure the consistency of the Union's external action". Indeed "consistency" reflects the functional logic of the new arrangement, with the High Representative straddling what have hitherto been two different policy processes with their own institutions, bureaucratic cultures and to some degree mutual suspicions.

The aim of dealing with external action as a coherent set of policies is further seen in another innovation in the Lisbon Treaty, by giving the High Representative the support of a European External Action Service (Article 27, Treaty on European Union, paragraph 3). The Service draws its personnel from the General Secretariat of the Council (the existing source of administrative support) and the Commission's staff (both in Brussels and abroad) and officials seconded from Member State foreign ministries. This new extended and amalgamated unit cooperates with the national foreign ministries which continue to support their respective foreign ministers.

All of this clearly amounts to an obvious change in existing patterns of institutional structures and policy processes. But its significance for the future of the Union may not be so clear-cut. Two mutually exclusive types of criticism have emerged in debates on the Lisbon Treaty. In the first approach, it is argued that the potential for streamlining a cumbersome policy process may not be realised. The High Representative is seen as a split personality, overloaded with responsibilities and likely to run foul of entrenched bureaucratic cultures in an excessively complex system. Even with regard to the core representative duties, there seems to be a blurred division of labour with the new-style President of the European Council. If these potential difficulties are to be overcome, much will depend on the personal capacity of the first holder of the new office.

A second type of criticism is found in the view that the High Representative is not too weak to fulfil the designated role, but rather that he or she is too strong. In this view, the High Representative will acquire the prerogatives of the foreign minister of a conventional federal state. Did not the rejected Constitutional Treaty of 2004 describe the new post as the "Union Minister for Foreign Affairs"? However, the implied analogy neglects several important facts. The High Representative does not replace the Member State foreign ministers, who remain accountable to their own governments and parliaments. They too make proposals to the Council and the High Representative acts only on their agreed mandate, under a voting regime which rests on the principle of unanimity.

The Common Security and Defence Policy

The Lisbon Treaty gives a fuller picture of "security and defence" than previous treaties, contained in Section 2, Chapter 2 of Title V of the amended Treaty on the European Union. Article 42, paragraph 1 provides an overview of what is described as "an integral part of the common foreign and security policy". Much of this reflects existing practice, but since it is the first time some of it appears in a treaty it merits further attention.

In the context of previous referendum debates in Ireland, the implication of EU membership for the national policy of "military neutrality" has been the major issue in this policy area. Both Article 24, paragraph 1 and Article 42, paragraph 2 contain an aspiration to a "common defence" that is generally understood to imply a mutual defence clause similar to that of a military alliance like NATO. Though there is a variation in the way this is expressed, the aspiration can only be realised by a unanimous decision of the Member States. Even where Article 42, paragraph 7 spells such a commitment out more explicitly, using wording taken from the now redundant treaty of the Western European Union, it is qualified in such a way as to remain in aspirational form. The key phrase is that this "shall not prejudice the specific character of the security and defence policy of certain Member States" and "shall respect" (i.e. defer to) the mutual defence obligations other Member States have in the context of the NATO alliance. This formula, first seen in the Maastricht Treaty of 1992, has not changed.

> "The common security and defence policy shall include the progressive framing of a common Union defence policy. This will lead to a common defence, when the European Council, acting unanimously, so decides. It shall in that case recommend to the Member States the adoption of such a decision in accordance with their respective constitutional requirements.
>
> The policy of the Union in accordance with this Section shall not prejudice the specific character of the security and defence policy of certain Member States and shall respect the obligations of certain Member States, which see their common defence realised in the North Atlantic Treaty Organisation (NATO), under the North Atlantic Treaty and be compatible with the common security and defence policy established within that framework."

Article 29.4.9 of the Constitution – inserted by the terms of the amendment approved in the second referendum on the Nice Treaty and replicated in the Bill published by the Government as the basis for the referendum on the Lisbon Treaty – provides that the state "shall not adopt a decision taken by the European Council to establish a common defence ......where that common defence would include the State". Thus it is firmly established that should a situation arise in future where it was proposed to establish a common defence it would not involve this country unless it was approved by the Irish people in a further referendum.

If it does not actually provide a "common defence" what then is the purpose of the security and defence policy? That is described succinctly as "peace-keeping, conflict prevention and strengthening international security in accordance with the principles of the

United Nations Charter". The scope of the policy is spelled out more fully in Article 43, paragraph 1, which extends the original description, the so-called "Petersberg tasks" contained in the Maastricht Treaty in 1992.

"The tasks referred to in Article 42(1), in the course of which the Union may use civilian and military means, shall include joint disarmament operations, humanitarian and rescue tasks, military advice and assistance tasks, conflict prevention and peace-keeping tasks, tasks of combat forces in crisis management, including peace-making and post-conflict stabilisation. All these tasks may contribute to the fight against terrorism, including by supporting third countries in combating terrorism in their territories."

The new formulation of policy scope reflects the increased complexity of international crisis management as experienced during the nearly two decades since the European Union as such was established. The fullest rationale for the Common Foreign and Security Policy is contained in an agreed strategy document, "A Secure Europe in a Better World", published in December 2003. This identifies five key threats – terrorism, proliferation of weapons of mass destruction, regional conflicts, state failure, and organised crime – and makes the point that "in contrast to the massive visible threat in the Cold War, none of these threats is purely military; nor can any be tackled by purely military means". The EU, with a comprehensive range of economic, humanitarian, political and military instruments, is equipped to meet such threats. It adds to the national efforts of its Member States a collective diplomacy based on what is often called "soft power" (as opposed to the traditional notion of "hard power" derived from military dominance). However, in order to play this role effectively, it is argued that the EU needs to be more active, more capable and more coherent.

The Lisbon Treaty deals with the fundamental issue of providing the necessary means for such a policy, in terms of both civilian and military capabilities. Apart from the obvious limitations arising from finite resources and the competing demands made on them at the national level, the realisation of the EU's potential depends on just what the Member State is obliged to do. Article 42, paragraph 3 embodies a very loosely defined commitment, saying that Member States "shall make civilian and military capabilities available to the Union". However, there is no stated level of contribution and no way in which the Union can enforce sanctions against what might be perceived as a recalcitrant Member State; ultimately Member States decide their own contributions.

In 2004 a European Defence Agency was established by the European Council (a decision requiring unanimity) in order to encourage a consensus on what capabilities are required and how best to achieve them. The Agency has been given a treaty base in Articles 42, paragraph 3 and Article 45. Participation is voluntary and the agency is in effect a device to identify realistic targets and encourage a continual process which depends on national decisions with a dash of peer pressure.

In practice, the latest development in organising military capabilities is the establishment of small standby forces called "battle groups" – task forces of a minimum of 1,500 personnel, capable of stand-alone operations and deployable after 5-10 days. Since the beginning of 2007 two such groups have been on call for periods of six months. Ireland contributes some 100 troops to the Nordic group, led by Sweden, currently on standby for the first six months of 2008. The battle group concept involves a high level of preparation and training, which traditional peacekeeping operations in the UN context are unable to avail of.

There is an implicit recognition in the Lisbon Treaty that not all Member States will be willing or able to contribute at the same level, in the provision for permanent structured cooperation (Article 42, paragraph 6, Article 46 and Protocol). This allows Member States which want to adhere to a more demanding level of military capabilities to do so within an arrangement with its own rules and criteria of membership. This additional "opt-in" commitment does not alter the overall rules about deploying military forces in CSDP missions, and is in effect an optional extra to do with the generation of military capabilities. It is expected that the French government will propose an initiative under this rubric later this year.

Of course, the critical decision to be made in the security and defence context is not so much about capabilities but whether to deploy a mission in any specific case. Here the Lisbon Treaty makes no change to the existing rule of unanimity, which is emphasised as absolute for decisions with military implications (Article 48, paragraph 7). Nor is there any change to the Member State's right to decide whether or not to participate in a particular mission. In Ireland's case this national decision is circumscribed by the "triple lock" provision, formally appended to the Treaty of Nice in the "Seville Declaration". This requires that any deployment of national forces outside the state must be under UN authorisation, formally approved by the government and endorsed by the Dáil. Given the intergovernmental nature of this policy area, parliamentary oversight of CSDP missions falls as much within the ambit of national parliaments as of the European Parliament. This is particularly the case for Member States participating in a military mission, since operating expenditure falls to them, not to the Union.

Although the common security and defence provisions in the Lisbon Treaty have been agreed on the basis of previous treaties, a clearer picture of this relatively new aspect of EU policy may be seen in the way these rather abstract legal commitments have been translated in to actual operations. The European Union deployed its first missions under the European Security and Defence Policy, a police task force in Bosnia and a military force in the Former Yugoslav Republic of Macedonia in 2003. Since then, 21 missions have been agreed, forming part of the EU's response to a wide variety of demands for peacekeeping and humanitarian assistance in areas of conflict in Europe, Africa and Asia.

In some cases these operations are on a small scale, involving perhaps just a dozen personnel from EU Member States helping in the reform of police, judicial or administrative systems. In others, the requirement may be for a substantial military force to provide protection for refugees or a sufficient degree of stability to hold elections. In all cases the policy framework is designed to balance civilian and military contributions, and to place them in the broader diplomatic context, involving the United Nations or other regional organisations.

About three quarters of the missions are civilian in character. For the most part these involve police personnel from Member States in a monitoring and mentoring role in situations where local police forces have difficulty in providing effective policing. The EU does not replace local police, but works with them or with police missions from other regional organisations, as is the case of assistance to the African Union in Darfur. "Rule of law" missions have a somewhat broader brief, with regard to the provision of professional advice and training of personnel in prison services and the administration of justice in general. There has been Irish involvement in 5 of the current civilian operations and 2 in the completed ones.

The military missions are usually on a larger scale, being faced with the difficult task of providing political stabilisation. Operation Althea, is still in place in Bosnia at a force strength of 2,500. In Africa, Operation Artemis in 2003 consisted of a force of about 2,000 troops sent to the Democratic Republic of the Congo at the behest of the United Nations, pending the much delayed deployment of an agreed UN force. The EU force was able to deploy in substantial numbers in about three weeks, and to hand over to the larger UN force some three months later. Three years later EUFOR Congo, a 3700-strong force, provided a secure environment to hold elections in the east of the country. At a broader level, the EU-African Union summit in Lisbon in December 2007 has agreed a joint strategy to develop security cooperation between the European Union and the African Union on a more systematic basis.

The two most recently agreed EU missions illustrate both the need for complex measures of conflict resolution and the difficulties in providing them. Following Kosovo's declaration of independence the largest civilian operation yet agreed, a police and rule of law mission, is being put together against the background of diplomatic confrontation and potential violence. In the context of actual violence and the vulnerability of up to a quarter of a million refugees on the border between the Darfur region in Sudan and Chad a large military mission, with significant Irish involvement, is being deployed to protect refugees and allow for humanitarian assistance to reach them. The EU contributions are part of a broader attempt, along with the UN, NATO (Kosovo) and the African Union (Darfur), to prevent persistent conflicts spreading further. There is necessarily a degree of risk involved, and the formation of the missions has exposed limitations in capabilities and political will. Action of this sort provides no panacea, but the alternative - inaction – may be seen as a greater risk in the longer term.

The Lisbon Treaty and the EU in the World Arena

The Lisbon Treaty makes three main changes to the way in which the European Union relates to the rest of the world. First, it reflects a more holistic approach to the wide spectrum of policies under the heading of external action. It then changes the institutional structure, in the post of High Representative of the Union for Foreign Affairs and Security Policy and the European External Action service, in order to maintain consistency of purpose across the policy spectrum. Finally, it spells out more fully the rules for the most recently devised part of that spectrum, the Common Security and Defence Policy.

All of these changes are evolutionary in character. They are pragmatic extensions of the legal base agreed in previous treaties, and do not alter the fact that the Union does not replace the Member States in the international sphere, but rather works with them. This complex arrangement has no historical precedent or parallel in the contemporary world, and for that reason it is often difficult to grasp what changes to a legal text like the Lisbon Treaty really mean. Putting them in the much broader context of a changing world may give us a better perspective to assess their significance.

It is clear that the underlying patterns of power and influence in world politics are undergoing profound transformation. The emergence of new power centres (China, India, Brazil) and the difficulties of old ones, together with the uneven impact of economic globalisation, fuelled by technological change, are only the most obvious indicators. But the consequences of these fundamental trends are rarely clear; it is to be expected that that in the short term they will interact in surprising and often threatening ways. "Events" will always challenge the best-laid plans of those in political authority.

Effective responses are increasingly beyond the capacity of individual states – hence the potential utility of a collective entity like the European Union. But to realise such potential the Union itself has to harness the political will of 27 Member States, with their own historical traditions, interests and internal political tensions. This is where its institutional structures and policy processes matter, and where we may find the meaning of the reforms contained in the Lisbon Treaty.

7

Treaty of Lisbon:
Freedom, Security & Justice

John Handoll

Introduction

In the area of freedom, security and justice, the Lisbon Treaty is at the same time innovative and rather conservative, giving Member States concerned about the encroachment of Union powers a level of protection not seen in many other areas of Union activity. In retaining its semi-detached status, Ireland continues to be able to strike the balance it desires between engagement and non-participation in areas threatening the Common Travel Area and its common law tradition particularly in the area of criminal law.

The Lisbon Treaty abolishes the two-pillar structure

A key achievement of the new Treaty is the abolition of the two-pillar structure for freedom, security and justice. Title V of Part 3 of the Treaty on the Functioning of the European Union will embrace the EC Treaty provisions on "visas, asylum, immigration and other policies related to the free movement of persons" and the Treaty on European Union provisions on "police and judicial cooperation in criminal matters".

The new Title thus contains a number of general provisions and specific provisions on (*a*) policies on border checks, asylum and immigration; (*b*) judicial cooperation in civil matters; (*c*) judicial cooperation in criminal matters; and (*d*) police cooperation.

Policies presented in a clearer and better-structured way

A welcome attempt has been made to present each of these policies in a clearer, more structured, way. It is certainly the case that a casual reader of the new provisions will have a better idea of what is involved than would have been the case in reading the old Treaty provisions.

Stand-still, "catch-up" and innovation

Many of the new provisions repeat those of the previous treaties. However, there have been some important substantive and procedural changes.

In some respects, these provisions have simply "caught up" with policy developments since the launch of the 1999 Tampere programme, reflecting the changing nature of the freedom, security and justice agenda since the signing of the Amsterdam Treaty. This is the case, for example, for immigration and asylum policy. Having a clear and unambiguous Treaty basis for implementing current Union policy is clearly desirable.

In other respects, the new provisions are innovative. The criminal justice provisions are broader than before: witness, for example, the possible creation of a European public prosecutor. In terms of decision-making, the increased use of the co-decision procedure in place of Council decision-making should strengthen democratic accountability and reduce blockages. This is seen as an important achievement of the Lisbon Treaty. However, in relation to judicial cooperation in criminal matters in particular, there are a number of areas where extension of Union activity to new areas will require not only unanimity in the Council but also the assent of the European Parliament.

Enhancement of the rule of law and fundamental rights

Although still constrained in some respects, the Court of Justice will have greater powers of judicial review than before. This development, welcomed by the Irish Government, augurs well for the observance of the rule of law, and the application of fundamental rights law, in these areas.

National sensitivities are taken into account, elements of
intergovernmentalism remain

At the same time, national sensitivities are taken into account and not a few traces of the "intergovernmental" approach remain. The frontiers of Union and Member State competence have been better delineated in order to protect areas of retained national power. In relation to judicial cooperation in civil and criminal matters, the central principle of mutual recognition is designed to reassure Member States that their individual legal systems will be respected. In especially sensitive areas – such as family law and the creation of a European Public Prosecutor – the Council will be the sole legislator acting by unanimity.

In some criminal justice areas, a Member State concerned about the consequences of the "ordinary" legislative procedure can apply an "emergency brake" by referring the matter to the European Council: if a consensus cannot be achieved, a body of at least nine Member States can then decide to establish enhanced cooperation (referred to colloquially as the "accelerator clause"). Such an accelerator clause also enables enhanced cooperation where the Member States cannot achieve unanimity in establishing a European Public Prosecutor's Office.

The European Council will have a key Treaty-defined role. Generally, it is to define the strategic guidelines for legislative and operational planning within the area of freedom, security and justice. In relation to certain areas of judicial cooperation in criminal matters and police cooperation, the European Council may be asked to try to achieve consensus in certain cases where a Member State has concerns about effects on its criminal justice system and in other cases where unanimity in the Council cannot be achieved. In both cases, the use of the highest political body in the Union can help to "oil the wheels" of decision-making where there may be acute national sensitivities.

Similar concerns underlie the provision for taking measures under which Member States, in collaboration with the Commission, will conduct objective and impartial evaluation of the implementation of the Union policies in Title V, in particular in order to facilitate full application of the principle of mutual recognition. The European Parliament and national parliaments are to be informed of the content and results of the evaluation. This mechanism is without prejudice to provisions for sanctioning Member State failure to comply with Union law.

Ireland continues to be "semi-detached" but will, where possible, be constructively engaged
Ireland, together with the UK, will continue its policy of semi-detachment from all of the Title V areas. The general "out/opt-in" protocol will continue in expanded form, as will the Schengen and internal market protocols. However, provided that the key concerns of protecting the Common Travel Area and the Irish legal system (especially in relation to criminal justice) are addressed, the present Government policy is one of constructive engagement. Given their obvious importance and relevance, these are separately addressed below.

The Protocols

Under the current Treaty arrangements, there are two Protocols which affect the participation of Ireland in the area of freedom, security and justice. First, the UK/Irish "out/opt-in" Protocol. Second, the Schengen Protocol. Reference should also be made to the "Internal Market" Protocol allowing Ireland and the UK to retain the benefits of the Common Travel Area at the expense of continuing frontier controls with the other Member States. Each of these is addressed below.

The UK/Irish "Opt-Out/Opt-In" Protocol
The existing "Protocol on the position of the UK and Ireland", which excludes these two Member States from participating in the adoption of Community measures in relation to visas, asylum and other policies related to free movement of persons until either of them "opts-in" to specific measures has been amended and retitled

the "Protocol on the position of the UK and Ireland in respect of the Area of Freedom, Security and Justice". The amended Protocol will thus now apply to the whole of Title V, including former third pillar areas of judicial cooperation in criminal matters and police cooperation.

The rationale for the exclusion varies between areas of activity. In relation to immigration and asylum, the principal reason is the desire to protect the Common Travel Area. In relation to the area of judicial and police cooperation, Ireland and the UK share concerns about respect for the core elements of their shared common law tradition. The UK has decided for exclusion and Ireland has reluctantly followed on the basis that it – together with the smaller common law jurisdictions who have not opted-out – will not have the necessary clout in decision-making.

However, the Irish Government has declared that it will participate to the maximum extent it deems possible and that it will, in particular, opt into police cooperation measures. It will review the operation of these arrangement within three years of the Lisbon Treaty's entry into force.

There are a number of technical amendments reflecting the broader scope of Title V of Part 3 of the Treaty on the Functioning of the European Union and the definition of the qualified majority needed for decision-making in the absence of the UK and Ireland.

The Protocol is to apply to measures *amending* an existing measure by which the UK and/or Ireland are/is bound. In essence, if there is no notification to opt-in in relation to the amending measure and the Council determines that this would make the application of the (amended) measure inoperable for other Member States or the Union, the existing measure will cease to be binding upon or applicable to the UK and/or Ireland, as the case may be, and the direct financial consequences of the ending of participation may have to be borne by the Member State concerned. This may put some moral, and even financial, pressure on Ireland to continue to participate in areas it has already signed up to.

The Schengen Protocol

The current Schengen Protocol is retained with a number of amendments.

The Schengen *acquis* – which is composed of a number of free movement/border control provisions – is now fully integrated into the framework of the EU. The UK and Ireland do not, because of their position on frontier controls (which is, for Ireland, driven by the desire to maintain the Common Travel Area), participate in all of the *acquis*. However, each of them may request to take part in some or all of the *acquis* (Ireland has already made a request for partial participation) and any request is to be decided on by the 25 "Schengen" Member States and the requesting Member State.

A somewhat complex procedure has been introduced in relation to Irish or UK participation in proposals and initiatives to build upon the *acquis*. As is currently the case, where Ireland or the UK has *not* notified the Council that it wishes to participate, the authorisation given under the "enhanced cooperation" provision of Article 329 of the Treaty on the Functioning of the European Union will be deemed to be granted where either of them wishes to participate. However, where Ireland or the UK is thus deemed to have given notification, it may within three months notify the Council that it does not wish to participate and it will then not take part in its adoption.

There is then a process for suspending the procedure for building on the *acquis* so that the Council, and if necessary the European Council, can decide on the extent to which the non-participating Member State can continue to benefit from the Council Decision allowing it to participate in the relevant part of the Schengen *acquis* in the first place.

It should be noted that the Council/European Council is to "seek to retain the greatest possible measure of participation of the Member State without seriously affecting the practical operability of the various parts of the Schengen *acquis*, while respecting their coherence". In the absence of a decision, and where the measure building on the *acquis* is adopted, the original Decision will cease to apply to the extent and under the conditions decided by the Commission. In essence, Ireland cannot adopt an a la carte approach where this might affect the integrity of the developing *acquis*.

The Internal Market Protocol
The current Protocol on the application of Article 14 of the Treaty Establishing the European Community to the UK and to Ireland is to be substantially retained. Ireland will thus continue to be able to impose frontier controls for as long as the Common Travel Arrangements are maintained. By the same token, the other Member States will continue to be able to exercise frontier controls from persons seeking to enter their territories from Ireland and the UK.

Security

A suite of general provisions addresses the issue of "security" in a way that accommodates national prerogatives in the area. First, a Council standing committee is to be set up in order to promote and strengthen operational cooperation in internal security. Second, repeating an existing provision, Article 72 of the Treaty on the Functioning of the European Union states that Title V "shall not affect the exercise of the responsibilities incumbent upon Member States with regard to the maintenance of law and order and the safeguarding of internal security". Third, Member States may organise between themselves and under their responsibility forms of cooperation and coordination they deem appropriate between departments of their administrations responsible for safeguarding national security.

Financing of Terrorism

A new provision in Article 75 provides that, where necessary to achieve the freedom, security and justice objectives set out in Article 67, the European Parliament and the Council are, as regards preventing and combating terrorism and related activities, to define a framework for administrative measures with regard to capital movements and payments. Regulations made in accordance with the ordinary legislative procedure are to cover matters such as the freezing of funds, financial assets or economic gains belonging to, or owned or held by, natural or legal persons, groups or non-State entities. The Council, acting on a proposal from the Commission is to take measures to implement this framework. The acts taken are to include necessary provisions on legal safeguards.

In contrast to the UK (which has nonetheless stated its intention to fully participate), the "out/opt-in" Protocol does not apply to Ireland in relation to this new provision.

Policies on Border Checks, Asylum and Immigration

Article 67.2 provides that the Union "shall ensure the absence of internal border controls for persons and shall frame a common policy on asylum, immigration and external border control, based on solidarity between Member States, which is fair towards third-country nationals". The Treaty reference to a common policy formalises the policy framework agreed by the European Council in Tampere in October 1999 and developed in the Hague Programme. Reference to the fundamental concept of solidarity (or burden-sharing) and the idea of fairness towards third country nationals also give Treaty recognition to the Tampere approach.

The EC Treaty contains provisions on "burden-sharing" in relation to refugees and displaced persons. This has been replaced by a provision applying to the whole of Chapter 2 of Title V, providing that the policies of the Union and their implementation are to be governed by the principle of solidarity and fair sharing of responsibility, including its financial implications, between Member States. Union acts are, where necessary, to give effect to this principle.

Border Checks

In relation to border checks, the Union is to develop a policy: (*a*) to ensure the absence of internal border controls; (*b*) to carry out checks on persons crossing, and efficient monitoring of, external borders; and (*c*) to gradually introduce an integrated management system for external borders.

Measures to implement this policy are now all to be taken by the European Parliament and the Council under the ordinary legislative procedure. The scope of existing EC Treaty provisions is increased in relation to the common policy on visas and short-stay residence permits, checks at external frontiers and the absence of internal border controls. Measures are now expressly provided for in relation to intra-Union travel of third-country nationals for short periods to the gradual establishment of an integrated management system for external frontiers.

In a departure from the position under the EC Treaty, the Council may now, in order to facilitate the union citizenship right of free movement and residence and where the Treaties have not provided the necessary powers, adopt provisions on passports, identity cards, residence permits or the like. The Council is to act unanimously under a special legislative procedure, after consulting the European Parliament. Such a power was excluded under Article 18.3 of the EC Treaty and the change involves an extension of Union competence, although Member States have an effective veto.

A new provision states that the above provisions do not affect the competence of the Member States on the geographical demarcation of their borders, in accordance with international law.

The "out/opt-in" Protocol applies to Ireland and the UK in respect of these provisions and the current "Internal Market" Protocol is to be substantially retained (see above). Ireland will thus continue to be able to impose frontier controls for as long as the Common Travel Arrangements are maintained. By the same token, the other Member States will continue to be able to exercise frontier controls from persons seeking to enter their territories from Ireland and the UK.

Asylum

In relation to asylum, Article 78 of the Treaty on the Functioning of the European Union provides a clearer legal basis for the developing common policy on asylum, subsidiary protection and temporary protection applying to third-country nationals (and stateless persons). It is made clear, as under the EC Treaty, that the policy must accord with the 1951 Geneva Convention and 1967 Protocol and other relevant treaties. The Lisbon Treaty has introduced a specific reference to compliance with the principle of non-refoulement (that is, that nobody be returned to a place where his or her life or freedom could be threatened, or where he/she faces a risk of persecution).

Replacing the Council as sole legislator, the European Parliament and the Council acting in accordance with the ordinary legislative procedure, are to adopt measures for a common European asylum system. These replace the rather more modest EC Treaty provisions which seek to allocate responsibility between Member States for determining asylum applications, to require minimum standards and to promote a measure of burden-sharing. Under the Treaty on the Functioning of the European Union the common system is to comprise: (a) a uniform status of asylum; (b) a uniform status of subsidiary protections; (c) a common system of temporary protection for displaced persons; (d) common procedures for granting and withdrawing asylum or subsidiary protection status; (e) criteria and mechanisms for determining which Member State is responsible for considering an application for protection; (f) standards on reception conditions for applicants; and (g) partnership and cooperation with third countries to manage inflows of applicants for protection.

As in the EC Treaty, the TFEU allows the Council to take provisional measures to deal with emergencies caused by the sudden inflow of third country nationals into one or more Member State/s. The existing six-month limit on the duration of such measures will be lifted and the European Parliament has now to be consulted.

Immigration

In relation to immigration, the Lisbon Treaty provides for the development of a common immigration policy, formalising the

Tampere approach as developed under the Hague Programme. This policy is "aimed at ensuring, at all stages, the efficient management of migration flows, fair treatment of third-country nationals residing legally in Member States, and the prevention of, and enhanced measures to combat, illegal immigration and trafficking in human beings".

Replacing the Council as sole legislator, the European Parliament and the Council acting in accordance with the ordinary legislative procedure, are to adopt measures in a number of areas. The first area – conditions of entry and residence, and standards on procedures for issue by Member States of long-term visas and residence permits, including those for the purpose of family reunification – is virtually identical to the existing EC Treaty provision. The definition of the rights of legally resident third-country nationals, an important part of the Tampere project, is given explicit treaty expression: this includes free movement (and incorporating an EC Treaty provision) residence in other Member States.

EC Treaty provisions on illegal immigration and residence are essentially reproduced, with a reference to "unauthorised" instead of "illegal" residence and the introduction of specific powers in relation to "removal", in addition to the repatriation of persons residing without authorisation. There is now a specific basis for measures to combat human trafficking, particularly of women and children, which should have important implications for Ireland since it has now decided to sign up to the international agenda in this area. The Lisbon Treaty also introduces a specific legal basis for the conclusion of readmission agreements with third countries.

EU powers in relation to the integration of legally-resident third-country nationals are also addressed in a new provision enabling the European Parliament and the Council, acting in accordance with the ordinary legislative procedure, to provide incentives and support for Member State action. That migrant integration policy is seen as an essentially national preserve is reflected in the express exclusion from such incentive and support measures of harmonisation of the laws and regulations of the Member States.

It is also made clear that the Treaty Article on immigration is not to affect the right of Member States to determine the "volumes" of admission to their territory of third-country nationals coming from third countries in order to seek work.

Judicial Cooperation in Civil Matters

Article 67.4 of the Treaty on the Functioning of the European Union provides that the Union is to "facilitate access to justice, in particular through the principle of mutual recognition of judicial and extrajudicial decisions in civil matters.

Article 81.1 requires the Union to "develop judicial cooperation in civil matters having cross-border implications, based on the principle of mutual recognition of judgments and of decisions in extrajudicial cases". Such cooperation may include measures approximating Member States' laws and regulations. The overarching principle of mutual recognition is new and is designed to reassure Member States that their individual civil law systems will be respected. However, there is now an explicit recognition that, where there are "cross-border implications", approximation measures may be adopted.

Measures necessary for the proper functioning of the internal market

The European Parliament and Council, acting under the ordinary legislative procedure, are to adopt measures in a number of areas, in particular when they are necessary for the proper functioning of the internal market. In contrast to the position under the EC Treaty, the legislators are no longer limited to measures necessary for such functioning.

Some of these areas are already covered in the EC Treaty provisions: (*a*) the mutual recognition and enforcement of judgments and extra-judicial decisions; (*b*) the cross-border service of documents; (*c*) the compatibility of rules on conflict of laws and jurisdiction; and (*d*) cooperation in taking evidence. Measures are also to be taken in the newly-specified areas of effective access to justice, eliminating obstacles to the proper functioning of civil proceedings (including promoting the compatibility of Member States' rules on civil procedure), developing alternative methods of dispute resolution and supporting judicial training.

Family Law

New provisions specifically address the sensitive area of family law with cross-border implications. Measures in this area are to be established by the Council, acting unanimously after consulting the European Parliament. The Council may, subject to a "veto" by any national Parliament (in itself a novel feature), unanimously adopt a "passerelle" decision allowing certain aspects of family law to be adopted by the ordinary legislative procedure. These requirements for unanimity – and the power given to national parliaments – should give reassurance to Member States with strong constitutional traditions centred on the family, including Ireland, that their interests will be protected.

Judicial Cooperation in Criminal Matters

The current provisions on judicial cooperation in criminal matters, contained in Title VI of the existing Treaty on European Union are to be replaced by provisions in the Treaty on the Functioning of the European Union (Title V, Chapter 4). Notwithstanding the shift to a single Treaty framework, the new criminal justice framework contains important protection even for those Member States committed to the common project. Ireland can, of course, choose to stay outside, with the "out/opt-in" Protocol extended to cover this area.

Article 67.3 of the Treaty on the Functioning of the European Union states that the "Union shall endeavour to ensure a high level of security through measures to prevent and combat crime, racism and xenophobia, and through measures for coordination and cooperation between police and judicial authorities and other competent authorities, as well as through the mutual recognition of judgments in criminal matters and, if necessary, through the approximation of criminal laws".

Acts referred to in this Chapter, and measures of administrative cooperation falling within this area, are to be adopted on a proposal from the Commission or (reflecting particular Member State concerns) on the initiative of a quarter of the Member States.

Member State concerns are also seen in the statement that national parliaments ensure that such proposals and initiatives comply with the principle of subsidiarity.

As an overarching principle, ensuring respect for national criminal law systems, Article 82.1 states that judicial cooperation in criminal matters in the Union shall be based on the principle of mutual recognition.

Member State Concerns

There are then no less than six separate sets of provisions reflecting different degrees of Member State concern.

The Irish Position

The position of the Irish Government in relation to judicial cooperation in criminal matters reflects the UK decision not to participate in justice measures (in contrast to its position in the defunct Constitutional Treaty). The Foreign Minister, Dermot Ahern, has stated that, had the UK decided fully to participate "the combined negotiating weight of Ireland and Britain would have been sufficient to ensure respect for the essential features of our shared common law tradition", with the absence of the UK, "as one of a handful of small Member States with a common law tradition, it could have been very difficult for Ireland acting alone to shape future proposals in a direction palatable to us".

General measures

First, the European Parliament and the Council, acting under the ordinary legislative procedure, are to adopt measures to: (*a*) ensure Union-wide recognition of judgments and judicial decisions; (*b*) prevent and settle conflicts of jurisdiction between Member States; (*c*) support judicial training; and (*d*) facilitate cooperation between judicial and equivalent authorities in relation to criminal proceedings and enforcement of decisions. All save the judicial training area are covered in the TEU, though the idea of *settling* conflicts of jurisdiction is new.

Facilitating mutual recognition and judicial cooperation in matters with a "cross-border" dimension

Second, the European Parliament and the Council may, by adopting directives under the ordinary legislative procedure, establish "minimum rules" in a number of areas to the extent necessary to facilitate mutual recognition and judicial cooperation in criminal matters "having a cross-border dimension". The needs to respect national systems is seen in the requirement to use directives, in the limitation to activity with a cross-border dimension and in the expressly-stated requirement that such rules "shall take into account the differences between the legal traditions and systems of the Member States".

It is, however, recognised that there may be approximation of national laws and regulations in these areas. They are: (*a*) the mutual admissibility of evidence between Member States; (*b*) the rights of individuals in criminal procedure; (*c*) the rights of victims of crime; and (*d*) any other specific aspects of criminal procedure identified in advance by the Council in a decision, adopted unanimously with the consent of the European Parliament.

There are two important additional national protections. First, Member States may maintain or introduce a higher level of protection for individuals than the minimum rules. Second, a Member State concerned that a draft directive would affect fundamental aspects of its criminal justice system may suspend the process by referring the draft to the European Council. Where, after discussion, there is consensus in the European Council, the draft is within four months to be referred back to the Council and the suspension lifted. However, if there is disagreement within the same four month period, it is open to at least nine Member States to establish enhanced cooperation in the area covered by the draft directive.

Definition of criminal offences and sanctions

Third, the European Parliament and the Council may, by adopting directives under the ordinary legislative procedure, establish "minimum rules" concerning the definition of criminal offences and sanctions in areas of particularly serious crime with a cross-border dimension. Such a dimension will result either from the nature/impact of such offences or "from a special need to combat them on a common basis". This covers crimes in the areas of terrorism, human trafficking and sexual exploitation of women and children, illicit drug trafficking, illicit arms trafficking, money laundering, corruption, counterfeiting of means of payment, computer crime and organised crime. As crime develops, other areas may be included by the Council, deciding unanimously with the consent of the European Parliament.

Provision is also made for directives establishing "minimum rules" for defining criminal offences and sanctions in areas where the approximation of Member States laws and regulations is essential to ensure the effective implementation of a Union policy in an area subject to harmonisation measures.

A Member State concerned that a draft directive would affect fundamental aspects of its criminal justice system may suspend the process by referring the draft to the European Council. Where, after discussion, there is consensus in the European Council, the draft is within four months to be referred back to the Council and the suspension lifted. However, if there is disagreement within the same four month period, it is open to at least nine Member States to establish enhanced cooperation in the area covered by the draft directive.

Crime prevention

Fourth, the European Parliament and the Council, acting under the ordinary legislative procedure, may establish measures to promote and support Member State action in the field of crime prevention. Any harmonisation of national laws and regulations is excluded.

Eurojust

Fifth, there are provisions on Eurojust. Article 85.1 of the Treaty on the Functioning of the European Union states that its "mission shall be to support and strengthen coordination between national investigating and prosecuting authorities in relation to serious crime affecting two or more Member States or requiring a prosecution on common bases, on the basis of operations conducted and information supplied by the Member States, authorities and by Europol". The European Parliament and Council are to adopt regulations under the ordinary legislative procedure determining Eurojust's structure, operation, fields of action and tasks.

It tasks may include: (*a*) the initiation of criminal investigations, and the proposing of initiation of prosecutions by national authorities; (*b*) the coordination of such investigations and prosecutions; and (*c*) the strengthening of judicial cooperation. The regulations are to determine arrangements for involving the European Parliament and national parliament in the evaluation of Eurojust's activities.

It is made clear that in any prosecutions, without prejudice to specific provisions in relation to the European Public Prosecutor (see below), formal acts of judicial procedure are to be carried out by the competent national officials.

European Public Prosecutor

Finally, initially at least in order to combat crimes affecting the financial interests of the Union, the Council may unanimously adopt regulations under a special legislative procedure establishing a European Public Prosecutor's Office. The consent of the European Parliament must be obtained.

In the absence of unanimity in the Council, a group of at least nine Member States may suspend the process by referring the draft to the European Council. Where, after discussion, there is consensus in the European Council, the draft is within four months to be referred back to the Council and the suspension lifted. However, if there is disagreement within the same four month period, it is open to at least nine Member States to establish enhanced cooperation in the area covered by the draft directive.

The Office would be responsible for investigating, prosecuting and bringing to judgment (where appropriate in liaison with Europol) the perpetrators of, and accomplices in, offences against the Union's financial interests. It is to act as prosecutor in the competent courts of the Member States.

The Council regulations are to determine the general rules applicable to the Office, the conditions governing the performance of its functions (including judicial review), rules of procedure and rules governing the admissibility of evidence.

There is a widespread, though not universal, belief that the establishment of a European Prosecutor is necessary to assure effective protection of the Union's *own* financial interests. The Council may, by means of a unanimous decision and with the consent of the European Parliament, extend the powers of the Office to include serious crimes having a cross-border dimension. The need for unanimity should reassure certain Member States that there will be no creeping extension of European prosecutorial power and it is noteworthy that there is no procedure for automatic enhanced cooperation in relation to proposals for such an extension.

Any Irish concerns about the immigration of an "alien" prosecutor into the Irish legal system are more than adequately addressed by the "out/opt-in" protocol.

Police Cooperation

The current provisions on police and judicial cooperation in criminal matters, contained in Title VI of the present Treaty on European Union are to be replaced by provisions in the Treaty on the Functioning of the European Union (Title V, Chapters 1, 4 and 5).

Although police cooperation is covered by the "out/opt-in" Protocol, it should be noted that Ireland has declared that it will participate, "to the maximum extent possible", in measures in this area. This reflects its current position and the future debate will doubtless centre on the limits of the possible.

Acts referred to in this Chapter, and measures of administrative cooperation falling within this area, are to be adopted on a proposal from the Commission or on the initiative of a quarter of the Member States. Member State concerns are also seen in the statement in Article 69 that national parliaments ensure that such proposals and initiatives comply with the principle of subsidiarity.

Article 87.1 requires the Union to "establish police cooperation involving all the Member States' competent authorities, including police, customs and other specialised law enforcement services in relation to the prevention, detection and investigation of crime". Four specific areas of action are identified.

Former TEU areas of cooperation
First, the European Parliament and the Council, acting under the ordinary legislative procedure, may take measures concerning: (a) the collection, storage, processing, analysis and exchange of relevant information; (b) support for training, and cooperation on staff-exchanges, equipment and crime-detection research; and (c) common investigative techniques in the detection of serious forms of organised crime. In substantive terms, these provisions replicate those in the existing treaties.

Operational cooperation between national authorities
The Council may also, acting unanimously and with the consent of the European Parliament, take measures concerning *operational cooperation between the national authorities*.

The need for unanimity is tempered by the possibility for enhanced cooperation. In the absence of unanimity in the Council, and only for acts which do not constitute a development of the

Schengen *acquis*, a group of at least nine Member States may suspend the process by referring the draft to the European Council. Where, after discussion, there is consensus in the European Council, the draft is within four months to be referred back to the Council and the suspension lifted. However, if there is disagreement within the same four month period, it is open to at least nine Member States to establish enhanced cooperation in the area covered by the draft directive.

Europol
Article 88.1 defines Europol's mission as being "to support and strengthen action by the Member States' police authorities and other law enforcement services and their mutual cooperation in preventing and combating serious crime affecting two or more Member States, terrorism and forms of crime which affect a common interest covered by a Union policy". The European Parliament and Council are to adopt regulations under the ordinary legislative procedure determining structure, operation, fields of action and tasks.

Europol's tasks may include: (*a*) the collection, storage, processing, analysis and exchange of information; and (*b*) the coordination, organisation and implementation of investigative and operational action carried out jointly with the Member States' authorities or in the context of joint investigative, where appropriate, in liaison with Eurojust. The regulations are to determine the procedures for the scrutiny by the European Parliament and national parliament of Europol's activities.

National concerns are addressed by the requirement that any operational action by Europol is to be carried out in liaison and in agreement with the authorities of the Member State/s whose territory is concerned. The application of coercive measures is to be the exclusive responsibility of the competent national authorities.

Operations in other Member States
Finally, the Council, acting unanimously under a special legislative procedure and after consulting the European Parliament, is to lay down the conditions and limitations under which national judicial and police authorities may operate in the territory of another Member State in liaison and agreement with the authorities of the latter.

8

Key Policies – Energy and Environment

Joe Curtin

Introduction

Although climate change is a relatively new policy challenge and despite the fact that it is not mentioned in the EU or EC Treaties, it has become a key policy area for the EU. This may be because the climate change problem is global in nature and necessitates structured cooperation between sovereign states to overcome the "prisoners dilemma" which has, to a certain extent, stymied efforts to address the challenge. The EU as an international organisation with a global role, experienced in cultivating cooperation between Member States and with an established institutional framework to develop policy, is well equipped to overcome blockages of this nature both between individual Member States and on the international stage.

Though the EU is responsible for only 10% of global GHG emissions, it has become the global leader on climate change through its ground breaking emission reduction commitments, first agreed at the March European Council, 2007, and subsequently developed by the European Commission in its package of implementation proposals, published on 23 January, 2008 (see Text Box 1). If agreed these proposals would not only necessitate radical restructuring of Member States' economies but would also profoundly influence the direction of international negotiations on a successor agreement to the Kyoto Protocol – agreed in 1997 and commiting all developed countries – expected in Copenhagen in December 2009. Professor Dieter Helm of Oxford University described the package as "one of the most radical proposals to come out of Brussels ... on a par with monetary union".[1] Ongoing negotiations between European leaders and their representatives, Commission officials and Members of the European Parliament will determine the exact shape of the final outcome with a conclusive agreement expected by April 2009.

Box 1

EUROPEAN CLIMATE CHANGE PROPOSALS

The 2007 March European Council had agreed that:

- The EU would reduce emissions by 20% on 1990 levels by 2020 (30% in the case of an international agreement involving "comparable" emissions reductions from other developed countries).

- The EU would consume 20% of energy from renewables by 2020.

- The EU would aim to achieve 20% improvement in energy efficiency by 2020.

- The EU would produce 10% of transport fuels from biofuels by 2020.

European leaders invited the European Commission to propose how these objectives might be achieved. In January 2008, the European Commission followed up with a package of proposals, the main elements of which are: proposals on effort sharing of renewables and emission targets – Ireland received among the most onerous targets – and a proposal on the post-2012 design of the emissions trading scheme.[2]

Because the words "climate change" are used for the first time and an entire new Energy Title has been added, advocates of the Lisbon Treaty argue that the Union's power and capacities to tackle climate change will be enhanced considerably. Critics have contended that the mere mention of climate change is of no real significance and that the Energy Title is nothing more than a formulation of competences that the Union has already developed under internal market and environment provisions. For these reasons, it is valid, if not essential, to pose the question: will the Lisbon Treaty affect or alter the way climate change policy is conceived, decided upon, or implemented in the EU? If so, what are the implications for EU Member States and the international climate change regime?

In order to address these competing perspectives, it is useful to divide climate change policy-making into two separate categories – internal and external policy-making – and describe how policy is formulated in each. What exactly the Treaty proposes in each area will then be set out and the implications evaluated.

Internal Policy Making

Actors and Rules in Internal European Climate Change Policy-Making
Directives and regulations relating to climate change policy-making fall under the environment chapter of the EC Treaty (Arts 174-176). Under the Environmental Title, qualified majority voting in the Council and the co-decision procedure is used for the adoption of legislative acts. The European Parliament thus plays a co-equal role in legislation with national governments.[3] However, several exceptions to the use of qualified majority voting exist, meaning that decisions taken in these areas must be taken unanimously. Proposals with fiscal implications require unanimity – a proposal on an EU-wide carbon tax in 1992 opposed by the UK, Ireland, France, Spain and Portugal failed to garner the unanimous support it required – as do measures affecting Member States' energy mix.

In practice, agreement is needed by a high proportion of participants across the spectrum of EU institutions for climate change policy to be adopted.

In the areas of climate change policy where the EU has a role, the Directorate General (DG) Environment of the European Commission is responsible for drafting legislation, with its Climate Change and Air Directorate given the lead. In several areas with implications for climate change, such as education and awareness, policy oversight and coordination, planning, transport and infrastructural development, competences remain largely in the hands of Member States and the Commission and the European Parliament's role is marginal.

Implications of the Lisbon Treaty

Overall, though the Lisbon Treaty includes a number of significant revisions which merit discussion, it is not anticipated that the reforms contained within it will radically alter the way that the EU designs, decides on or implements internal climate change policy. Several aspects of the new Energy Title XXI in the Treaty on the Functioning of the European Union (see: text box 2) could have indirect implications for EU climate change policy. Article 194.1, which refers to the establishment of an internal market for energy, references "the need to preserve and improve the environment" and goes on to commit Union policy to "promote energy efficiency and energy savings and the promotion of new and renewable forms of technology".

Although, arguably, EU policy is already committed to the promotion of renewables and energy efficiency, these articles offer a clear legal basis outside the political agreements at European Councils for policies consistent with the achievement of these objectives. Were the political climate to change, these amendments may prove significant.

Box 2

TITLE XXI: ENERGY

Article 194

1. In the context of the establishment and functioning of the internal market for and with regard for the need to preserve and improve the environment, Union policy on energy shall aim, in a spirit of solidarity between Member States, to:

   a. ensure the functioning of the energy market;
   b. ensure security of energy supply in the Union; and
   c. promote energy efficiency and energy savings and the development of new and renewable forms of energy; and
   d. promote the interconnection of energy networks.

2. Without prejudice to the application of other provisions of the Treaties, the European Parliament and the Council, acting in accordance with the ordinary legislative procedure, shall establish the measures necessary to achieve the objectives in paragraph 1.

   Such measures shall be adopted after consultation of the Economic and Social Committee and the Committee of the Regions. Such measures shall not affect member state's right to determine the conditions for exploiting its energy resources, its choice between different energy sources and the general structure of its energy supply, without prejudice to Article 192.2(c).

3. By way of derogation from paragraph 2, the Council, acting in accordance with a special legislative procedure, shall unanimously and after consulting the European Parliament, establish the measures referred to therein when they are primarily of a fiscal nature.

Take for example Energy Efficiency: policies which improve the efficient use of energy have implications for climate change because less energy is required to sustain a given level of economic activity; and thus emissions are reduced. The EU Energy Efficiency Action Plan, agreed on 23 November 2006 requires of Member States the production of National Energy Efficiency Action Plans to set out how 20% energy efficiency savings are to be achieved by 2020 (Ireland's consultation was launched in October 2007). However, unlike the case with renewables, no legally binding agreements have been or will be entered into by Member States. Again, the Treaty basis for policy might prove significant and would add an additional layer of protection were the political climate to change and the determination to tackle climate change to recede.

It is also significant that underlying all of the objectives listed in Article 194.1 is the commitment to "preserve and improve the environment". Although the Commission has made it clear that it considers the sustainability objective to underpin the others, it is significant that this perspective now has a legal basis overarching all internal market legislation.

External Climate Change Policy Making

Rules Governing External Policy Making in the EU
International environmental policy-making is described as an area of "mixed competences". This means that individual Member States have competences to negotiate in international bodies and to conclude international agreements (a right enshrined in Article 174.4 of the EC Treaty). In fact, both the European Union and its Member States were signatories to the Kyoto Protocol, leading to some ambiguity as to who was ultimately responsible for implementation. Positions adopted prior to UNFramework Convention on Climate Change negotiations must therefore be based on consensus. Positions are prepared by the EU's working party on International Environmental Issues (IEI), which meets twice a month, and the Council of Environment Ministers or the

European Council – if necessary – adopts final positions. The Presidency has responsibility for drafting the EU's position and representing the EU at negotiations as part of the "troika" consisting of the Presidency of the Council, the Commissioner for External Relations and the High Representative of the Common Foreign and Security Policy. Given the requirement for consensus, the Presidency plays an important role in moving negotiations forward at EU coordination meetings – attended by climate change delegations and representatives of the Commission – which take place during UNFCCC negotiations on a daily basis.

The Lisbon Treaty

The Lisbon Treaty contains provisions which may influence external EU climate change policy making. Article 191.1 commits the EU to: "promoting measures at international level to deal with regional or worldwide environmental problems, *and in particular combating climate change*". For the first time combating climate change is explicitly stated as an EU Treaty objective. Although this reference to combating climate change is limited to the international level, it is possible that a proactive ECJ could take a maximalist approach and use this Article to challenge other EU laws. The Commission could also use this reference to challenge Member States' policy that is incompatible with "combating climate change".

Precedents in the area of environmental legislation do exist where an activist ECJ has made rulings with potentially profound implications. For example, the judgement in case C-176/03 Commission v Council, held that although "as a general rule, neither Criminal law nor the rules of criminal procedure fall within the Community competence", such lack of express competence did not "prevent the Community legislature … from taking measures which relate to the criminal law of the Member State which it considers necessary in order to ensure that the rules are fully effective". This ruling for the first time allowed the Communities access to criminal law to enforce environmental protection in a manner which was certainly not foreseen by Member States.

Box 3

Environment Title XX

Article 191.1

Union Policy on the environment shall contribute to the pursuit of the following objectives:

    a. Preserving, protecting and improving the quality of the environment,

    b. Protecting human health,

    c. Prudent and rational utilisation of natural resources,

    d. Promoting measures at international level to deal with regional or worldwide environmental problems, and in particular combating climate change.

Article 218 outlines how international negotiations would be undertaken and has implications for how the EU would approach international climate change negotiations. It states that: "The Council shall authorise the opening of negotiations, adopt negotiating directives, authorise the signing of agreements and conclude them", and "the Commission.....shall submit recommendations to the Council, which shall adopt a decision authorising the opening of negotiations and, depending on the subject of the agreement envisaged, nominating the Union negotiator or head of the Union's negotiating team". The nominee would replace the Presidency as the lead EU negotiator at climate change negotiations. It would be the Union negotiator who would propose an agreement to the Council for decision.

Conclusions

Although the words "climate change" only appear in the Treaty of Lisbon on one occasion, there are several areas which have the potential to influence the internal and external climate change policy-making process in the EU. The new Energy Title, XXI, though for the most part a formalisation of policies that the EU has taken on under its internal marked and environmental competences, nevertheless solidifies and strengthens the direction the EU has taken. Promotion of renewables and energy efficiency in particular are established in the Treaties for the first time. For international negotiations, the Commission may play an increasing important role, with the ECJ looking on to ensure outcomes compatible with Art. 191.1.

References

1. Helm, D. (2008) *The EU Climate Change Package: Even More Radical than it Looks,* www.dieterhelm.co.uk
2. Curtin, J. (2008) *IIEA Energy and Climate Change Policy Brief,* www.iiea.com
3. Weale (2005) *Environmental Rules and Rule Making in the European Union.*
4. *Consultation on National Energy Efficiency Action Plan,* October 2007.

9

Key Policies – The Economic Dimension

David Croughan

Most of the key policy issues relating to economic governance, sectoral and social policies are contained in Part 3 of the Treaty on the Functioning of the European Union, which concerns Union Policies and Internal Actions. There are only a small number of changes of substance relating to economic governance contained in the Treaty though this chapter outlines, for completeness, a summary of the main principles on economic policy that are retained intact.

On economic and monetary policy, it is important to refer briefly to the Treaty on European Union (TEU). Thereafter, the chapter refers solely to the Treaty on the Functioning of the European Union.

Economic and Monetary Policy

The Treaty on European Union in Article 3.3 states that the Union shall establish an internal market. It redefines and mainly restates its objectives to work for the sustainable development of Europe based on balanced economic growth and price stability, a highly competitive social market economy, aiming at full employment and social progress and a high level of protection and improvement of the quality of the environment.

A reference to "free and undistorted competition" contained in the Constitutional Treaty was deleted, raising some concerns that competition policy might be diluted but, in mitigation of these concerns, the Protocol on the Internal Market and Competition mentions a "system ensuring that competition is not distorted."

However, Article 3.5 also states ambiguously, that in relations with the wider world, "the Union shall uphold and promote its values and interests and contribute to the protection of its citizens." This protection could be interpreted in a number of ways including consular protection or protection from terrorism, but has been used in France as a reference to protection against perceived threats of globalisation.[1]

Article 4.3 lays down a marker for co-operation and states that "Member States shall in full mutual respect assist each other in carrying out tasks which flow from the Treaties." This underpins the co-operation necessary for the successful implementation of the Broad Economic Policy Guidelines and the Lisbon Agenda on Competitiveness (not to be confused with the Lisbon Reform Treaty).

Treaty on the Functioning of the European Union (TFEU)

The provisions governing Economic and Monetary Policy are contained in Part 3, Title VII of the Treaty on the Functioning of the European Union. Chapter 1 deals with Economic Policy, Chapter 2 with Monetary Policy, Chapter 3 with Institutional Provisions, including a greater role for the euro zone Member States and Chapter 4 with the Transition countries.

The changes to economic governance are limited, given the sensitivity of Member States on their right to run their own economic affairs. This Title updates the Treaties by introducing the use of the euro as the single currency and many of the amendments apply only to those Member States that have adopted the euro, where there is a modest strengthening of the rules of governance. Euro zone countries have been given some powers to pursue policies as distinct from those Member States which have not adopted the euro.

Economic Policy

The Treaty restates the obligation of Member States to regard their economic policies as a matter of common concern and maintains the power of the Council on a recommendation from the Commission to formulate and adopt broad economic policy guidelines for the Member States. The Council will continue to monitor developments in each Member State based on reports from the Commission.

The Commission is given a new power to address a warning to a Member State which pursues policies not consistent with the broad guidelines. The Council acting on a qualified majority, excluding the Member State concerned, may address and publish the recommendation of the Commission.

On a proposal from the Commission, the Council may decide in a spirit of solidarity to take measures if difficulties arise in the supply of certain products notably in the area of energy.

The terms of the Stability and Growth Pact are restated. Member States shall avoid excessive government deficits, the reference values of which are laid down in the Protocol as 3% for the ratio of planned or actual government deficit to GDP and 60% of the ratio of government debt to GDP. The Commission shall monitor the developments of the budgetary situation and stock of government debt with a view to identifying gross errors. If a Member State does not fulfil the requirements, the Commission may prepare a report if it is of the opinion that there is a risk of an excessive deficit. The Commission is given a new power, if it thinks that an excessive deficit exits or may occur, to address an opinion to the Member State and to inform the Council.

On a Proposal from the Commission (which has more weight than a recommendation) the Council will decide whether an excessive deficit exists. Where the Council decides that a deficit does exist it shall without due delay adopt the recommendations of the Commission to end the situation. If a Member State does not take effective action within the period laid down, the Council may make the recommendation public. If effective action is still not taken after a period of closer scrutiny, the Council can decide to apply the sanctions that already existed in the treaties, namely: to publish specified information before issuing bonds; invite the EIB to reconsider its lending policy; to require the Member State to make a non-interest-bearing deposit for as long as the excessive deficit exists; or to impose a fine. The Council will take such decisions acting on a recommendation from the Commission and according to QMV of the other Member States. Any changes to the Protocol on Excessive Debt Procedures requires unanimity.

Monetary Policy

The Lisbon Treaty makes no significant changes to the execution of monetary policy. The primary objective of the European System of Central Banks (ESCB) to maintain price stability is restated. Without prejudice to this objective, the ESCB shall support the general economic principles outlined in Article 3 of the Treaty on European Union stated above. This again represents no change in policy.

The tasks of the ESCB are to define and implement monetary policy, to conduct foreign exchange operations, to hold and manage the foreign reserves of Member States and to promote the smooth operation of payment systems. It also contributes to the smooth conduct of policies relating to prudential supervision of credit institutions and the stability of the financial system. The Council may unanimously, after consulting the European Parliament and the European Central Bank, confer special tasks to the European Central Bank with regard to prudential supervision of credit and non-insurance financial institutions. This represents a downgrading of the European Parliament's role from consent to consultation.

The European Central Bank has the exclusive right to authorise the issue of euro banknotes within the Union. Member States may issue euro coins subject to the approval of the European Central Bank of the volume of the issue. On a proposal from the Commission, after consulting the European Parliament and the European Central

Bank, the Council may adopt measures to harmonise the denominations and technical specifications of all coins. Such measures do not constitute legislative acts and this represents a downgrading of the European Parliament's role from consent to consultation.

The Statute on the ESCB and the European Central Bank are contained in the Protocol. The European Parliament and the Council, following a recommendation from the European Central Bank after consulting the Commission, may amend specified Articles of the Statute through co-decision. Unanimous voting by the Commission has been dropped.

The European Parliament and the Council by co-decision shall lay down the measures necessary for the use of the euro as the single currency, after consultation with the European Central Bank.

Institutional Provisions

The European Central Bank, mindful of its independence, had sought to have the Treaty distinguish it from an Institution of the Union, though clearly linked to it. The Member States, however, decided not to change the wording on the basis that the Treaty's provisions are strong enough to safeguard its status. The Articles establishing the remit of the European Central Bank and the ESCB are reiterated in Chapter 3 Title VII of the Treaty. The only change of significance is that the President, Vice-President and other members of the Executive Board will be elected by QMV of the European Council rather than by unanimity.[2]

The Economic and Financial Committee is established in order to promote coordination of the policies of the Member States. This Committee took over from the Monetary Committee, which was dissolved at the start of the third stage of monetary union. The Treaty reiterates the tasks originally performed by the Monetary Committee which were to deliver opinions either at the request of the Council or Commission or under its own initiative, to review and report regularly on the economic and financial situation of Member States, to advise the Council and to examine at least once a year the situation regarding capital movements and payments.

Euro Group of Finance Ministers

In an entirely new provision Article 114 and the related Protocol formally recognises the informal Euro Group of Finance ministers. The Euro Group of Finance ministers already meets the day before Ecofin Council meetings to discuss issues relating to the euro area. The Euro Group's inclusion in the Treaty, however, enhances its standing by recognising the desirability of developing ever closer coordination of economic policies within the euro area. It also recognises the need to lay down special provisions for enhanced dialogue between Member States whose currency is the euro. The meetings remain informal but will be attended by the Commission, with an invitation to attend for the European Central Bank. The ministers of the Euro Group will elect, by a majority, a president for two and a half years.

In order to secure the euro's place in the international monetary system, the Council of Finance Ministers on a proposal from the Commission will establish common positions on matters of particular interest for economic and monetary union within the competent international financial institutions and conferences and ensure unified representation within them. Only members of the Council representing Member States whose currency is the euro may vote on such matters by QMV.

Transitional Provisions

A significant rewriting of the articles relating to the transition provisions, which are now obsolete, was required. For the purposes of the articles relating to the transition period, Member States means Member States whose currency is the euro and Member States with a Derogation mean those states in respect of which the

Council has not decided they have fulfilled the necessary conditions for the adoption of the euro. A current example is that of Lithuania which was not admitted to the Euro Group in 2007 while Slovenia was approved.

Certain provisions such as the adoption of the broad economic guidelines which concern the euro area, coercive means of remedying excessive deficits, or the appointment of the Executive Board of the European Central Bank do not apply to such Member States. At least once every two years at the request of a Member State with a Derogation, the Commission and the European Central Bank shall report to the Council on progress of Member States with a Derogation in fulfilling their obligations regarding the achievement of economic and monetary union. The reports shall include the compatibility of the national legislation of these Member States as well as the achievement of a high degree of convergence.

There are four criteria specified in Article 117 and developed in the Protocol. The criteria are: price stability judged by reference to no more than 1.5% higher than the three best performing Member States; sustainable government financial position; observance of normal fluctuation margins provided by the exchange-rate mechanism for at least two years without devaluing against the euro; the durability of convergence achieved reflected in long-term interest rates. The Council shall act within six months of a recommendation of a qualified majority of Member States whose currency is the euro.

The Commission shall investigate the position of a Member State with a Derogation which is in difficulties as a result of a disequilibrium in its balance of payments, and which may jeopardise the functioning of the internal market. It will recommend remedial actions to be taken by the Member State, and may recommend to the Council the granting of mutual assistance if the measures prove unsuccessful.

Employment and Social Policy

The provisions governing employment and social policy are in Part 3, Titles VIII to XI.

Title VIII deals with employment. There are no new provisions in the Reform Treaty but a reiteration of the aims of the Union to develop a co-ordinated strategy for employment, in particular relating to promoting a skilled, trained and adaptable workforce responsive to change. This links back to Article 3 of the Treaty on European Union objectives to work for the sustainable development of Europe based on balanced economic growth and price stability, a highly competitive social market economy, aiming at full employment and social progress. The Treaty reiterates that promoting employment is a "common concern" of the Member States, which should coordinate their actions in this respect.

Each year the European Council will consider the employment situation based on a report from the Council and the Commission. Following the conclusions of this report the Council will, after due consultation with the European Parliament, draw up guidelines for the Member States and each year the Member States must report on the principal measures taken to implement the policies indicated in the guidelines. These articles underpin much of the reform under the Lisbon Agenda (not to be confused with the Lisbon Reform Treaty) aimed at making the EU "the most dynamic and competitive knowledge-based economy in the world...".

The Treaty provides for the Council to establish an advisory Employment Committee to promote coordination between Member States.

Provisions relating to Social Policy are contained in Title IX. Most of the text is a reiteration of the existing Treaties. The European Parliament gains some enhanced powers. The Union and Member States have as their objective the promotion of employment and improved living and working conditions. In taking measures to achieve this, however, account is taken of the diverse nature of national practices, especially in the field of contractual relations.

In a new article the Union recognises and promotes the role of the social partners and shall facilitate dialogue between them. The Tripartite Social Summit for Growth and Employment shall contribute to social dialogue. This clause will be subject to the simplified revision procedure set down in Article 33 of the Treaty on European Union.

Article 153 lists a number of fields of social policy where the Union shall support and complement the activities of the Member States. These are unchanged from the present treaty provisions and cover such matters as health and safety, social security and protection, a wide range of workers' rights, employment of third country nationals, equality between men and women and combating social exclusion.

The European Parliament and the Council may adopt measures designed to encourage co-operation but excluding any harmonisation of the laws and regulations of the Member States. The European Parliament and Council in accordance with the ordinary legislative procedure, following due consultation, may adopt by means of a directive minimum requirements for the gradual implementation of the activities so long as they avoid imposing administrative, financial and legal constraints on the development of SMEs. However in matters relating to social security and social protection, protection of workers whose employment contract is terminated, representation and collective defence of the interests of workers and employers and conditions of employment of third country nationals, unanimity is required.

The European Social Fund

Title X reiterates the purpose of the European Social Fund, which is administered by the Commission to improve employment opportunities of workers by increasing their geographic mobility within the Union and to facilitate their adaptation to industrial changes through vocational training and retraining. Implementing regulations relating to the Fund shall be adopted by co-decision.

Educational, Vocational Training, Youth and Sport

Title XI reiterates the former Treaty articles in contributing to the development of quality education by encouraging cooperation and where necessary by supplementing Member State actions, including support for vocational training. The aim is to develop a European dimension to education and languages and encourage mobility of students and teachers and recognition of diplomas and periods of study. In a new aim the Treaty includes a new European dimension to sport by promoting fairness and integrity. The Union and Member States will foster cooperation with third countries in both education and sport. After due consultation, incentive measures excluding any harmonisation shall be adopted by co-decision.

Infrastructure Sectoral Policy and Trans-European Networks

The Articles dealing with these policy areas are found in various Titles of Part 3 and also in Part 5 Title II on Common Commercial Policy.

Title XV reiterates that, in the interests of citizens, economic operators and regional and local communities deriving the full benefit of the area without internal frontiers, the Union shall contribute to the establishment and development of trans-European networks in the areas of transport, telecommunications and energy infrastructures.

These provisions may take on a new significance in the context of rapidly changing priorities and opportunities in the energy field. Within a system of open and competitive markets, the Union shall promote interconnection and interoperability of national networks as well as access to such networks, in particular taking account of the need to link island, landlocked and peripheral regions to the central regions of the Union. Measures in pursuit of these aims shall be adopted by co-decision.

Industry

Title XVI reiterates that the Union and Member States shall ensure that conditions necessary for the competitiveness of the Union's industry exist. In accordance with a system of open and competitive markets their actions shall be aimed at speeding up industrial structural change, encouraging an environment favourable to initiative and the development of SMEs and fostering the better exploitation of innovation, research and technological development. Member States shall coordinate their action, where necessary and in an extension of its remit, the Commission may promote initiatives aimed at the establishment of guidelines and indicators, the organisation of best practice and prepare the necessary elements for periodic monitoring and evaluation.

This is an example of the application of the Open Method of Co-ordination which is characteristic of the Lisbon Strategy. The European Parliament shall be kept fully informed. After due consultation, specific measures to support Member States to achieve these objectives may be adopted by co-decision, but excluding the harmonisation of the laws and regulations of the Member States.

Economic, Territorial and Social Cohesion

Title XVII reiterates the promotion of harmonious development through the Structural Funds, the European Investment Bank and other existing Financial Instruments. The Treaty clarifies areas of priority. Particular attention shall be paid to rural areas, areas affected by industrial transition, and regions which suffer from severe and permanent natural or demographic handicaps such as the northernmost regions with very low population density and island, cross-border and mountain regions.

If specific actions prove necessary outside the Funds, the European Parliament and the Council after due consultation may adopt such actions. The European Parliament and Council shall define the tasks, priority objectives and the organisation of Structural Funds. Implementing regulations relating to the European

Regional Development Fund will now be subject to co-decision by the European Parliament and the Council. Governance of the European Agricultural Guidance and Guarantee Fund Guidance Section and the European Social Fund will continue as before.

Research and Technological Development and Space

Title XVIII has been amended to include Space. The objectives under this title have been extended in the particularly incoherent Article 179 as follows. The Union shall have the objective of strengthening its scientific and technological base by achieving a European research area in which researchers, scientific knowledge and technology circulate freely and encouraging it to become more competitive, including in its industry, while promoting all the research activities deemed necessary by virtue of other Chapters of the Treaties.

The Treaty reiterates the Union's purpose to encourage undertakings, research centres and universities in their R&D activities and shall support their efforts to cooperate with one another, aiming notably at permitting researchers to cooperate freely across borders. In a further new emphasis, the Commission may take any useful initiative aimed at the establishment of guidelines and indicators, the organisation of exchange of best practice, and the preparation of the necessary elements for periodic monitoring and evaluation, or in other words to utilise the Open Method of Co-ordination. The European Parliament shall be kept fully informed.

A multiannual framework programme and measures necessary for the implementation of the European Research area shall be adopted by co-decision.

In a further extension of its aims the Union shall draw up a European Space Policy. It may promote joint initiatives, support research and coordinate efforts needed for the exploration and exploitation of space. The European Parliament and the Council shall take the necessary measures, which may take the form of a

European space programme, excluding any harmonisation of the laws and regulations of the Member States. It shall establish appropriate relations with the European Space Agency.

Internal Market

The Treaty recognises in Title I the expiry date of the 1992 deadline for completing the internal market by expanding the stated aim of establishing or ensuring the functioning of the internal market.

There is no change of substance to articles referring to the Free Movement of Goods or the Customs Union. The Treaty reiterates that the European Parliament and the Council shall take measures to strengthen customs cooperation between Member States. It further reiterates there will be no quantitative restrictions on imports and exports except on the grounds of public morality, public policy or public security. It reiterates that Member States shall adjust any state monopolies of commercial character to ensure no discrimination on conditions of sale or purchase between nationals of Member States.

Agriculture and Fisheries

Title II is amended to include Fisheries with Agriculture to define a Common Agriculture and Fisheries Policy. In practice, the EU has a common fisheries policy. This title extends the internal market to agriculture, fisheries and trade in agricultural products. There is a shift in relation to the rules of competition in the production and trade of agricultural products and the common organisation of agricultural markets and the pursuit of the objectives of a common agriculture and fisheries policy to the European Parliament and the Council. The Council, however, without the Parliament shall adopt measures on fixing prices, levies, aid and quantitative limitations and allocation of fishing opportunities.

Free Movement of Persons, Services and Capital

Chapter 1 of Title III relates to workforce and the free movement of labour. In a shift to co-decision the European Parliament and the Council after due consultation shall issue directives or make regulations with regard to free movement of labour.

The European Parliament and the Council shall adopt measures in the field of social security to provide freedom of movement of employed and self employed workers. This formerly required a unanimous decision of the Council. However, there is a so called "emergency brake" where a Council member declares that a draft legislative act would affect important aspects of its social security system including scope, cost and financial structure it may request the matter is referred to the European Council which acting by consensus may refer the draft back to the Council, take no action, or request the Commission to submit a new proposal.

Chapter 2 of this title reiterates the prohibition of restrictions on the freedom of establishment of nationals of a Member State in the territory of another Member State. The codecision procedure is extended to the Right of Establishment.

Chapter 3 of this title reiterates the prohibition of restrictions on the freedom to provide services within the Union. As before services in the field of transport and banking and insurance have separate articles. The co-decision procedure by the European Parliament and the Council is extended to these articles. Free movement of capital to and from third countries involving direct investment, provision of financial services or the admission of securities to capital markets are also moved to the co-decision procedure.

Chapter 4 relates to capital and payments. The Council acting unanimously and after consulting the European Parliament may adapt measures which constitute a "step back in Union law" as regards the liberalisation of the movement of capital to or from third countries. The European Parliament in this article gains consultation rights.

In an entirely new article, the Council acting unanimously may adopt a decision stating that restrictive tax measures adopted by a Member State concerning one or more third countries are to be considered compatible with the Treaties insofar as they are justified by one of the objectives of the Union.

Transport

Title V relates to Transport Policy. In the main, the Reform Treaty reiterates common rules applicable to international transport between Member States, the conditions under which non-resident carriers may operate and safety. These Articles move to the co-decision procedure. However, account shall be taken of cases where the application of measures may have a serious effect on the living standards or level of employment in certain regions. This is no longer subject to a unanimous decision by the Council.

Competition, Taxation and Approximation of Laws

Rules on competition, state aids and tax provisions are dealt with in Title VII.

Chapter 1 deals with rules applying to undertakings and state aid. The chapter largely reiterates existing rules applying to undertakings in regard to price fixing, market rigging or abuse of dominant position. It also reiterates that any aid granted by a Member State which distorts, or threatens to distort competition is prohibited. In a new amendment, within five years of entry into force of this Treaty, the Council acting on a proposal from the Commission may, by QMV, adopt a decision to repeal provisions allowing the Federal Republic of Germany measures to compensate for economic disadvantage caused by the division of Germany.

Tax Provisions

Chapter 2 deals with tax provisions. Articles 94 and 95 reiterate that any Member State is prohibited from imposing directly or indirectly internal taxation on the products on other Member States in excess of that on similar domestic products. In accordance with a special legislative procedure, unanimously and after due consultation, the Council may adopt provisions for the harmonisation of legislation concerning turnover taxes, excise duties and other forms of indirect taxation to ensure the functioning of the internal market and to avoid the distortion of competition.

The Treaty of Lisbon and taxation – a clarification

Occasional ill-informed comment has suggested that ratification of the Treaty of Lisbon would somehow place Ireland's corporation tax rate of 12.5% under threat. Nothing could be further from the truth. The Treaties form the legal basis of the Union, define the areas of governance that fall within the competence of the Union, and lay down rules and procedures to exercise that competence. Article 4 of the TFEU states: "In accordance with article 5, competences not conferred upon the Union in the Treaties remain with the Member States." Nowhere in the Treaties, including the Treaty of Lisbon, is there mention of direct taxation and in particular corporation tax. This means that matters relating to direct taxation remain, as they always have remained, within the exclusive competence of each Member State.

EU President Barroso on a visit to Dublin on April 17-18 2008, referring to the Treaty of Lisbon, underlined this: "We will have more qualified majority voting, which should help to speed up decision-making. However, here in Ireland, knowing that taxation is a sensitive issue, I would like to underline the fact that the Lisbon Treaty does not change the rules on taxation. They remain subject to unanimity, giving each Member State a veto. Nothing can be agreed on taxation issues without Ireland's consent and nothing can be imposed on Ireland."

This is confirmed by decisions of the European Court of Justice in such cases as C-446/03, Marks and Spencer and

C-196/04, Cadbury Schweppes. Both judgements state that "according to settled case-law, although *direct taxation falls within their competence*, Member States must none the less exercise that competence consistently within Community law." In the case of Marks and Spencer, the Advocate General stated in his opinion that "First, the limits flowing from Community law apply only to the competences *exercised* by the Member States. The Member States thus remain free to determine the organisation and conception of their tax system and to determine the need to allocate between themselves the power of taxation. Secondly, in the absence of harmonisation of national laws in this field, the difficulties ensuing for economic operators as a result of mere differences in tax regimes as between Member States are outside the scope of the Treaty." In the Cadbury Schweppes case the Advocate General stated "... in the absence of Community harmonisation it must be accepted that there is competition between the tax regimes of the various Member States.... It may be regrettable that competition operates between the Member States in this field without restriction. That is, however, a political matter."

Any change in this existing position would therefore require a further amendment to the Treaties, again only possible through unanimous agreement of the Member States and, in the case of Ireland, probably another referendum. Ireland therefore maintains its veto over any proposed changes in direct taxation. The European Union can do nothing to compel a change in Irish domestic policy on corporate taxation. This is confirmed by the Treaty of Lisbon, which secures the power of the Irish State to set its own corporate tax rate for the foreseeable future. A further Treaty revision would be required to alter this position, which would undoubtedly require approval of the electorate in a referendum.

The Confusion arising out of a likely proposal to introduce a Common Consolidated Tax Base (CCCTB)

There is absolutely no connection between the Lisbon Reform Treaty and a proposal to introduce a common consolidated corporate tax base (CCCTB). This was on the Commission's agenda before the Treaty was drafted. In 2000, the European Commission under the Lisbon Strategy (not to be confused with the quite separate Lisbon Reform Treaty) laid down an action and development plan to make the European Union "the most dynamic and competitive knowledge-based economy in the world...". As part of this plan, Commissioner Kovacs introduced the notion of a CCCTB.

The French government is expected to promote this proposal vigorously when the Presidency of the Union passes to France in the second half of 2008. Indeed, President Nicolas Sarkozy and French Finance Minister Christine Lagarde have been quite explicit about their intentions.

However, the Reform Treaty, if ratified, confirms the existing position that direct taxation remains outside the competence of the European Union. Therefore, any attempt to introduce direct taxation, such as the introduction of a CCCTB, requires unanimous agreement. Ratification or not of the Treaty of Lisbon makes absolutely no difference to this position. Given the Irish Government, as well as a significant number of other Member States, oppose CCCTB it is not possible for this proposal to succeed. It is likely, however, that Ireland's principled stance against the introduction of a CCCTB would meet with more understanding if Ireland supported the more efficient administration of the Union by voting to ratify the Treaty.

It is possible under the system of Enhanced Cooperation that if at least eight Member States wish to proceed to introduce CCCTB in their *own* jurisdictions they may do so provided a qualified majority of all Member States gives its approval. The Treaty of Lisbon increases the necessary number of Member States to nine, making Enhanced Cooperation a little harder to achieve. It is worth noting that enhanced cooperation has never been used in the European Union.

Approximation of Laws

The articles in Chapter 3 in the main reiterate that the European Parliament and the Council may adopt measures for the approximation of provisions laid down by law, which are aimed at the establishment and functioning of the internal market. However, a Member State on the grounds of public morality, public policy, public security or protection of the environment, shall notify the Commission if it deems it necessary to maintain national provisions. Notwithstanding this, the Council in accordance with a special legislative procedure may unanimously after due consultation issue a directive for the approximation of such laws.[3]

Most importantly, there is a new legal basis adopting legislation concerning EU-wide intellectual property rights protection and for establishing a centralised Union-wide authorisation, coordination and supervision arrangement. This will be effected through the European Parliament and the Council. However, the Council, acting unanimously, after consulting with the European Parliament, shall establish language arrangements for European intellectual property rights.

Common Commercial Policy (CCP)

Part 5, Title II lays down the principles and procedures of the common Commercial Policy which is an exclusive competence of the Union. The former Article 133 has been restructured.

Article 207 brings Foreign Direct Investment (FDI) within the Common Commercial Policy. This change was introduced in the Convention text "in recognition of the fact that financial flows supplement trade in goods and today represent a significant share of commercial exchanges." The Commission requested the change, apparently to provide a basis for negotiations on a multilateral investment treaty in the WTO as there is no prospect of such a treaty emerging from the present Doha Round. The new Article now also includes the commercial aspects of Intellectual Property.

A change to co-decision involves the European Parliament in the process of adoption of legislation. In negotiating with one or more states or international organisations, the Council and the Commission shall be responsible for ensuring that agreements negotiated are compatible with internal Union policies and rules. The Commission shall conduct negotiations in consultation with a special committee appointed by the Council; it will report regularly to the Committee and the European Parliament on progress of the negotiations.

The Council shall act by QMV in most areas but it will act unanimously in the fields of trade in services, the commercial aspects of Intellectual Property and Foreign Direct Investment. The Council shall also act unanimously in the field of cultural and audiovisual services, where agreements risk prejudicing the Union's cultural and linguistic diversity, and in the fields of trade in social, education and health services where agreements risk seriously disturbing the national organisation of such services and prejudicing the responsibility of Member States to deliver them.

Article 207.6 provides that the exercise of the competences conferred by the article in the field of the Common Commercial Policy shall not affect the delimitation of competences between the Union and the Member States, and shall not lead to harmonisation of legislative or regulatory provisions of the Member States insofar as the Treaties exclude such harmonisation.

References

1. Zuleeg, F. (2007) *Challenge Europe – The People's Project?* pp 34-40, European Policy Centre.
2, *Statewatch.*
3. European Convention, Explanatory Note on Common Commercial Policy, CONV 685/03.

10

Enlargement and Europe's Neighbours

Andrew O'Rourke

The Lisbon Treaty does not change the existing basic provision that membership of the Union shall be open to all European States which respect its values and are committed to promoting them.

Criteria for Accession

Any European country which respects the principles of liberty, democracy, respect for human rights and fundamental freedoms, and the rule of law may apply to become a member of the Union. The Treaty on European Union sets out the conditions (Article 6, Article 49).

Applying for EU membership is the start of the long and rigorous process. The official starting point is that a country submits an application – although this invariably arises out of an already strong bilateral relationship with the EU. A valid application triggers a sequence of EU evaluation procedures that may – or may not – result in a country eventually being invited to become a member. The speed with which each country advances depends solely on its own progress towards our common goals.

The application from a country wishing to join is submitted to the Council. The European Commission provides a formal opinion on the applicant country, and the Council decides whether to accept the application. Once the Council unanimously agrees a negotiating mandate, negotiations may be formally opened between the candidate and all the Member States. This is not automatic, though. The applicant country must meet a core of criteria before negotiations start.

The so-called "Copenhagen criteria", set out in December 1993 by the European Council in Copenhagen, require a candidate country to have:

- stable institutions that guarantee democracy, the rule of law, human rights and respect for and protection of minorities;

- a functioning market economy, as well as the ability to cope with the pressure of competition and the market forces at work inside the Union;

- the ability to assume the obligations of membership, in particular adherence to the objectives of political, economic and monetary union.

In 1995 the Madrid European Council further clarified that a candidate country must also be able to put the EU rules and procedures into effect. Accession also requires the candidate country to have created the conditions for its integration by adapting its administrative structures. While it is important for EU legislation to be transposed into national legislation, it is even more important for the legislation to be implemented and enforced effectively through the appropriate administrative and judicial structures. This is a prerequisite of the mutual trust needed for EU membership.

In addition, the EU must be able to integrate new members; it needs to ensure that its institutions and decision-making processes remain effective and accountable; it needs to be in a position, as it enlarges, to continue developing and implementing common policies in all areas; and it needs to be in a position to continue financing its policies in a sustainable manner.

Candidates

Countries that are candidates for the EU are Croatia, the Former Yugoslav Republic of Macedonia and Turkey. Potential candidate countries are Albania, Bosnia, Montenegro, Serbia and Kosovo.

However, the incorporation into the Treaties of the Charter of Fundamental Rights, the proposed accession of the Union to the European Convention on Human Rights and the expansion of the statement of the Union's values reinforces the obligation of candidate countries to "respect the values" of the Union.

The normative bar for membership has thus been raised. In particular, the reference to the "rights of persons belonging to minorities" and to "equality between men and women" establishes additional specific conditions to be met by future new members.

Otherwise, current negotiations for membership, with Croatia and Turkey, will be unaffected by the Lisbon Treaty and will continue on the basis of the existing mandates and of the stringent political and economic criteria which candidates are required to meet before accession treaties can be agreed and submitted for ratification to the Member States and for the consent of the European Parliament.

The institutional changes made in the Treaty of Nice were essential to allow the enlargement of the Union to proceed in 2002. Subsequent discussion on the future of the Union revealed a consensus among Member States, including the new Member States, that further institutional change was necessary in order to ensure the greater effectiveness of a Union of 27 and more members and to enable it to play a full role in dealing with new policy areas and new world-wide challenges.

The amendments contained in the Lisbon Treaty should remove for the foreseeable future any concerns that inadequate institutions might be a barrier to the pursuit by the Union of its enlargement policy. This policy has been of major importance in expanding across Europe the area of peace and prosperity and of respect for human rights and the rule of law, in consolidating democracy in former dictatorships (Greece, Spain, Portugal) and in strengthening the transition of Central and Eastern European countries to democratic market economies.

At present, the enlargement policy of the Union does not extend beyond the two countries negotiating for membership and the countries of the Western Balkans. In all these countries the prospect of closer integration with the Union, which is already being actively pursued through Stabilisation and Association Agreements, provides an essential support for political and economic reforms. The expectation is that, through this policy, the area of peace and stability on the Union's borders will be further extended and dangerous instability and its inevitable consequences, also in Member States, avoided.

The perspective of closer relations with the Union is also an important factor in encouraging progress towards higher standards of democracy and good governance in countries in the "neighbourhood" of the enlarged Union, further east and south. The Treaties provide that the Union shall develop a special relationship with such neighbouring countries, aiming to establish an area of prosperity and good neighbourliness, founded on the values of the Union and characterised by close and peaceful relations based on cooperation. The Union's present active policy of political and economic engagement with these countries will therefore continue and will, it is hoped, be enhanced by the changes introduced in the Lisbon Treaty and intended to provide increased coherence for Union action at the international level.

European Neighbourhood Policy

Definition

The European Neighbourhood Policy (ENP) was developed in 2004, with the objective of avoiding the emergence of new dividing lines between the enlarged EU and our neighbours and instead strengthening the prosperity, stability and security of all concerned. In this way, it also addresses the strategic objectives set out in the December 2003 European Security Strategy.

The European Neighbourhood Policy (ENP) was first outlined in a Commission Communication on Wider Europe in March 2003, followed by a more developed Strategy Paper on the European Neighbourhood Policy published in May 2004. This document sets out in concrete terms how the EU proposes to work more closely with these countries. As part of its report on implementation, in December 2006 and again in December 2007, the Commission also made proposals as to how the policy could be further strengthened.

The EU offers our neighbours a privileged relationship, building upon a mutual commitment to common values (democracy and human rights, rule of law, good governance, market economy principles and sustainable development). The ENP goes beyond existing relationships to offer a deeper political relationship and economic integration. The level of ambition of the relationship will depend on the extent to which these values are shared. The ENP remains distinct from the process of enlargement although it does not prejudge, for European neighbours, how their relationship with the EU may develop in future, in accordance with Treaty provisions.

Finally, it is worth noting that in a greatly enlarged and more diverse Union there is a new provision allowing the voluntary withdrawal of a member; this is in addition to existing provisions dealing with the risk of or the actual existence of a serious breach by a Member State of the Union's values which could lead to the suspension of certain of that Member State's rights, including voting rights. These provisions recognise the commitment of the enlarged Union to its stated values and the obligation of every Member State to uphold and advance those values

11

Final Provisions

Gavin Barrett

Introduction

Some of the most important stipulations of the foundational treaties of the European Union are to be found in their so-called final provisions. This chapter examines briefly the most significant changes which the Treaty of Lisbon effects to these provisions.

The most significant amendments effected by the Treaty of Lisbon to the Final Provisions of the Treaty on European Union are four in number: (i) the conferring of legal personality on the European Union; (ii) the alteration of the steps required to be taken in order to amend the Treaties in the future; (iii) provision being made for the possibility of Member States leaving the Union and (iv) the expansion of the jurisdiction of the European Court of Justice.

The most significant amendment effected by the Treaty of Lisbon to the General and Final Provisions of the EC Treaty is (v) the amendment of the so-called "flexibility" clause.

All five of these amendments are discussed briefly in the text that follows.

The Conferring of Legal Personality on the European Union

The new Art. 47 of the Treaty on European Union will provide simply that "the Union shall have legal personality". This is a significant, but not revolutionary step. The Treaty on European Union has in any case for long implicitly conferred legal personality on the European Union: an international organisation can only conclude international agreements if it has legal personality – and Art. 24 of the existing Treaty on European Union confers power on the Union to conclude international agreements both in the common foreign and security policy field and in the field of police and judicial cooperation in criminal matters.

The main advantage of expressly conferring legal personality on the Union is the procedural one that it will facilitate the conclusion by the European Union of agreements in *all* areas in which it has competence. Other consequences will include giving the Union a clearer profile for the Union *vis-à-vis* both its own citizens and third States.

It should be noted that the mere conferring of legal personality on the European Union alone does not provide any answer to the question of the legal nature of the European Union since a variety of entities varying from international organisations to confederal and federal entities have enjoyed such status.

The Alteration of the Procedures for Amending the Treaties

The Treaty of Lisbon alters the procedures for amending the constitutive Treaties, which are at present set out in Art. 48 of the existing Treaty on European Union. Under that article as it now stands, any Member State Government or the Commission is entitled to submit proposals to the Council for the amendment of the Treaties. If the Council, after consulting the European Parliament and, where appropriate, the Commission (and if institutional changes in the monetary area are involved, the European Central

Bank) then delivers an opinion in favour of calling an intergovernmental conference, such a conference is convened for the purpose of determining by common accord the amendments to be made to those Treaties. The amendments then enter into force after being ratified by all the Member States in accordance with their respective constitutional requirements.

Overall, the existing procedure differs only slightly from what international law would require in any case were there no Art. 48. In practice, implementing its requirements is a lengthy, drawn-out process, too cumbersome to be used every time a technical provision in the treaties needs to be amended and otherwise lacking both transparency and (arguably) sufficient democratic input and control.

The new "amendment procedure" set out in a new Art. 48 of the Treaty on European Union seeks to address such difficulties. It will replace the old single-lane road for treaty change with a four-track procedure for treaty amendment. In the first place (constituting, it might be said, the slow track) there will be the so-called "ordinary revision procedure" which is to be the main or solemn procedure for amending the Treaty.

The new "ordinary" procedure will be like the present procedure – but with some additions designed to address concerns about its opaqueness. Secondly, there will be three separate so-called "simplified revision procedures". Each of these "simplified revision procedures" constitutes an effort to provide an accelerated procedure compared to the rather lumbering "ordinary" amendment process – regarded as too cumbersome for technical amendments.

The existing Article is doubly respectful of state sovereignty in that it imposes a requirement that all amendments to the Treaties be agreed upon unanimously, and then accepted by their national parliaments. None of the new procedures proposed under the Treaty of Lisbon deviate in substance from this double-unanimity requirement. As will be seen, all three of the simplified revision procedures are notable for their effective maintenance of a power to veto Treaty amendments not only in the hands of all Member States but also on the part of national parliaments.

The Proposed Ordinary Revision Procedure

The proposed ordinary revision procedure is an enhanced and extended form of the existing procedure. Under it, the process of revision of the Treaties will take place in four steps. First – as under the existing Article – any Member State Government or the Commission will be able to submit to the Council proposals for the amendment of the Treaties. So too, and for the first time, however, will be the European Parliament. This is an upgrade of this institution's role: Parliament, although it has influenced and stimulated Treaty reform in the past, has never had the capacity to initiate it formally.

The proposals will then be submitted to the European Council by the Council and national Parliaments have to be notified of them. Again, this represents some change. Neither the European Council nor national parliaments had any explicit role under the original version of Art. 48, although it can scarcely be doubted that heads of State and Government – who are members of the European Council – kept a close eye on the process of Treaty reform. Of course, national parliaments would always have been involved later in the process of ratification, but their being made aware of the *initial* proposals – even if this is a limited level of involvement – certainly represents an improvement in terms of openness and democratisation.[1]

The second step in the new amendment process will be that, the European Council, after consulting the European Parliament and the Commission, adopts by a simple majority a decision in favour of examining the proposed amendments, the President of the European Council will be required to convene a Convention. The Convention – composed of representatives of the national Parliaments, the Heads of State or Government of the Member States, of the European Parliament and of the Commission, and the European Central Bank in the case of institutional changes in the monetary area – will examine the proposals for amendments and adopt by consensus a recommendation to an intergovernmental conference.

Under the proposed new Art. 48, it is provided that the European Council may decide by a simple majority not to convene a convention "should this not be justified by the extent of the proposed amendments." In this case, the European Council is to define the terms of reference for an intergovernmental conference. However, this decision may be reached only after obtaining the consent of the European Parliament. Any risk that the European Council might overuse, for the sake of political convenience, its discretion to leapfrog the convention stage is thus deliberately checked by giving the European Parliament a veto over the taking of this step. Philadelphia-style conventions seem likely to be with us to stay in any process of Treaty revision, therefore.

The third step in the process in the proposed "ordinary revision procedure" will be that a conference of representatives of the governments of the Member States is to be convened by the President of the Council for the purpose of determining by common accord the amendments to be made to the Treaties. The fourth and final step will be that the amendments are to enter into force after being ratified by all the Member States in accordance with their respective constitutional requirements. Neither step three nor four represents a change from the existing provisions.

The Member States have taken care to ensure that even in the wake of the Lisbon Treaty coming into force, they will remain very much in control of this main procedure for revising the Treaties. Hence the main powers in the ordinary revision procedure lie with those institutions in which individual Member State interests are most vigorously defended – *viz.,* the European Council and the Council of Ministers.

The First Simplified Revision Procedure

The existing process of amendment of the constitutive treaties has always been an awkward and cumbersome means of amending highly technical provisions of the constitutive Treaties. The case for a simplified revision process for at least some of the provisions which are of lesser importance has for long been strongly arguable. The Treaty of Lisbon will introduce such a process, with what we may call the first simplified revision procedure, which is designed to facilitate easier amendment of those Treaty provisions which concern issues more technical than constitutional in nature.[2] More specifically, it will permit easier amendment of Part Three of the Treaty on the Functioning of the European Union, to be styled "Union policies and internal actions".

The first simplified revision procedure will operate as follows. First, the Government of any Member State, the European Parliament or the Commission will be entitled to submit to the European Council proposals for revising all or part of the provisions of Part Three. Next, the European Council – acting by unanimity after consulting the European Parliament, the Commission, and the European Central Bank in the case of institutional changes in the monetary area – will be able to adopt a decision amending all or part of the relevant provisions. This decision will not enter into force until it is approved by the Member States in accordance with their respective constitutional requirements.

The procedures, although simplified, will still represent a formidable obstacle to amendment of the Treaties where they apply. The requirement of unanimity will continue to apply, giving each one of the currently-27 Member States an effective veto over any amendment. Moreover, approval of the decision by Member States in accordance with their constitutional requirements will be required. This will involve at least parliamentary ratification in all states and in Ireland, for example, could conceivably involve a referendum. However, the requirement of the convening of an intergovernmental conference (and a convention) is at least dispensed with, and also the technical requirements of a formal ratification process. Once the approval of the last Member State takes place, the decision to amend the Treaties under the simplified procedure may enter into force.

PART THREE OF THE TREATY ON THE FUNCTIONING OF THE EUROPEAN UNION

Second and Third Simplified Revision Procedures – An Introduction

Two further simplified revision procedures are laid down by the new Art. 48.7. These second and third simplified revision procedures are sometimes referred to as general *passerelle* clauses. *Passerelle* clauses constitute a route whereby a decision-making procedure stipulated in the Treaties – unanimity or a special legislative procedure – can be transformed to a less heavy or cumbersome process – qualified majority vote or the ordinary legislative procedure – without going through the ordinary process of Treaty amendment. The image conjured up by the term *passerelle* is thus one of a convenient bridge, or shortcut, leading from a place of cumbersome, awkward procedural requirements to a place where procedural requirements are less burdensome. What is new about the Treaty of Lisbon scheme is not the existence of *passerelle* clauses – several of these are to be found in the existing Treaties – but rather that this *passerelle* system has been generalised. The bridge or *passerelle* has been widened. The Member States were probably emboldened in agreeing to the expansion of the system by the knowledge that in practice the *passerelles* in the existing Treaties have tended hardly ever to be used.[3]

The deployment of the second and third simplified revision procedures is subjected to a number of restrictions. First (as is the case with all three of the simplified revision procedures), the European Council decision to switch to qualified majority voting or co-decision, as the case may be, must be unanimous. Secondly, the European Parliament is also given a power of veto over any deployment of the second or third simplified revision procedures. The Parliament's consent, moreover, must "be given by a majority of its component members", and not merely a majority of those members who vote, which would be an easier requirement to meet. Thirdly, any initiative taken by the European Council to switch to qualified majority voting or co-decision, as the case may be, is required to be notified to the national parliaments. If any national parliament makes known its opposition within six months of the date of such notification, the decision shall not be adopted. Fourthly, both the second and third simplified revision procedures are to be specifically precluded from being applied to a number of particularly sensitive provisions of the Treaty on the Functioning of the European Union, such as those relating to the Union's own resources, the flexibility clause and suspension of rights resulting from membership of the Union.

233

Some Further Observations Specifically on the Second Simplified Revision Procedure

The membership of what has become the European Union continues to expand. With the addition of each new Member State the difficulty increases of arriving at any decision that the Treaties require to be taken by unanimity. Because of this, every amending Treaty from 1986 onwards has sought to increase the level of qualified majority voting at Council level and to reduce the level of voting by unanimity. Notwithstanding this, the number of decisions which will involve a Treaty-imposed requirement of a unanimous Council vote even after the Treaty of Lisbon enters into force remains strikingly high, with each instance involving the danger that the Union will be unable to exercise its competence to act in the relevant policy area.

Faced with the seemingly inevitable need to amend any Treaty legislative basis requiring a unanimous Council vote if it is ever seriously proposed to attempt to deploy that provision (and yet confronted by an inability to secure agreement on the elimination of unanimity voting in these areas), the Member States accepted, *inter alia*, the compromise of the second simplified revision procedure. This simplified revision procedure is to apply where either the Treaty on the Functioning of the European Union or Title V of the Treaty on European Union provides for the Council to act by unanimity in a given area or case. The relevant provision stipulates that the European Council may adopt a decision authorising the Council to act by a qualified majority in that area or in that case.

Two important limits on the second simplified revision procedure are that (*a*) it applies – as has already been noted – only with regard to the Treaty on the Functioning of the European Union and to Title V of the Treaty on European Union (i.e. the Title which concerns external action and the common foreign and security policy). Further, (*b*) it may not be used to authorise the use of qualified majority voting in relation to decisions with military implications or those in the area of defence.

Some Further Observations Specifically on the Third Simplified Revision Procedure

The third simplified revision procedure will apply where the Treaty on the Functioning of the European Union provides for legislative acts to be adopted by the Council in accordance with a so-called "special legislative procedure" (which involves, in the normal case, the final decision on the adoption of legislation being taken by the Council of Ministers). Art. 48.7 provides that where this is the case, the European Council may adopt a decision allowing for the adoption of such acts in accordance with the so-called "ordinary legislative procedure" (involving co-decision by the Council of Ministers and the European Parliament on whether legislation should be adopted).

The third simplified revision procedure is thus a *passerelle* clause which simplifies further switches away from such special legislative procedures in favour of the use of co-decision (or, as it is now to be known, the "ordinary legislative procedure"). It thereby continues the trend towards co-decision which has prevailed since the introduction of this legislative process by the Treaty of Maastricht (a trend which has evolved because co-decision is regarded as the most democratically acceptable means of lawmaking in a Union in which a need for some form of majority voting within the Council is required by efficiency concerns).

The Possibility of Withdrawing From the European Union

One of the most significant articles to be inserted into the Treaty on European Union is the new Art. 50. Its core – Art. 50(1) – is deceptively short, providing simply that "any Member State may decide to withdraw from the Union in accordance with its own constitutional requirements". Whatever about its future practical effects, what Art. 50 says about the nature of the European Union should not be underestimated. It has been pointed out that a right of withdrawal normally exists in confederations of states but never in federal states. One writer has used this to conclude that "this provision on withdrawal could be seen as clarifying a basic issue, *i.e.,* that the Union is actually a voluntary association between states which remain sovereign as to the question of whether or not they remain in that association".[4]

Under the Treaties in their pre-Lisbon form, the existence of any such right had always been left deliberately unstated as a matter of Community or Union law. Although certain Treaty articles as well as certain dicta of the Court of Justice could be argued to lean against a right of withdrawal, in practice, the Member States always appear to have regarded themselves as having the right of withdrawal from the process of European integration. For example, the 1975 referendum in the United Kingdom on the question of whether the United Kingdom should remain in the Common Market was clearly predicated on the assumption of the existence of the right of that State to leave should it wish to do so.

Of course, the reality is and always has been that should any Member State decide that it no longer wishes to remain part of the Union, the Union has never had any means at its disposal to prevent this from happening. In 1985, Greenland – which, in constitutional terms, is a self-governing province of Denmark – actually did secede from the then European Communities. The argument could thus be made that because of this, the adoption of Art. 50 will constitute less a concession to intergovernmentalism than a Treaty-level recognition of reality.

The existence of a provision like Art. 50 has been described as an important political signal against the notion that the Union is a rigid entity which it is impossible to leave, and a reminder that membership of the European Union is the outcome of a freely consented-to decision, and not – as some of its critics would seek to claim – a sentence to imprisonment in a penal colony. Art. 50 is meant to confront opponents of the European Union of the ongoing reality of democratic acceptance in each and every Member State of that state's membership of the European Union. It clarifies that membership of the Union is an ongoing freely-made choice (the logic being that the contrary can not be convincingly argued to be the case if each Member State retains an expressly-stated right to leave the Union). Such a reminder has been argued to have been rendered more urgent by the need to reassure the peoples of the central and eastern European Member States of the European Union, all of which were involved in the past in international arrangements not of their population's choosing.

Art. 50 seems unlikely to be invoked in the foreseeable future. More than a half-century since the beginnings of what has evolved into the European Union, during which time a multitude of political and economic crises have been weathered by both the Union and its Member States, no Member State has ever found it to be in its interests even to contemplate seriously secession, let alone to take such a drastic step.

The Procedure for Withdrawing from Membership of the Union

The remaining five sections of Art. 50 – sections 2 to 6 – deal with the modalities of such a withdrawal – in essence, what one might call the divorce procedures – in the event of this article ever being invoked by a Member State. Specifically, what is to happen is that a Member State which decides to withdraw is to notify the European Council of its intention. In the light of the guidelines then provided by the European Council, the Union is required to negotiate and conclude an agreement with that Member State which both sets out the arrangements for the state's withdrawal, and takes account of the framework for its future relationship with the Union. (The withdrawing Member State is not, of course, to participate in the discussions of the European Council or in decisions concerning it.)

Negotiations are not to be permitted to drag on indefinitely: there is to be no question of a Member State's desire to leave the Union being stymied by the failure, deliberate or otherwise, by the Union to reach agreement with it. Thus, under Art. 50, finality is ensured *via* a provision that the Treaties are to cease to apply to the

State in question from the date of entry into force of the withdrawal agreement or, failing that, two years after the notification to the European Council of its intention to withdraw from the European Union – unless the European Council, in agreement with the Member State concerned, unanimously decides to extend this period.

Expanded Jurisdiction for the European Court of Justice

The European Court of Justice has played a key role in shaping the nature of the European Community legal order, ensuring the rule of law and vital features of the Community legal system ranging from its uniformity throughout the territories of the Member States to the fact that Member States are held to the commitments which they undertake at European level. The role which the Court has played has been important in terms of regulating relationships between Member States. But it has also been important in terms of the protection of the individual under Community law.

One of the most significant of the existing final provisions of the Treaty on European Union has been Art. 46, which limited the applicability in the context of that Treaty of Treaty provisions concerning the European Court of Justice. Up until now, it has provided that the various provisions concerning the powers of the Court of Justice and their exercise would apply only in limited circumstances outside the Community context (which broadly speaking relates to the single market and monetary union). In particular, such provisions applied to the Treaty on European Union's provisions on police and judicial cooperation in criminal matters only under conditions provided for by the existing Art. 35 of the Treaty on European Union (which, *inter alia*, requires Member States to opt in to the jurisdiction of the Court of Justice to give preliminary rulings). The provisions of the Treaty on European Union concerning the common foreign and security policy fall completely outside the jurisdiction of the Court at present.

The existing Art. 46 of the Treaty on European Union is simply to be deleted when the Treaty of Lisbon comes into force. However, some of its restrictions are resurrected elsewhere in the amended Treaties. The most significant effect of the deletion will be that – subject to exceptions detailed in Article 275 of the Treaty on the Functioning of the European Union in respect of police operations and national security – the entire area of justice and home affairs will finally be brought under the jurisdiction of the Court of Justice – a step which seems an appropriate, welcome and long overdue increase in the protection of individual rights. It should also result in better enforcement of Member State obligations as this policy area will no longer be exempted from the possibility of Commission proceedings being brought for failure on the part of Member States to fulfil their legal obligations. The expansion of the Court's judgment in this respect has thus been correctly characterised as "good news for the rule of law, the uniform application of EU law and the protection of individual rights."[4]

The deletion of the existing Art. 46 will result in only a small (albeit significant) increase in the Court's jurisdiction in the common foreign and security field. This is because the Treaty of Lisbon inserts other provisions elsewhere in the Treaty on European Union, the effect of which is to continue the exclusion of the Court from the common foreign and security policy field. Limited exceptions, however, are established: hence, for example, the Court is given jurisdiction to review the legality of decisions providing for restrictive measures against natural or legal persons.

Amendment of the So-Called "Flexibility" Clause

Apart from the changes which it effects to the Final Provisions of the Treaty on European Union, the Treaty of Lisbon also effects a number of amendments to the General and Final Provisions of the Treaty Establishing the European Community (now, of course, to be rebranded the Treaty on the Functioning of the European Union). Of these amendments, the most important (and the only one it is proposed to deal with here) is the generalisation to Union level of the so-called "flexibility clause".

The legal system of the European Community has for long been based on the principle of conferral, according to which the Community and its institutions have no inherent powers, but rather enjoy only those powers which have been conferred upon them. With the coming into force of the Treaty of Lisbon, the express application of this principle will be expanded, and hence the limits of *Union* (rather than Community) competences provided to be generally governed by the principle of conferral. The principle of conferral has always itself been subject to limits which restrict its impact, however.[5]

One broad such limit has been provided for in the Treaty Establishing the European Community, in the form of the provision in Art. 308 (originally Article 235 of the Treaty of Rome itself) that

> ... if action by the Community should prove necessary to attain, in the course of the operation of the common market, one of the objectives of the Community, and this Treaty has not provided the necessary powers, the Council shall, acting unanimously on a proposal from the Commission and after consulting the European Parliament, take the appropriate measures.

Art. 308 has been a useful instrument in the Community's legislative toolbox, since if the Article did not exist, Member States would be forced to go through the cumbersome and time-consuming procedure required to agree and ratify an international treaty or convention regulating the problem in question. Because of the considerable scope it would otherwise give for circumventing Treaty restrictions of Community action, however, Art. 308 has been subjected to considerable restrictions. Most famously, the Court of Justice held in its *ECHR* ruling that what is now Art. 308 could not

... serve as a basis for widening the scope of Community powers beyond the framework created by the provisions of the Treaty as a whole and, in particular, by those that define the tasks and the activities of the Community. On any view, Article [308] cannot be used as a basis for the adoption of provisions whose effect would, in substance, be to amend the Treaty without following the procedure which it provides for that purpose.[6]

Further, measures taken under Art. 308 must not be contrary to an express prohibition contained in the Treaty. This would also seem to be a logical corollary of the latter sentence just quoted from the ruling of the Court. The normal requirement of respect for subsidiarity – which applies wherever the Community acts in areas which do not fall within its exclusive competence – has also applied up until now in relation to the use of Art. 308.

The wording of Art. 308 itself has also imposed a series of restrictions of varying degrees of significance on the use of the so-called "flexibility clause".

In practice, the level of use to which Art. 308 has been put by the Community legislator has gone through a series of phases. From 1958 to 1972, during the first phase of the Community's existence, Art. 308 was used on average a mere five times a year. This rose, however, from 1972 to 1986 to an average of 27 times a year, and from 1987 to 1993, to 30 times a year. In the wake of the coming into force of the Maastricht Treaty, as might be expected with the expansion in the legal bases available for legislative action, its use fell away to about 20 occasions each year. Overall, Art. 308 may be described as having produced a fairly light, although not insignificant, stream of Community legislation.

The Impact of Lisbon

Under the Treaty of Lisbon, the single paragraph of text that currently makes up Art. 308 is to be replaced by a new four-paragraph Article (renumbered Art. 352). The first paragraph extends the Article to the Union generally – with some modifications. The three new paragraphs both highlight pre-existing restrictions to the deployment of the "flexibility clause" and add others which go beyond those which have just been seen to have applied to date in the Community context.

The most striking feature of the new Art. 352 is its continuity with the provisions of the existing Art. 308. Four significant changes in the wording may be pointed out however. The first three of these are consequent on the new European Union – rather than, as heretofore, European Community – context in which Art. 352 will operate post-Lisbon.

Hence, first, the new Art. 352.1 will apply where action by the *Union* (not, as up to now, the Community) is necessary to attain one of the *objectives set out in the Treaties* (not, as up to now, objectives of the Community). This broadens the scope of the new Article in two respects. First, and most obviously, it will confer a power on the Union as a whole and not merely, as up to now, on one part of it only. Secondly, the objectives which will be capable of being attained *via* the deployment of Art. 352.1 will be broader, since what will be referred to post-Lisbon will be the objectives of the *Union* rather than merely (as before) the objectives of the *Community*.

A second change consequent on the new European Union-wide context in which Art. 308 will operate post-Lisbon is that what would otherwise become an excessively limiting factor that an objective be required to be attained "in the course of the operation of the common market" is replaced by the less constrictive formulation that the objective be required to be attained "within the framework of the policies defined in the Treaties".

A third change in the wording of Art. 352 is the reference to the [EC] Treaty not having provided the necessary powers being replaced by a reference to the *Treaties* not having done so. This actually involves a considerably broadened restriction on the use of the "flexibility clause", since the situations in which the (post-Lisbon) Treaties provide for a power to act will obviously be far broader than those in which the (pre-Lisbon) EC Treaty alone did so. In each case in which such a power is provided for, the Art. 252 flexibility clause cannot be deployed.

A fourth major change which will introduced by the Treaty of Lisbon – and one which is not directly consequent on the new European Union context of the operation of Art. 352 – is the introduction of a requirement to obtain the consent of the European Parliament (an institution which up to now has needed only to be consulted). This will give this institution a new right to veto any recourse to the flexibility clause, in the wake of the coming into force of the Treaty of Lisbon. This constitutes at the same time an increase in the level of democratic control which exists on the deployment of the "flexibility clause" and a significant additional hurdle to be overcome should use sought to be made of it.

So much for Art. 352.1. Of the three extra paragraphs which are to be added to Art. 352 by the Treaty of Lisbon, one effectively merely highlights an existing restriction on the use to which the flexibility clause may be put. One creates major restrictions on the scope of the Article's application and one in effect does both of these things – *i.e.,* it both highlights existing restrictions on the use of the "flexibility clause" and creates a new restriction. Art. 352.4 in particular provides for major restrictions on the scope of application of Art. 352. Broadly speaking, what the Member States have done is to rule out the deployment of the flexibility clause in relation to matters coming within the common foreign and security policy. This is a highly significant restriction on the expansion of the scope of Art. 352 to the European Union field generally. It is one which – combined with the availability of a broad range of alternative legal bases – may have the effect of keeping any increase in the scale of deployment of Art. 352 within fairly narrow bounds.

Finally, the new Art. 352.2 expressly requires the Commission to draw national Parliaments' attention to proposals based on Art. 352, using the subsidiarity-monitoring procedure (a procedure introduced under the Treaty of Lisbon, which will be capable at least in theory, of producing consequences as serious as that of legislative initiatives being entirely blocked).

References

1. Barrett, Gavin ed. (2008) *National Parliaments and the European Union,* Dublin, Clarus Press.
2. Burgorgue-Larsen, Levade and Picot eds (2007) *Traite etablissant une Counstitution por l'Europe – Tome I,* Bruylant.
3. See however Council Decision 2004/927/EC which applied the co-decision procedure to the adoption of certain measures in the field of free movement of persons.
4. Piris, J-C. (2006) *The Constitution for Europe – A Legal Analysis,* Cambridge University Press.
5. Hartley, T. (2007) *The Foundations of European Community Law, sixth edition,* Oxford University Press.
6. European Court of Justice, *Opinion 2/94 Accession of the Community to the European Convention for the Protection of Human Rights and Fundamental Freedoms* (1996) ECR I-1759.

12

Europe after Lisbon

Tony Brown

The Presidency Conclusions of the European Council meeting on 14th December 2007 stated that

> the Lisbon Treaty provides the Union with a stable and lasting institutional framework. We expect no change in the foreseeable future so that the Union will be able to fully concentrate on addressing the concrete challenges ahead, including globalisation and climate change....[1]

The European Convention

The European Convention was asked, in the Laeken Declaration, to address the expectations of Europe's citizens. Highlighting key policy areas such as cross-border crime, combating poverty, migration and asylum and – even in 2000 – climate change, the declaration argued that citizens wanted a common approach to "transnational issues which they instinctively sense can only be tackled by working together".[2]

The second plenary session of the European Convention in March 2002 took up this aspect of the Laeken mandate. In a long debate, with more than 80 interventions, a virtual agenda for the EU emerged which set the scene for the later Working Groups and which, looked at today, shows the essential continuity in the substance of the Convention's work, the text of the Constitutional Treaty, the messages from the period of reflection and the content of the Treaty of Lisbon.

This agenda highlighted: the shared values of European democracy; the equality of the Member States; rule of law and human rights; incorporation of the Charter of Fundamental Rights; solidarity; transparency and accountability; institutions and procedures; subsidiarity; an enhanced role for national parliaments; enlargement; policies to cope with globalisation; action on the environment; co-operation on defence; the area of security and justice; policies to deal with terrorist threats and migration.

The Convention debate also reflected a degree of concern about over-regulation by both Brussels and national authorities and voices were heard suggesting that there should be an openness to scale down EU action in certain fields.[3]

In this chapter a number of the pressing issues facing the European Union are briefly addressed. This agenda is global in its range and exacting in its impact on the decision-making and implementation capability of the Union.

Speaking at Berlin's Humboldt University, President Mary McAleese addressed the question of Ireland's perspectives on "Europe in the Coming Times" in striking terms:

> Exercising our independence and our sovereignty we chose to join the European Union. It is in some ways our lodestar as we seek to plot a course through a changing world. We hope to see the Union develop its full potential as a prosperous knowledge economy, as a peaceful, common homeland, as a champion of good values and good practice within the Union and around the world, as a witness to the power of partnership in diversity and to the benefits that come from ending conflict and beginning consensus, as a friend to the world's poor and overlooked.[4]

The EU Institutions

The Treaty provisions for institutional reform and restructuring give rise to important questions about the future efficiency and effectiveness of EU decision-making and activities. In each of the Union's institutions it will be necessary to adapt rapidly to changes in structures, systems and personalities.

Of immediate concern will be the capacity of the EU institutions to adapt to the changes – in terms of structures and individual positions – introduced in the Treaty. The arrival of the permanent President or Chairman of the European Council and of the High Representative for Foreign Policy and Security Policy will offer the opportunity for more coherence in policy and action but will demand great clarity in the demarcation of responsibilities and good interpersonal relations. The High Representative will have some work to do in rationalising the efforts of Council and Commission services.

The Council of Ministers will have to adapt to a new regime with team presidencies, permanent presidents of the Foreign Affairs and Euro Group Council formations and the need to meet in public when legislating. The Commission will be reduced in size and the necessary arrangements for rotation and for ensuring proper sensitivity to the interests of Member States without a national at the table will require early and well-judged decisions. The new status of the Commission President, elected by the Parliament on a proposal from the European Council, taking into account the results of the European Parliament elections, may have significance for the direction of policy.

Issues will arise in connection with decision-making, QMV voting arrangements and the extension of the co-decision system. The European Parliament has gained in terms of power and influence and must arrange its business to live up to this added responsibility. The Treaty provisions on National Parliaments and Subsidiarity will provide challenges for the systems in both Brussels and the national capitals. There is a new emphasis in this treaty on the regional aspects of European integration, on territorial cohesion and, in institutional terms, on the role of the Committee of the Regions.

The Union's Future Financing

The compromise agreement on the Financial Perspectives for 2007-2013 has ensured that important EU policies can be carried forward following enlargement. However, concerns continue about the level of funding for the new Member States, including Bulgaria and Romania, and for the Union's capacity to match its policies to a changing environment.

The proposed 2008 budget review will be of significance and emphasis is likely to be placed on setting new priorities e,g. R&D funding and cohesion funding for new members in place of the current emphasis on the CAP. This will prove controversial for countries with large farming interests. The attitude of net contributors – old, like Germany, the UK and Netherlands, and new, like Ireland – will be critical. The concept of solidarity remains high on the Union's rhetorical agenda but is clearly under pressure.

Priority must be devoted to economic development, growth and job creation. Widespread feelings of economic and social insecurity in a globalised economy were clearly evident in the French and Netherlands referendum campaigns. Economic governance is a critical policy priority as is the relevance of the energy and environment agenda where inevitable cost factors can be offset by the technological opportunities which are emerging.

Energy and the Environment

The sheer scale of the issues arising at global level in relation to Environment and Energy is fully recognised by both the EU institutions and the individual Member States.

The 2007 Spring European Council unveiled a new Energy Policy for Europe which included a formula for achieving demanding environmental targets by 2020. The European Commission in its report on Climate Change in September 2007 accepted that the planet is facing irreversible climate change unless action is taken quickly and indicated the EU's clear response in the shape of an integrated Energy and Climate Change policy.[5] This policy was set out in the terms of a seven point package launched in January 2008, covering the key issues of Emissions Trading, binding Emissions Reduction targets, targets for Renewables and Biofuels, state aids for environmental protection, Carbon capture and clean coal and Energy Efficiency Action Plans.[6]

The EU has been committed to a policy stance balancing internal and international policies and programmes. Integrated EU energy markets and creative links between energy policy and policies such as research, agriculture and trade can contribute to the fight against Climate Change, greater security of energy supply and continued economic growth. Internationally, the EU has led the way in connection with the Kyoto Protocol and now seeks to increase global co-operation on the key issues.

These pressing issues give rise to important considerations of EU Foreign and Security Policy. The 2008 Spring European Council received a joint paper from the High Representative, Javier Solana, and the European Commission on "Climate Change and International Security" which identified Climate Change as "a threat multiplier which exacerbates existing trends, tensions and instability." The UN estimates that all but one of its appeals for emergency humanitarian aid in 2007 were climate related. The report concludes with reference to the challenges for the EU:

> The EU is in a unique position to respond to the impacts of climate change on international security, given its leading role in development, global climate policy and the wide array of tools and instruments at its disposal. Moreover, the security challenge plays to Europe's strengths, with its comprehensive approach to conflict prevention, crisis management and post-conflict reconstruction, and as a key proponent of effective multilateralism.[7]

The European Council instructed the institutions to develop appropriate responses to the issues raised in this report and to link its findings to the review of the 2003 European Security Strategy and to the search for intensified co-operation with third countries and regions. The Union's relationship with the Russian Federation is critical in this connection. The evolving EU New Neighbourhood policy has a significant energy component in particular in respect of the Caucasus region (Georgia, Armenia).

With recognition of the scale of the Climate Change and Energy challenge must come a realisation that adversity can be turned into advantage and opportunity. The European Union is well positioned to be the world leader in creating what may become a new industrial revolution. "Being first to market will position the European Union as a leader ... giving it the commercial edge in the export of green technological know-how and equipment around the world. Producing a new generation of renewable energy technologies ... will have an economic multiplier effect that stretches well towards the mid decades of the 21st century."[8]

This whole area is one where the importance of achieving and maintaining agreed common strategies cannot be overestimated. Progress on emissions reduction depend on agreement to targets and commitment to implementation. Both elements carry potential political risk for governments at a time of economic and financial uncertainty. Full implementation of the wide-ranging Commission package will be a major test of the capacity of the enlarged European Union.

Globalisation and Change

Globalisation and Interdependence are dominant issues which form the background to all economic and social policy debates. The EU is variously depicted as the only political force to counter the negative impacts of free markets and footloose capital or as the main proponent of those phenomena. The European Council of December 2007 adopted a Declaration on Globalisation which highlighted the importance of the lasting institutional framework set in the Lisbon Treaty in improving the capacity to achieve consistency in the Union's internal and external policies.[9]

The linked issues of trade and development are of obvious relevance, notably in the WTO Doha Round and its implications for the agriculture and services sectors. The perceived challenge from China and India is often seen in terms of cost and wage pressure and job dislocation but it is more likely that the long-term threat is from the high educational and research standards in those countries. Positive responses, in innovation and applied science, can offer market opportunities for Europe, including Ireland.

This puts a spotlight on the role of the European Central Bank whose mandate, centred on price stability, is increasingly questioned. Attention is also directed to the future implementation of the Stability and Growth Pact, in particular in the context of the potential expansion of the Eurozone following enlargement. Future economic growth is related to the working of the Internal Market which needs further reform. A focused regime for development and regulation of the huge services sector is clearly important

Enlargement

It has been argued that enlargement has been the EU's greatest historic achievement as it has spread stability, security, prosperity and democracy across most of the continent – from Greece in 1981 to the former Soviet provinces in the Baltic and the Balkans. The expansion from 15 to 27 Member States between May 204 and January 2007 has been achieved with a high level of success but with continuing challenges and opportunities.

As the Swedish Foreign Minister, Carl Bildt , has remarked "one of the main lessons of the 50 years since the Treaty of Rome is that each enlargement has not only made our Union into a stronger factor for peace and stability on our own continent: it has also added to its global weight."[10]

The European Council in December 2004 decided to open

accession talks with Turkey and Croatia while Macedonia has been given candidate status. While Croatia is likely to complete its negotiations and become the 28th Member State, perhaps in 2010, the position in respect of Turkey remains highly controversial and it is impossible to give any clear indication of the outcome.

The current debate on enlargement is centred on so-called absorption capacity of the EU. However, clear commitments have been given to the states of the Western Balkans (Albania; Bosnia and Herzegovina; Serbia; Montenegro) on their future EU membership. The emergence of Kosovo as a new entity in the region adds a further dimension. The Union's commitments must be honoured if there is not to be a reversion to conflict and division in the region.

The European Council, in December 2006, agreed an enlargement strategy based on the concepts of consolidation, conditionality and communication combined with the capacity of the Union to integrate new members. "To sustain the integration capacity of the EU the acceding countries must be ready and able to fully assume the obligations of Union memberhip and the Union must be able to function effectively and to develop. Both these aspects are essential for ensuring broad and sustained public support which should also be promoted through greater transparency and better communication."[11]

Expansion to 27 Member States gives rise to issues such as the security of a Union with new borders and longer term relationships with new neighbours: Ukraine, Caucasus etc. Relations with the Russian Federation will centre on energy supply and security. The EU's New Neighbourhood Policy is being developed to deal with these matters in a structured way through targeted bilateral arrangements.

Justice and Home Affairs

The Justice and Home Affairs area has a crowded agenda with many items of real concern to citizens – human rights, police and judicial co-operation, anti-terrorism policy, external border control, asylum policy, common migration policy and efforts to combat international crime and trafficking.

The Hague Programme of 2004, dealing with asylum and migration, justice issues and the fight against cross-border crime is of great importance and there is urgency in relation to implementation. A debate is on-going about the possibility of extending Qualified Majority Voting in these areas on the basis that there must be no unnecessary constraints on the Union's capacity to deal with issues which directly affect the security and well-being of many European communities and individuals.

The creation of an area of "freedom, security and justice" is a positive aspiration for the European Union which directly reflects the fundamental values set out in the treaties and re-emphasised in the text of the draft Constitutional Treaty. Central to the achievement of this policy goal is the implementation of the 1999 Tampere Programme, amended in part at the Hague. Tampere set out a comprehensive programme of measures to be put into practice jointly by the Member States. These included enhanced mutual recognition of judicial decisions in both civil and criminal matters. The evolving Europol network of police co-operation was complemented by the creation of Eurojust, a unit composed of national prosecutors charged with ensuring the proper co-ordination of national prosecuting authorities and supporting criminal investigation in cases of organised crime.

EU-level co-operation in JHA matters is crucial. The introduction of the European Arrest Warrant has proved important in denying shelter and leeway for highly mobile criminals. There is a need to follow up all initiatives to create structures and systems that can deliver results in areas from the enforcement of civil judgments to the prevention of child abduction and from joint action to deal with terrorist atrocities such as those in London and Madrid to decisions on tackling vehicle crime with cross-border implications.

In all of these considerations the centrality of democratic norms and human and civil rights must be recognised and fully vindicated. In a Union of Values there can be no place for back-sliding on basic rights even in the face of terrorist threats. Any moves to diminish fundamental rights and freedoms would constitute a major and inexcusable victory for the terrorist cause.

For Ireland, the implementation of the opt-out/opt-in provisions set out in a Protocol to the Treaty will require sensitive responses to what is likely to be a rapidly evolving EU system. The indication by Ireland that the provisions will be reviewed in three years gives rise to a need for close monitoring of developments.

Social Europe and the Lisbon Agenda

The Lisbon Agenda brings together key policy concerns: building a knowledge economy, sustainable development, social cohesion and environmental protection. It was designed as a pragmatic, non-ideological package focused on real opportunities for Union while fully respecting subsidiarity. The Open Method of Co-ordination was initially hailed as a flexible path to progressive policies. However, there is genuine concern on aspects of the progress made to date, notably in respect of social cohesion and combating poverty.

Reviews of the Lisbon Agenda highlight the urgency of economic reform in key EU Member States to ensure competitiveness in the context of globalisation. Emphasis is placed on the need for enhanced training and up-skilling provisions and for greater investment in the fields of R&D and innovation. Social cohesion and inclusion policies must be brought back into the mainstream of the Lisbon Agenda. Targeted policy initiatives such as the 2010 European Year for Combating Poverty and Social Exclusion will be of importance.[12]

Attention is turning to the successful models of development in the Nordic states, notably Finland and Denmark (with its unique "flexisecurity" policy for retraining and enhancing skills). While not necessarily transferable, they demonstrate that social protection and economic flexibility are not mutually exclusive.

The French and Netherlands referendum campaigns revealed serious concerns about the focus and direction of social policy in Europe. The intensity of debate on the nature and future of the European Social Model (or Models) has been heightened by the recent controversies over the Services Directive and the Laval and Irish Ferries cases.[13] The issue of the competences of the Union and the individual Member States in the social field, which was debated but not finally resolved by the Convention, remains contended.

The controversies mentioned above turn attention to the prospect of intense political debate on the balance between the economic and social dimensions of European integration. The debate in the European Parliament on the Services Directive clearly demonstrated that policy development in the EU is changing. This proposal generated a genuine debate which engaged public opinion in many Member States. This welcome advance will be repeated in the period ahead not least in the field of social policy.

Demographic trends in ageing European societies are of critical importance. These are given added priority by the emerging pressures of internal migration and immigration. It is clear that emerging public attitudes towards migration issues, often with undertones of racism, represent a challenge to political leadership. Responses must deal with a complex mix of labour market policies, social provision, integration measures and policing.

Foreign Policy and Security

This general heading covers the fields of Common Foreign and Security Policy and European Security and Defence Policy. The provisions of the Treaty are of great relevance in all of these areas e.g. the proposals for new structures in both CFSP and ESDP, including the introduction of the position of High Representative of the Union for Foreign Affairs and Security Policy.

The EU is playing an important role in international diplomacy, maintaining peace and security in the Balkans; monitoring the Gaza border and supporting the Aceh peace progress; playing a key role in the Middle East process and the Iran nuclear standoff. There is a need for understanding and realism about what the EU is doing on the ground. Stability and Security are objectives of policy which resonate with the political, economic and social needs and aspirations of EU citizens.

With military and police missions in the Balkans and Africa the Union is increasingly active in the field of peace-keeping where relations with the UN are crucial. The controversial issue of "battlegroups" – which will provide the Union with modern capability in the broad field of crisis management – can be seen in this wider context. The Lisbon Treaty provision for enhanced military capabilities has been translated by some as a commitment to increase expenditure on armaments at the expense of socially desirable activities. It can equally be argued that what is in mind is spending better rather than spending more. Modern military operations are complex, demanding sophisticated rather than largescale equipment and technologies. The lengthy delay in deploying the mission to Chad because of the lack of logistical and "heavy lift" capability among the EU states involved have provided a clear example of the basic requirements for effective implementation of even the most urgent tasks.

Among the main issues of concern for CFSP /ESDP are EU-US relations, assisting Africa in the search for answers to the great problems of famine and epidemic disease and ensuring that Human Rights remain a clear focus of policy.

The role of the EU, as the world leader in Development Co-operation, remains a central priority with an emphasis on effectiveness and the capacity for rapid and co-ordinated response to humanitarian crises. The Lisbon Treaty contains important commitments, notably by setting "as its primary objective the reduction, and in the long term, the eradication of poverty." This is accompanied by the provision that any Union policies that affect developing countries must take account of the stated objectives of development policy. Sensitive questions arise in connection with the link between development and migration – as highlighted by the many tragic instances of loss of life among desperate men, women and children attempting to reach Malta or the Canaries by sea from the African coast. A response to this complex issue must involve effective immigration policies and infrastructures and focused development policies aimed at reducing the 'push' factors of unemployment, famine and hopelessness.

The Treaty also includes a chapter on Humanitarian Aid which commits the Union to concerted action in the face of natural and man-made distasters. This involves the establishment of a European Voluntary Humanitarian Aid Corps.

Long-term development calls for policy responses across a broad front – aid, trade, education, investment and governance – in which the EU can make a difference. The new emphasis on developing civilian responses to crisis situations will call for action at both Union and national level. The Irish Government has started to create relevant structures. Controversies exist in relation to aspects of policy such as the Economic Partnership Agreements currently under negotiation, for example in respect of the level of administrative capacity in poorer countries, and these merit close political attention.

The practical implementation of these commitments will require clarity and openness in the management and co-ordination of programmes and activities. The new institutional arrangements for the Union's external action will be of relevance in this connection with two issues of particular significance.

Changes in the configuration, and chairmanship, of the Council and the reduction in the membership of the European Commission give rise to questions about the place of Development Co-operation, in particular within the Commission which has traditionally included a Commissioner with responsibility for Development.

The proposed bringing together of the Council and Commission functions has led to concern among interested parties that the Union's considerable budgetary resources in the Development field might be subject to changed priorities. The treaty's insistence on the need for consistency between key policies is of importance as is the highlighting of development and, in particular, the primary aim of eradicating poverty among the main objectives of the Union's External Action. These provisions add up to a benchmark for analysis and monitoring of both policy and performance.

Ireland, with its increasing scale of financial commitment to development, will have a growing opportunity to influence both EU policies and national strategies in the countries with which Irish Aid interacts.

Disconnect between the EU and European citizens and voters: Democratic Deficit

The so-called democratic deficit exists fundamentally at home, in the national political and media systems. It increasingly appears that the political leadership in Western Europe – especially in the older EU Member States – no longer sends out signals saying that the EU is a good thing. They, like many of their citizens, seem to have lost their historical perspective, not to mention their courage. Commissioner Olli Rehn has deplored the "deficit of European thinking in national capitals…".

Irish political debate still relegates EU affairs to specialist committees and is slow to mainstream EU matters. Decrying "Brussels" remains a mainstay of Irish political discourse. There is an urgent need to see what can be done to to stimulate and assist Irish politicians to deal realistically and positively with EU issues. And, there are serious questions about the role of the media in covering EU matters in terms other than seeking short-term controversy and falling for the "straight banana" line of UK tabloids.

Lack of basic information about the EU has had the cumulative effect of weakening the EU. This implies a challenge to the education system and the curriculum. History is a neglected school subject. The key lies in developments in the areas of education, information and media, which will require the availability of authoritative material as an input to debate. The National Forum on Europe is doing much to close this gap.

At the level of both the EU institutions and the national governments (and opposition parties) there is the challenge of coherent public communication. Both must consult and engage in public debate before undertaking major initiatives. Implementation of EU policies must be explained and made fully transparent. Accountability is essential and must be founded on effective national structures, such as accessible parliamentary committees, and interaction with wider, civil society.

The Reflection Group

Looking at the extensive and evolving agenda of the EU leads inevitably to consideration of the long-term direction and prospects of a Union of 27 and eventually more than 30 Member States. Can this entity of almost 500 million people find the shared political will to fulfil the high purposes set out in the opening articles of the amended Treaty on European Union? Can it match those aspirations with policies and programmes appropriate to the needs of the 21st century? Above all, can it move forward across the broad front identified here with the full understanding and support of the people?

The decision of the European Council in December 2007 to establish a Reflection Group on Europe's Horizon 2020-2030 shows that there is a recognition of the challenges ahead. The Berlin Declaration on the 25th Anniversary of the Treaty of Rome concluded that "with European unification a dream of earlier generations has become a reality. Our history reminds us that we must protect this for the good of future generations."[14]

The Reflection Group has been charged with identifying the key issues and developments which the Union is likely to face and to analyse how these might be addressed. A wide range of such issues is proposed for consideration, including the European Model of economic success and social responsibility, competitiveness, sustainable development, global stability, migration, energy and climate change, global insecurity and the fight against crime and terrorism.

In a paragraph interpreted by some as referring indirectly to the question of Turkish membership, the Group is asked to "take into account likely developments within and outside Europe and examine in particular how the stability and prosperity of both the Union and the wider region might best be served in the longer term."

The establishment of the Reflection Group was originally proposed by French President, Nicolas Sarkozy, who referred to the familiar list of Europe's challenges and argued that "we have no more time to lose if we are to deal with them. We have no more time to lose if we are to ensure that the people can regain confidence in Europe. We have already lost enough time."[15]

The Group will be chaired by the former Spanish Premier, Felipe Gonzalez with two Vice Chairpersons – Dr Vaira Vike-Freiberga, former President of Latvia and Jorma Ollila, Chairman of Nokia – and with six further members to be identified and appointed later this year. The Group will not address institutional or budgetary matters. The content of the Lisbon Treaty is to be taken as the framework for the Group's work.

The Group is to report by June 2010.

The Reflection Group may turn out to be overburdened by the breadth of its mandate and unlikely to deliver much of importance, other than meeting French concerns about an ever wider EU. On the other hand there may be a genuinely useful purpose in providing a focus for strategic reflection as the Union contends with its many current concerns.

The European Union has been through a period of frustration and introspection just as the world environment experienced change at an unparalleled pace and intensity. The agreement on the Lisbon Treaty holds out the hope of a lengthy period without the distraction of institutional wrangling. Attention can be devoted to the day-to-day concerns of Europe's citizens and neighbours. But, there is still a need to find space for reflection on fundamentals.

Jean Monnet wrote that he always believed in Franklin Roosevelt's saying "where there is no vision, the people perish." It is rarely a mistake to return to Monnet.

References

1. European Council (2007) Presidency Conclusions, December 2007.
2. European Council (2001) Laeken Declaration on the Future of the European Union.
3. European Convention (2002) Note on Plenary Meeting, 21 and 22 March 2002. CONV 14/02.
4. President Mary McAleese (2008) Address to the Humboldt University, Berlin.
5. European Commission (2007) Combating Climate Change: the EU Leads the Way, Brussels, September 2007.
6. European Council (2008) Presidency Conclusions, March 2008.
7. European Council (2008) Climate Change and International Security, Paper fom the High Representative and the European Commission, March 2008.
8. Rifkin, Jeremy (2008) Presentation to the Institute of International and European affairs, April 2008.
9. European Council (2007) Declaration on Globalisation, December 2007.
10. Bildt, Carl (2007) "Heed Our History: Widen the Union" in European Union: the Next Fifty Years, *Financial Times Business*, March 2007.
11. European Council (2006) Presidency Conclusions, December 2006.
12. European Commission (2007) Statement on the European Year for Combating Poverty 2010, Brussels, December 2007.
13. ETUC (2007) Statement on the Laval Case, Brussels, December 2007.
14. Declaration on the Occcasion of the 50th Anniversary of the Signature of the Treaties of Rome, Berlin, 25th March 2007.
15. Sarkozy, Nicolas (2007) Speech to the European Parliament,Strasbourg, 13 November 2007.

13

Implications for Ireland

Brendan Halligan

Section One: Context

As is normally the case with a treaty of this sort, the Treaty of Lisbon is a series of amendments to already existing treaties and, as widely acknowledged, is difficult to follow. So, for ease of reference and in order to remove any ambiguity as to what the people are voting on, the methodology employed in the following analysis is to use the text of "The Consolidated Version of the Treaties as amended by the Treaty of Lisbon" as published by the Institute. This is how the text would actually read if the Lisbon Treaty is ratified. In popular parlance it is also called the Reform Treaty because its main purpose is to improve the functioning of the European Union and, at the same time, to clear up any ambiguities about the respective powers of the Union and its Member States.

The preamble to the Treaty of Lisbon explains that its express purpose is to enhance the efficiency and democratic legitimacy of the Union and to improve the coherence of its action. If adopted, it would complete the process of reforms initiated by the Single European Act (1987) and continued by the treaties of Maastricht (1992), Amsterdam (1997) and Nice (2001) in response to new global economic challenges and the imperative of admitting central European states into membership. The Lisbon Treaty is intended to bring this process of reform to an end, at least for a generation according to the Heads of State and Government in their joint statement in December 2007 having agreed the final text.

This particular treaty has the great merit of combining all existing treaties and the amendments agreed by the 2007 Intergovernmental Conference into two complementary treaties, which are to be of equal value. The first, the Treaty on European Union, defines what the Union is. The second, the Treaty on the Functioning of the European Union, defines how the Union works. The new treaties attempt to live up to the aims of enhanced legitimacy, efficiency and coherence by introducing clarity where it was needed and by making necessary improvements where essential. The result is a more simplified structure in that, for example, the confusing division between the European Community and European Union is to be ended.

In broad terms, the first treaty deals with how the Member States have decided to pool sovereignty with each other and this is done by defining the competences they wish to confer on the Union and those they wish to retain for themselves. The second treaty, on the other hand, sets out the policies which the Member States will pursue in common and indicates how they will arrive at decisions and, in many cases, make law by which they will be bound. The one exception to this schema are the provisions governing the Union's external action and its Common Foreign and Security Policy, which are contained in the Union treaty because of their intergovernmental nature.

There are good reasons for believing that the reform of the common institutions has, indeed, come to a natural end. The list of prospective members is short and if admitted to membership they can be accommodated within the new institutional arrangements agreed in Lisbon. No further change in their composition or role is contemplated. That being the case, a consolidation phase is about to begin as it is generally conceded that a respite from institution building is urgently needed. The Union, after all, is now the largest economy in the world and the biggest trading block. It is a global leader in development aid and in the fight against climate change.

Its internal responsibilities and its external reach combine to make consolidation the over-arching priority for the decades ahead. The Lisbon Treaty is intended to give the Member States and their

Union the necessary breathing space to accomplish tasks which are well recognized as urgent. Whether it has succeeded in this ambition is the central focus of the analysis following, with particular emphasis on the implications for Ireland.

Methodology

The methodology adopted in this analysis is to follow the logic of the Laeken Declaration which set out the agenda for the final phase of the reform process and assigned it to the Convention which produced the Constitutional Treaty. By force of circumstances these same tasks were bequeathed to the Intergovernmental Conference convened in the wake of the Constitution's rejection; the Lisbon Treaty is the outcome.

It is best judged and evaluated by grouping the Laeken agenda items under the following five tasks:

(*a*) outlining the democratic principles and fundamental rights on which the Union is based;

(*b*) clarifying the nature and scope of the Union by defining which competences the Member States wish to confer upon it and those they wish to retain for themselves;

(*c*) simplifying the institutional structure of the Union and thereby making it more comprehensible to the citizens;

(*d*) ensuring transparency in decision-making and efficiency in action; and

(*e*) adding new tasks where deemed necessary to advance the common European interest.

It follows that the reference points for the following analysis are democracy and legitimacy, structural simplicity, transparency and efficiency. The implications for Ireland will be assessed in this broad framework, and so too the implications for the Union as a whole. The underlying assumption is that a functioning and successful Union is inherently good for all Member States and that their individual welfare is intrinsically linked with the welfare of the whole. This is particularly true of a small Member State like Ireland which has benefited so spectacularly from Union membership.

Section Two: Purpose and Nature of the European Union

In analysing the outcome of the Intergovernmental Conference the first question for consideration is whether the Lisbon Treaty reforms relating to competences would change the scope and purpose of the European Union in any fundamental sense. This was the approach taken by the Supreme Court in the Crotty judgment. The second is whether the contemplated reforms would add new policy competences to the Union which, in turn, would amount to significant change. The difference between these two approaches could be described, for ease of convenience, as that between the generic and the specific or, indeed, between powers and policies. It would make sense to begin with the foundations and to look first at the purpose and nature of the Union.

In addressing the generic issues relating to powers it is no surprise that these have been a rich source of controversy since Ireland first contemplated membership of the European Economic Community fifty years ago. They relate in the main to the purpose and nature of the organisation which decades later is now styled as a Union and whose membership has risen from six to twenty-seven countries. From the outset, differences of opinion, first about the European Community and now about the European Union, have depended on how people viewed the rationale and modus operandi of this new and unique international organisation, some recognising it as a novel experiment in sharing sovereignty, for which there was neither an analog nor precedent and others regarding it as a revival of the worst features of Europe's imperialist past, of which there had been too many distressing examples. This explains why, in the same debate, it is sometimes possible for the European Union to be hailed as the greatest peace experiment in history and simultaneously damned as an incipient federalist superstate or, alternatively, to be praised for being the first ever experiment in shared sovereignty based on interdependence while condemned for being a military superpower in the making. These depictions are polar opposites and, self-evidently, cannot both be true.

There are at least two methods of resolving these contradictions: observation and textual analysis. For example, the past half century can be examined and conclusions drawn: alternatively, the text of the consolidated treaties, as amended by the Lisbon Treaty, can be read and the implications assessed. Looking back at the history of the past fifty years, the evidence points one way: European countries, all of them sovereign and independent, founded on democracy and based on the rule of law, have sought to cooperate in the areas of economic, monetary, political, social and trade policy to their mutual advantage. Uniquely, they have done so on the basis of jointly making law, while also co-operating in more traditional modes of intergovernmentalism. Observation confirms that the Union they have voluntarily created is something novel, as its founders intended, and that its defining characteristic is the sharing of sovereignty in clearly defined policy areas for specific purposes.

Democratic Principles
In using the treaty text as the basis of analysis, the Treaty on European Union is the immediate reference point for evaluating whether significant changes have been introduced to the existing Union as a result of outlining the democratic principles and fundamental rights on which it is grounded. The text is short, running to fifty-five articles and taking up only 28 pages in the edition published by the Institute. Of these, the first twelve articles spell out the nature of the Union, its role and raison d'etre and the democratic principles on which it is based. If words mean anything, then the literal interpretation of these twelve articles is that the Union is in essence democratic, in ambition peaceful and in practice rule-bound (see Chapter Three).

What comes across from a comparison of the existing treaties and the consolidated text as amended by the Lisbon Treaty is that no changes are contemplated in the fundamental nature of the Union or in the principles on which it is founded. The Union remains a body "on which the Member States confer competences to attain objectives they have in common" (Article 1) and is founded on democratic values which are spelled out in Article 2. In fact, Article 3 puts paid to any charge of actual or incipient militarism since it states that "The Union's aim is to promote peace, its values and the well being of its peoples" and to contribute to a range of global objectives which include "the strict observance and development of international law, including respect for the principles of the United Nations Charter".

The immediate implication for Ireland and, indeed, for all the other Member States, is that the European Union is to continue in being, unchanged in either the principles on which it is based or objectives it is to pursue. The purpose and nature of the Union remain as they were.

Equality of the Member States
The equality of the Member States will continue as the bedrock of the Union and is guaranteed under Article 4. This is of vital importance to the small members, such as Ireland, for it ensures that the composition of the common institutions is to be based on equity and fairness. In fact, it has been a reassuring feature of the Union from its inception under the Coal and Steel Community (1951) that the smaller states were over-represented in each of the institutions. This principle is re-endorsed with respect to representation in the European Parliament, although strict equality is to apply to the composition of the Commission and, in some instances, to voting in the Council.

In addition to respecting the equality of Member States, the Lisbon Treaty marks a significant advance in respect for the fundamental rights of the citizen. Although adopted in 2000 and then appended to the Nice Treaty (2001) the Charter of Fundamental Rights of the European Union was not incorporated into the text of the treaties. This is now to be done in Article 6 which states that the Charter is to have the same legal value as the treaties. Furthermore, the Union, under the same article, is to accede to the European Convention for the Protection of Human Rights and Fundamental Freedoms, the full significance of which is spelled out in Chapters

267

Five and Seven. In short, the new Treaty on European Union would greatly enhance individual rights and freedoms within the Union and copperfasten its democratic nature.

This is underpinned by Articles 10 and 11 which, inter alia, lay down that every citizen has the democratic right to participate in the democratic life of the Union and that the institutions are to maintain an open, transparent and regular dialogue with representative associations and civil society.

The logic of these elaborations is carried to its conclusion in Article 7. Should the Member States determine that there is a clear risk of a serious breach of the Union's democratic values by an existing Member State then its voting rights will be suspended. This provision clearly establishes that it is a condition of Union membership that a country should respect the rule of law, human rights and fundamental freedoms. The more fundamental reference to respect for human rights and the rule of law is, of course, that relating to the conditions governing the admission of an applicant state into membership. This is covered in Article 49 by the simplest requirement that respect for the Union's fundamental values is a prerequisite for membership.

Conclusion

The overall conclusion to be drawn is that the essential nature and powers of the European Union will remain the same as before if the Lisbon Treaty comes into force. The Union will continue as an organization on which, according to Article 1 of the Treaty on European Union, the Member States have agreed to "confer competences to obtain objectives that they have in common". The limits of the competences are governed by the principle of conferral and competences not conferred upon the Union in the treaties remain with the Member States (Articles 5 and 4). The use of Union competences is governed by the principle of subsidiarity and proportionality. These three principles are the "constitutional" bedrock on which the Union rests. Together with the principles and objectives set out in accompanying articles they define the European Union as a system founded on law and intended to facilitate cooperation between European states in particular policy areas. This broad framework has been in construction for a long time.

The question posed at the start of this section was whether the Lisbon Treaty changed the scope and purpose of the European Union in any fundamental sense. The conclusion reached here is that it does not. It is equally important to examine the changes made to the institutions to see if this element of the reform process has introduced any changes of a fundamental nature.

Section Three: The Institutions

The starting point for this particular piece of analysis is the system of rules governing decision-making within the Union. They have always excited attention for the good reason that the Union is unlike any other international organisation in that it can not only make law but, in certain circumstances, can do so by a majority vote of its Member States. When presented in these terms it is understandable why the decision-making provisions, including the composition of the common institutions, should be subject to close scrutiny.

This is all the more necessary because the role and power of the three institutions involved in law making (Commission, Council and Parliament) has constantly evolved over the past fifty years in the light of experience. There has been a continuous trend towards transforming the Council of Ministers and the European Parliament into co-legislators which are on equal footing with each other. In this system of co-decision, both bodies act on the basis of majority voting, although the definition of what constitutes a majority can be complex enough. Nevertheless, the principle is clear.

On the other hand, the Member States have been resolute in confining certain sensitive policy areas to decision-making by unanimity, such as indirect taxation. Where unanimity is the working rule in the Council of Ministers then the European Parliament has no legislative role in the decision-making process, which remains inter-governmental in character. The issue for examination is whether the composition of the institutions, the relationship between them, and the manner in which they make decisions have been altered in a way that would affect the scope and purpose of the Union. Each institution will be examined in turn in the light of the Lisbon Treaty.

European Council

It is proposed that the European Council, consisting of the Heads of State and Government, should become an institution of the Union and is to have its own Chairman elected by the Council for a period of two and a half years. As stated in the Treaty text, the main task of the Chairman, styled as President of the European Council, will be to chair its meetings, ensure continuity in its work and facilitate cohesion and consensus among its members. This catalytic role is important since the main tasks of the European Council are to make policy (it does not make law) and to define the general political direction and priorities of the Union. The significance of this role can be appreciated when looking back, for example, at the major climate change initiatives taken over the past decade. All of them came via the European Council and many went beyond what had been anticipated at the time. So, the role of the Council President will be of significance to the future success of the Union.

The immediate implication of this amendment will be the end of the current form of rotating Presidency whereby the Prime Minister of one Member State presides over all European Council meetings. The rotating Presidency required each Prime Minister to act in turn as President of the European Council for a period of six months. The responsibilities were often demanding, as when the Taoiseach, Bertie Ahern, inherited a failed attempt to secure agreement on the European Constitution, and sometimes were ceremonial, as when the Taoiseach presided over the pageantry welcoming ten countries into membership of the Union. All that will be in the past if the Lisbon Treaty is approved.

The implications of the proposed change are straight-forward enough for this country. Whoever is Taoiseach will, as a matter of course, require a good working relationship with the President of the Council analogous to that with the Presidents of the Commission and the European Parliament.

Qualified Majority Voting

It has been said above that where decisions are made by majority voting under the co-decision procedure the Member States are sharing sovereignty and that where they use unanimity they are acting intergovernmentally and retain sovereignty. But the logic inherent in the system of creating ever closer unity among the peoples of Europe as set down in the preamble to the Treaty of Rome is that the boundary between the two is periodically shifted in the direction of shared sovereignty. The Lisbon Treaty is intended to bring this evolutionary process of moving from unanimous to majority voting to an end, at least for a generation ahead.

That expectation is the real political significance of the Lisbon Treaty. In bringing the reform process to finality, as the leaders hope, the Treaty introduces some innovations in the interest of greater transparency and legitimacy. Greater transparency in decision-making will be ensured by requiring the Council of Ministers to sit in public when framing new laws. Legitimacy will be deepened by bringing national parliaments into the process. Both measures had long been sought by those wanting to reduce the democratic deficit and can only be welcomed as an enhancement of the Union's democratic legitimacy.

Representation in Council

The rules governing the size of a majority in the Council of Ministers have also been altered. The philosophy behind qualified majority voting, as it has been since the beginning of European integration over half a century ago, is that the large Member States cannot dominate the small and the small cannot frustrate the large. Consequently, majorities or blocking minorities require coalitions of both large and small Member States. The Lisbon Treaty continues this principle but it establishes population size as the basis for weighting the vote of each country in place of the mathematical formulae used for the past half century. It seems capable of being extended to a Union of even thirty or more Member States (as is likely to happen).

The new system for calculating voting thresholds would still require coalitions of the large and small states to either pass or block legislation and has the merit of objectivity. The practical implications for the future arise not from a change in Ireland's relative voting strength but from the reality that the number of countries in the Council has quadrupled since Ireland's accession in 1973, thereby diminishing the influence of all Member States. This is the political consequence of a mathematical reality. Advancing the national interest in harmony with the general European interest will be more difficult as the Council gets bigger. All other Member States (even the biggest) face a similar challenge, of course, and the outcome clearly depends on the quality of the people chosen to represent the country in the common institutions and the clarity with which they and the government articulate national policy.

The Commission

The other institutional change ahead, should the new Treaty be ratified, is the composition of the Commission. The ever increasing number of Member States has put irresistible pressure on the principle that each should be able to appoint a Commissioner. That point was conceded, reluctantly it should be said, nearly a decade ago and a pragmatic solution has steadily won acceptance whereby the size of the Commission will correspond to two-thirds of the number of Member States. If this provision comes into force as a result of ratification then from 2014 onwards nine Member States would be without a Commissioner during each period of office, now set at five years. The implications of the loss of a Commissioner for one in every three terms of office would be no different in formal terms for Ireland than for any other Member State.

The periodic loss of a Commissioner is the price the Member States are willing to pay for ensuring that size does not compromise the efficiency of this key institution. It is a truism that an effective

Commission is of more importance to small Member States given its role as the guardian of the treaties and the protector of the European interest. If that viewpoint is accepted then the implications of the new rules governing the composition of the Commission would, on balance, be benign for a small country, such as Ireland.

The alternatives of a large Commission with an inner cabinet or a system of senior and junior Commissioners have been previously dismissed as inherently inequitable and politically dangerous. The formula advanced in the Lisbon Treaty has been in the making for a decade and is generally regarded as the best that can be devised.

European Parliament

The continuous trend towards enhancing the democratic legitimacy of the Union has essentially centered around the role of the European Parliament. Starting as an assembly composed of national parliamentarians with a dual mandate it was turned into a directly elected parliament in 1979. Eight years later it was given its first real legislative power on the basis of qualified majority voting being extended by the Single European Act to measures designed to complete the internal market. Each reform treaty since then has extended the scope of qualified majority voting and, hence, the role of the Parliament in the legislative process.

As a result of the Lisbon Treaty, "the adoption of all European Union legislation will be subject to a level of parliamentary scrutiny that exists in no other supranational or international structure". The European Parliament report on the Lisbon Treaty goes on to note that all European legislation will, with a few exceptions, be submitted to the dual approval of the Council and the Parliament.

Furthermore, the President of the Commission will be elected by the European Parliament, thus putting an end to the canard that the Commission was an unelected body. A new, simpler and more democratic budgetary procedure is to be introduced which ensures full parity between the Parliament and Council. Parliament's consent will be required for the approval of a wide range of international agreements signed by the Union. Agencies, such as Europol and Eurojust, will be subject to greater parliamentary scrutiny. Mention is made elsewhere of amended procedures for revising the treaties but particular reference is to be made here to the proposal that the Parliament will acquire powers to submit its own amendments during this process which in itself is a major democratic advance of the type envisioned by the Laeken Declaration.

This is a formidable list of increased powers for the directly elected members of the European Parliament. Under the Lisbon Treaty reforms the Parliament can be said to have finally come of age. Given the objectives set by the Lisbon Treaty in respect of enhanced democracy and legitimacy the proposals in relation to the European Parliament satisfy these requirements by placing the Parliament at the heart of the legislative process and at the centre of democratic control.

Conclusion

This scrutiny of the reform affecting the institutions has established that they have not been altered in a way that would affect the scope and purpose of the Union. On the contrary, the evidence points to a reinforcement of the democratic basis and a strengthening of the democratic legitimacy of the Union. The clarification of the division of competences between the Union and its Member States is a major achievement in terms of making the Union comprehensible to the citizen.

Section Four: Principal Innovations

Overview

Every treaty introduces a number of innovations which go beyond the simple amendment of a particular procedure. New procedures can be introduced or a move towards a greater pooling of sovereignty can be undertaken, usually on the grounds that a trial period at managing greater interdependence on an intergovernmental basis has proven satisfactory but could clearly be improved by moving to qualified majority voting.

The Lisbon Treaty follows this fashion and four innovations will be analyzed for their effect on the nature and scope of the Union. They relate to the area of freedom, security and justice, the strengthened role for national parliaments, the introduction of a new legal basis for the fight against climate change and simplified procedures for revising the treaties. Each will be analysed for its impact on Ireland.

The Area of Freedom, Security and Justice

The Third Pillar introduced by the Maastricht Treaty is to be ended. Under that arrangement, the Member States had decided to cooperate with each other in the areas of justice and home affairs on an intergovernmental basis but at Lisbon they advanced to the stage where they were willing to create an area of freedom, security and justice by pooling elements of their sovereignty in these policy areas and thereby resorting to the method of decision-making set out in the original Rome Treaty. The involvement of the European Commission, Parliament and Court of Justice would represent a profound commitment to sharing sovereignty in a highly sensitive policy area. Merging the Third Pillar with the old Economic Community to create a single Union would be a definitive move towards the simplification of the Union's structure that was set down at the beginning of the chapter as a benchmark against which to judge the Lisbon Treaty. In many ways it is the most significant change among the various reforms decided upon at Lisbon.

The provisions creating the area of freedom, security and justice are contained in the Treaty on the Functioning of the European Union and consist of 22 articles. They cover a range of issues of direct relevance to the citizens of Europe, such as the prevention and combating of terrorism, a common policy on asylum and immigration and, crucially, combating trafficking in persons, particularly women and children. This is a growing problem, especially in the context of open borders and self-evidently requires deep cooperation on the part of European states. The Treaty would make this possible in Article 79 by authorizing the Member States to make Union law on this matter, which would thereby create the legal and policy framework for fighting this heinous practice.

Judicial cooperation in civil matters, particularly where necessary for the proper functioning of the internal market, is to be introduced. Similar cooperation in criminal matters is to be secured which, inter alia, will provide for the rights of victims of crime and strengthen cooperation in the fight against crime, especially of the cross-border type.

Police cooperation is to be established in relation to the prevention, detection and investigation of criminal offences.

As explained in previous chapters, the creation of this area of freedom, security and justice posed certain problems for Ireland because our legal system based on the common law is different from that in most Member States. Consequently, it was decided that some measures would not automatically apply to Ireland and that Ireland would opt to participate on a case by case basis. The decision will be reviewed after three years. Meanwhile, the overall policy approach is to opt into measures in this area and this predisposition has been expressed in a Declaration appended to the treaties.

The implications for Ireland are that, on the one hand, the capacity of the Union to fight crime and terrorism would be greatly enhanced by the Lisbon Treaty reforms. The proposed measures are eminently sensible and, indeed, urgent, as in the case of human trafficking. On the other hand, the measures could pose problems for the legal system and a balance had to be struck between the two. For the period ahead, Ireland will retain a degree of flexibility in deciding the areas in which it can participate without prejudice to further modifications three years ahead.

National Parliaments

As is always the case with treaty reforms there are innovations which compensate for a perceived or actual loss of national influence elsewhere. On this occasion, the treaties are to be amended by giving national parliaments an explicit voice in what might be called the constitutional acts of the Union, in addition to a new role in the passage of ordinary legislation. Interestingly, Article 12 setting out the overall role for national parliaments is part of the provisions on democratic principles in the amended Treaty on European Union and precedes provisions on the common institutions. This sequence confers a solemn status on the constitutional standing of the national parliaments, one which is spelled out in a protocol appended to the Treaty.

In summary, national parliaments will be consulted in the pre-legislative phase whereby draft legislative acts will be forwarded to them for scrutiny, particularly in respect of compliance with the principles of subsidiarity and proportionality. When taken in conjunction with the clear delineation of the competences to be exercised by the Union, on the one hand, and the Member States, on the other, this amounts to a significant augmentation of the status and authority of national parliaments in the day to day life of the Union.

The implications are straightforward. The Oireachtas will have to be equipped with the necessary resources to scrutinize draft legislation emanating from the Commission with the attention it deserves, and needs. If there is to be any substance in the allegation that the Union suffers from a "democratic deficit" then henceforth that charge will have to be laid at the feet of national parliaments should they fail to measure up to the new demands being placed upon them. The full implications of this increased work-load on the Oireachtas will, no doubt, be studied by the government and the political parties.

Indeed that work-load could, on occasion, be added to in the constitutional sphere, as distinct from the on-going process of framing legislation. This would arise whenever a new simplified revision procedure is invoked to allow for the introduction of majority voting in the Council of Ministers in place of unanimity. It is not an open-ended invitation to amend either Treaty. Firstly, there has to be unanimity in the Council that the change should be made. This gives a veto to each government. Secondly, there has to be unanimity among national parliaments. This gives a veto to each parliament. Any national parliament has the right to block a proposed change in voting procedures. On examination, it can be seen, therefore, that the procedure, which is set out in two sections of Article 48 of the Union Treaty, corresponds with the normal process of negotiating and ratifying international treaties. As such, it will add to the weight of parliamentary oversight to be required at national level should the Lisbon reforms be adopted.

Climate Change

It would be misleading to view the Lisbon Treaty as an isolated stand-alone event divorced from what was happening in the Union and the wider world at the time it was being drafted. (Chapters One and Two set out the background and are an indispensable guide to what follows.) Since the beginning of the new millennium one of the issues progressively dominating the global agenda has been climate change and the European Union has led the response, set the pace, fashioned the policies, implemented emissions reduction measures, and pioneered new mechanisms, such as the Emissions Trading Scheme.

The Lisbon Treaty would for the first time give a treaty basis to the promotion and development of renewable energy and to the promotion of measures at international level to combat climate change. In fact, both would be part of Union policy and measures to promote renewable energy and climate change objectives would be agreed under the ordinary legislative procedure i.e. no country would be able to use a veto to block progress. This would give the Union the political means of achieving its objectives and the moral authority to recommend that others, such as the US and China, should follow suit.

The principal political implication of the Lisbon Treaty in respect of climate change is that Ireland would be part of the leadership group which is setting the pace for the rest of the world. Self-evidently, this would be an ethical role for this country to play and would provide opportunities for influencing global policy that would be denied to an EU outsider. For example, it is generally understood that the reference to climate change in the Lisbon Treaty is the result of an Irish initiative at the Intergovernmental Conference. No doubt, Ireland's seat at European Council and Council of Ministers could be similarly used with equal effect in pushing the Union's leadership role in the global arena, particularly in the negotiations on a successor agreement to the Kyoto Protocol.

On the domestic level, Ireland will be obliged under impending Union law to meet the emissions reduction target which is implicit in the Programme for Government. But in the event of an international agreement at Copenhagen in December 2009 then Ireland's national reduction target would be increased by approximately a half. It is doubtful whether such a target would ever have emerged from a purely domestic decision-making process. Indeed, the value of an external discipline in the emissions reduction area is analogous to the external fiscal disciplines which arose from compliance with the Maastricht Criteria as a precondition for membership of the EMU. The analogy will not be lost on those determined to lead Ireland towards a low carbon economy.

All in all, it can be inferred from the evolution of the Union's policy on climate change and the strengthening of the Treaty basis for measures intended to meet environmental and energy objectives that the Member States are embarking on a course of action from which there will be no return. If the Lisbon Treaty is ratified then the European Union's leadership role will receive enhanced legal standing in the international arena, and Ireland will be placed in the vanguard of the Union's attempt to forge a credible global response to the climate change challenge.

Revision of the Treaties

That said, a new concern of the generic variety surfaced upon the publication of the Lisbon Treaty text. It was alleged that the treaties would become self-amending if the Lisbon Treaty were ratified. In other words, the accusation was that the Heads of State and Government were trying to pull a fast one by devising a new amendment procedure which would by-pass national parliaments and electorates. The general thesis was that national elites were engaged in a secret plot to submerge their respective countries in a monolithic European state. A mechanism for amending the Treaties without recourse to the democratic process would be consistent with this overall belief.

The basis for this claim allegedly comes from the final provisions of the Treaty on European Union in which Article 48 deals at length with the procedure for revising the Treaties. Two methods can be employed: one styled the ordinary revision procedure and the other the simplified revision procedure. As the name suggests, the ordinary procedure is that conventionally in use for the amendment of an international treaty, although with the added embellishment of a Convention composed of national parliaments, the European Parliament and Commission and the Heads of States or Government, that will advise as to whether amendments should be sought or not. If the Convention deems them necessary and if they are agreed by the European Council then, as normal, they will be subject to ratification by the Member States in accordance with their respective constitutional requirements. So far, so good. The only change introduced by the Lisbon Treaty is an additional layer of democratic legitimation to be provided by the Convention.

The problem arises with the proposed simplified revision procedure. It can only be invoked, however, in respect of the second treaty, that on The Functioning of the European Union, and is confined exclusively to its Part Three, which covers economic, fiscal and social policies, as well as police and judicial co-operation, which are expressed in 171 articles.

The simplified procedure would consist of the Heads of State or Government unanimously agreeing to revise all or any of these articles. To state the obvious, this could hardly be done in secret. Not only that, but the procedure does not permit the Heads of State or Government to initiate a proposal for revision; in fact, they can only consider a proposal coming to them from the Government of a Member State, the European Parliament or the Commission. This restriction on their freedom of action would hardly permit them to act as a secret cabal. Instead, they are only to react to proposals generated from elsewhere and these are in turn limited under the procedure to proposals which do "not increase the competences conferred on the Union in the Treaties". As in the ordinary procedure, the decision will be subject to approval by the Member States in accordance with their respective constitutional requirements.

Article 48 also includes a procedure to allow for the substitution of qualified majority voting for unanimity without going through the major complication of summoning an Intergovernmental Conference (IGC). But "decisions with military implication or those in the area of defense" are specifically excluded from the procedure and are to remain subject to voting by unanimity. The use of this "general passerelle", as it is called, would be confined to the non-military aspects of the Common Foreign and Security Policy, social policy (employment law), fiscal matters relating to the environment, judicial co-operation in respect of family law and the multi-annual financial framework.

This procedure also introduces a new requirement into the ratification process by requiring national parliaments to be notified before the European Council adopts a decision. If any national parliament makes known its opposition within six months then the European Council cannot adopt a decision. In other words, every national parliament has a veto over the proposed revision.

What all this boils down to is that the only real difference between the ordinary and the simplified revision procedures is that one requires an Intergovernmental Conference (IGC) and the other does not. This is hardly the stuff of conspiracy. The allegation that the Lisbon Treaty would make the treaties self-amending is unfounded and is based on a misreading or misunderstanding of the revision provisions. The new simplified procedures hold no threat whatever to Ireland, nor to any other Member State for that matter.

Conclusion

The four principal innovations analysed above indicate that the Lisbon Treaty proposes substantial progress on enhancing the efficiency and coherence of the Union's action and of strengthing its democratic legitimacy. In each case, the progress would correspond to Irish national objectives, such as eliminating trafficking in women and children, extending the role of the Oireachtas in decision-making, fighting climate change and simplifying complex procedures.

Section Five – National Issues

Introduction
Every previous referendum has thrown up issues of the type described earlier as generic. Some are perennial, such as military neutrality. Others are once-off, such as fears over foreign direct investment.

This section analyses some of the main issues which surfaced in the debate on the Lisbon Treaty. It would be impossible to cover them all but the following are taken as a representative sample of those that might be called the more important.

Military Neutrality
One of the generic fears voiced in the 1972 referendum campaign was that Irish membership of the then EEC would compromise and even expunge Irish military neutrality. These fears were repeated when a Common Foreign and Security Policy emerged a decade later, were still in vogue in the 1990s and have once again been articulated as a criticism of the Lisbon Treaty. In examining the Union's security policy it is necessary to contextualise it, firstly, in the light of the first twelve articles of the Union Treaty mentioned earlier in the section on Democratic Principles and, secondly, in the light of the general provisions on the Union's external action, which are spelled out in two articles (22 and 23 of the Treaty on European Union). The logic applied by the Member States is that the common provisions guide the provisions on external action and that these, in turn, guide the provisions of the Common Security and Defence Policy. It's all rather like a series of Russian dolls. The Common Security and Defence Policy is an integral part of the Common Foreign and Security Policy which, in turn, is conducted in

accordance with the common provisions.

Two conclusions follow from an examination of the Treaty text. The first is that the Security and Defence Policy is focused on attempting to prevent or stabilise conflicts in the context of a political approach. Secondly, there will be a common defence only if the European Council unanimously decides so and if the Member States ratify that decision in accordance with their respective constitutional requirements. Furthermore, the policy may "not prejudice the specific character of the security and defence policy of certain Member States". This wording in Article 42 protects the Irish position on neutrality, as well as that of Austria, Finland, Sweden, Cyprus and Malta. In short, the status quo is undisturbed. Consequently, the Treaty of Lisbon cannot be invoked as a threat to Irish military neutrality.

It is worth noting that the strategic interests and objectives of the Union are to be identified by the European Council and that its decisions on these matters are to be unanimous (Article 22.1). In effect, this gives the Taoiseach of the day the right of veto over other Prime Ministers and Heads of State and this is but another way of saying the whole policy area remains intergovernmental in character, falls outside the ordinary legislative process and does not involve any law making (Article 31.1). In other words, sovereignty is not to be shared. In a few instances, the Foreign Ministers may take decisions by a qualified majority but this cannot apply "to decisions having military or defence implications" under Article 31.4.

In any event, there has been a constitutional prohibition on Ireland entering a common defence ever since the referendum on the Nice Treaty in November 2002. This prohibition will be carried forward in the wording of the constitutional amendment on which the electorate will vote in the forthcoming referendum. Article 29.4 of the constitution will then include a new subsection to the effect that the State will not adopt any decision taken by the European Council to establish a common defence "where that common defence would include the State". The impact of this is clear enough. Ireland's neutrality is constitutionally protected. When added to the maintenance of the status quo in the Treaty on European Union, the implications of the Lisbon Treaty are also clear enough. Irish military neutrality is respected by the Treaty and protected by the Constitution.

Corporate Taxation

A reference to corporate taxation is necessary as fears about enforced harmonisation being possible under the Lisbon Treaty surfaced after its publication. The legal situation is that the Lisbon Treaty does not change the status quo. The Union never had and does not have any competence in direct taxation, either personal or corporate. That situation will remain unchanged under the Lisbon Treaty. There is not, nor can there be, any legal basis within the treaties for the harmonization of corporate taxation either in respect of a common consolidated tax base or a minimum tax rate. Furthermore, the simplified revision procedure cannot be used to increase the competences conferred on the Union; that is quite clearly stated in the Lisbon Treaty text. Hence, it cannot be used to bring direct taxation within the ambit of the treaties, even if the Member States wanted to. They would have to use the ordinary revision procedure and proceed by way of an Intergovernmental Conference. The Irish government and electorate would each have a veto over the proposed amendment.

Fears of enforced harmonisation (a contradiction in terms) are sometimes based on the wording of Article 113 of the Treaty on the Functioning of the European Union which allows the Council of Ministers to adopt harmonisation measures "concerning turnover taxes, excise duties, and other forms of indirect taxation to the extent that such harmonisation is necessary to ensure the establishment and functioning of the internal market and to avoid distortion to competition". The wording of the article could hardly be more explicit. It is confined to indirect taxation only – in conformity with the wording of the original Treaty of Rome and the economic rationale for a functioning internal market. This whole question has been previously analysed by the Institute in two books, the most recent of which appeared only last year, and in which the legal basis for tax harmonisation was extensively examined. In both cases it was clearly established that direct taxation falls outside the treaties and is not a Union competence. These conclusions still hold under the Lisbon Treaty.

It is true that at present, with or without the Lisbon Treaty, some Member States could seek to use the existing provisions on enhanced cooperation to introduce a harmonised direct tax system applying only to them. Ireland would, of course, be free to opt out of such a scheme and could not be coerced into joining. Whether the other Member States would succeed in their attempt to avail of the enhanced cooperation mechanism remains to be seen. It is also true that sovereign states can enter into tax treaties with each other and this could lead at any time to new agreements on corporate taxation that would introduce elements of harmonisation amongst countries that happened to be Member States of the Union. But this is a matter of international law and has no bearing on the Lisbon Treaty.

Foreign Direct Investment

Finally, there is the claim that Ireland's capacity to attract foreign direct investment could be undermined by the Lisbon Treaty. This belief has arisen from a confusion between the Union's external trade relationships and the internal policies conducted by Member States. In any event, Ireland has a veto, in common with all other Member States, over agreements on external trade. Fears to the contrary are misguided. There are no inherent threats to our Foreign Direct Investment policies in the Treaty of Lisbon.

Conclusion

This section dealt with only a sample of the various fears which have surfaced about the Lisbon Treaty during the referendum debate. The analysis has concluded that in each case the status quo is not affected and that the Treaty does not introduce any threats to sensitive areas of the national interest.

Section Six: Implications of Rejection

The implications of the Lisbon Treaty for Ireland naturally depend on the outcome of the referendum. Ratification would give rise to a whole series of changes which have been identified and analysed in preceding chapters. By and large their implications are predictable since the aims of the negotiators were well known in advance and have been endlessly explained ever since. On the other hand, the implications of a rejection lie in the future and are open to conjecture. Nevertheless, it is possible to put various scenarios together on the basis of past experience and an understanding of how the Member States relate to each other in the daily working of the Union and, more importantly, what they expect of each other in terms of mutual solidarity.

Irrespective of the referendum outcome, however, a common thread joins the implications of either ratification or rejection. That thread is the legal nature of the Lisbon Treaty itself, indeed of any treaty, or contract, for that matter. This has been the starting point for similar analyses of previous treaties published by the Institute and it remains valid despite its lack of originality at this stage.

The key point for emphasis is that a treaty, according to the dictionary, is an agreement between two or more countries. In legal terms, it is a contract between sovereign states. Indeed, in the case of all the European treaties the signatories describe themselves as the "High Contracting Parties". It is in the nature of a contract that the parties enter into a set of reciprocal obligations from which they expect to derive mutual benefit but it is essential for the legality of a contract that it be negotiated in good faith, without duress, and that it be agreed freely and voluntarily. These requirements were met throughout the conduct and conclusion of the negotiations leading to the signing of the Treaty in Lisbon.

The international law on treaties goes further by requiring a process of validation whereby the text negotiated and concluded by a country's plenipotentiaries must be placed before its national parliament for endorsement. Ratification is therefore not complete until the treaty secures parliamentary approval. Irish constitutional requirements go further, however, in that the text of Bunreacht na hÉireann must be amended before Dáil Éireann can ratify a treaty relating to the European Union and that in turn requires the assent of the people by way of referendum. If the referendum is carried then the Irish Constitution will be amended accordingly.

No Plan B

As stated at the outset of the chapter, the implications of a rejection of the Lisbon Treaty have to be assessed against a number of objective realities. The first is the prolonged process of adjustment over the past three decades to successive enlargements (the number of members has more than quadrupled from six in the early seventies to twenty-seven at present, with more in prospect). The Lisbon Treaty is regarded as the final instalment of a series of reforms initiated by the Single European Act in 1987 and the Maastricht Treaty in 1992, final in the sense that there are no plans to revisit the make-up of the European Union for a generation.

In these circumstances, the immediate implication of the Lisbon Treaty being rejected by Ireland would be consternation among the other Member States because there is no fall-back position. There is no plan B – for the good reason that the Lisbon Treaty is plan B following the defeat of the Constitutional Treaty. At least when the European Constitution was rejected by France and the Netherlands the automatic response was to revert to the traditional form of treaty amendments, as are set out in the Treaty before us. But no such strategy is available on this occasion and the implications for this country would be determined by the degree of determination on the part of the other Member States to press on with the reforms agreed in Lisbon.

Simply put, the decision could be to go ahead without Ireland. That is a hard one to call because some other Member States might be unwilling to set the precedent whereby an existing Member State could forfeit its membership for failing to go along with new rules and procedures already agreed by its government and endorsed by all the other members.

In the past, Denmark was accommodated by a special deal concerning the Maastricht Treaty and Ireland in relation to the Nice Treaty. On the other hand, the Constitutional Treaty was simply dropped when rejected by France and the Netherlands. All these countries remain, as we know, in good standing as EU members.

But nothing is ever quite the same. The core of the Lisbon Treaty is the reform of the common institutions and the simplification of the decision-making processes. Crudely put, there is nothing from which Ireland could derogate, à la Denmark after it rejected the Maastricht Treaty. It would appear to be all or nothing, as in the case of France and the Netherlands, except that on this occasion there is no obvious fall-back position for the Union as a whole. The most likely outcome would be stalemate and the Union would be denied important new competences, like fighting climate change or dealing with trafficking in women and children.

There is no question but that the rejection of the new Treaty would provoke a backlash elsewhere in the Union against Ireland. That was the case after the first Nice referendum and the country's reputation was only salvaged by the skilful management of the situation by the government and through its success in having the Nice Treaty ratified at the second attempt. The Nice affair also provoked a reaction in some Member States who contrasted their solidarity with Ireland in the economic sphere with Ireland's lack of solidarity with them in the political arena. It requires little political acumen to conclude that had the situation continued Ireland's reputation and influence within the Union would have waned and could even have been fatally compromised. To argue that there would be no political price to be paid for rejecting the Lisbon Treaty is either disingenuous or consciously misleading. The political consequences would, as common sense suggests, be negative. At their worst they could be deeply wounding, long lasting and self-inflicted. There could be economic consequences if foreign investors believed that rejection had introduced a question mark over Ireland's continued participation in the internal market, and even the euro. This might be no more than perception – but in risk analysis perception is reality.

On previous occasions when faced with the implications of rejecting a new Treaty the Institute worked out a series of elaborate scenarios as to what might happen. For the purposes of simplicity they can be reduced as follows. Firstly, the other Member States would throw their hats at reform and leave the status quo intact. Secondly, they could offer Ireland some concessions, à la Denmark after Maastricht, and ask for the referendum to be re-run. Thirdly, Ireland could volunteer to hold a second referendum on the basis of clarifications or assurances, as with the Nice Treaty. Fourthly, Ireland could be invited to step aside, develop some uncharted external association with the Union and let the other Member States get on with the reform process. As of now, it is a matter of personal choice as to what scenario seems the more likely. But one thing is clear, none of these scenarios is without its down-side.

Conclusion

The implications of ratifying the Lisbon Treaty have emerged from the above analysis as politically benign and in conformity with the national interest. In contrast, the implications of rejecting the Treaty have emerged as entirely negative, both for Ireland and for the Union from which we derive so much benefit. The price to be paid for a rejection would be high in terms of Ireland's standing and status within the Union and our capital of goodwill would be dissipated at a stroke. Equally disturbing, the capacity of the European Union to act effectively on the world stage would be weakened at a time when leadership was most needed. For that eventuality, Ireland alone would be responsible.

Section Seven: Conclusion

Ratification of the Lisbon Treaty would not endanger any of the special provisions and safeguards previously secured by Ireland (neutrality, abortion, common travel etc). They all remain intact. Ratification would maintain the economic advantages (the Internal Market and euro) conferred by EU membership as well as the political influence that accrues from membership. Neither would the Treaty open the country to new threats, such as to the corporate tax system or to the foreign direct investment regime. There seems no evidence that the European Union is intent on becoming a military super power or a political super state, or both simultaneously. Rather, the Lisbon Treaty offers a vision in which the countries of Europe, united in common endeavour on the principle of democracy, can lead the world in the fight against common challenges, such as climate change and world poverty.

As on previous occasions, Ireland has a choice to make, not just for itself, but for the rest of the European Union as well. It is an awesome responsibility. This book has been intended as an aid in arriving at an informed decision on the future of the European Union and on the contents of the Lisbon Treaty.

The Institute of International
and European Affairs
(IIEA)

tron: Mary McAleese, President of Ireland

mité d'Honneur: An Taoiseach Bertie Ahern; Commissioner Charlie
cCreevy; Pat Cox; David Byrne; John Bruton; Garret FitzGerald; Albert
ynolds; Richard Burke; Padraig Flynn; Ray MacSharry; Michael O'Kennedy;
ter Sutherland

e Institute of International and European Affairs is an independent self-
verning body which promotes the advancement and spread of knowledge
the process of European integration and, in particular, on the role and
ntribution of Ireland within Europe.

e Institute provides a permanent forum for the identification and development
Irish strategic policy responses to the continuing process of European
tegration and to the wider international issues which impact on Europe. The
ain aim is to provide objective analysis of the key political, economic, social
d cultural issues for those charged with representing Irish views within the
ropean policymaking structures. This is done by facilitating policy discussion
th inputs from all relevant sectors, assembling information on key topics and
sseminating research results.

an independent forum, the Institute does not express opinions of its own.
e views expressed in its publications are solely the responsibility of the
thor(s).

e legal form of the Institute is that of a company limited by guarantee and
t having share capital. It is funded by annual membership subscriptions, from
mpanies, organisations, institutions and individuals. A number of founding
onsors enable the Institute to operate on a financially secure basis. It also
ceives an annual grant from the European Commission.

IIEA Foundation Members

The Institute is particularly indebted to its Foundation Members which enable it to operate independently on a financially secure basis.

AIB Bank plc
Bank of Ireland
Bord na Mona
CIE
Citybank Europe plc
Construction Industry Federation (CIF)
Cement Roadstone Holdings plc
Deloitte
DePfa-Bank plc
Diageo
Dublin Airport Authority
Electricity Supply Board
Enterprise Ireland
Failte Ireland
FBD Insurances plc
Forfás
Gecas
Glen Dimplex

Google
Goldman Sachs
IBEC
IDA
IFA
Merrill Lynch plc
National Treasury Management Agency
NTR plc
Pioneer Investments Management Ltd
RTE
Siemens Ltd
SIPTU
State Street International
Smurfit (Ireland) Ltd
Tourism Ireland
VHI
Waterford Crystal plc

IIEA Corporate Members

Accenture • Agriculture & Food, Department of • Airtricity • A & L Goodbody • All Party Oireachtas Committee on Constitution • Anglo Irish Bank • Attorney General/Chief State Solicitor's Office, Office of the • Aviareto Ltd • Arts, Sport & Tourism, Department of • Bord Gais • Central Bank of Ireland • Chambers of Commerce of Ireland • Church of Ireland Working Group on Europe • Central Statistics Office • Cipherion Translations • Commission for Communications Regulation • Commission for Energy Regulation • Committee on European Affairs of the Irish Episcopal Conference • Communications, Marine & Natural Resources, Department of • Competition Authority • Concern • Director of Public Prosecutions, Office of the • Director of Telecommunications Regulation, Office of the • Dublin European Institute • Defence, Department of • Dublin City Council • Education & Science, Department of • Embassy of Austria • Embassy of Australia • Embassy of Belgium • Embassy of Britain • Embassy of Bulgaria • Embassy of Canada • Embassy of Croatia • Embassy of the Czech Republic • Embassy of Estonia • Embassy of Finland • Embassy of Germany • Embassy of Greece • Embassy of Japan • Embassy of Latvia • Embassy of the Republic of Cyprus • Embassy of Romania • Embassy of Sweden • Embassy of the United States of America • Enterprise, Trade & Employment, Department of • Environment, Heritage & Local Government, Department of • Environmental Protection Agency • European Foundation for the Improvement of Living and Working Conditions • FÁS • Finance, Department of • Financial Services Ombudsman • Fingal County Council • Food and Safety Authority of Ireland • Foreign Affairs, Department of • Fujitsu Siemens • Greenstar • Health & Children, Department of • Higher Education Authority • IMPACT • Independent News and Media plc • INTO • Irish Distillers • Irish Times • INTO • Irish Life & Permanent plc • Justice, Equality & Law Reform, Department of • KPMG • Leargas • Local Governmental Management Services • McCann FitzGerald • Microsoft Ireland • National Grid • NESC • NorDubCo • Ombudsman, Office of the • PriceWaterhouse Cooper • Railway Procurement Agency • Revenue Commissioners, Office of the • Shannon Development • Social, Community and Family Affairs, Department of • South Dublin County Council • Taipei Representative Office in Ireland • Taoiseach, Department of the • Teagasc • Tesco • The Royal Danish Embassy • The Royal Netherlands Embassy • The Royal Norwegian Embassy • Thomson Prometric • Tipperary Rural Business Development Institute • Transport, Department of • Unicredito Italiano (Ireland) • United Drug • University of Dublin, Trinity College Dublin • Údarás na Gaeltachta • University College Cork • University College Dublin • Viridian • William Fry Solicitors